Turkey's New Geopolitics

A RAND Study

Turkey's New Geopolitics

From the Balkans to Western China

Graham E. Fuller
and Ian O. Lesser

with Paul B. Henze
and J. F. Brown

Westview Press

BOULDER • SAN FRANCISCO • OXFORD

A RAND Study

RAND books are available on a wide variety of topics. To receive a list of RAND books, write or call Distribution Services, RAND, 1700 Main Street, P.O. Box 2138, Santa Monica, CA 90407-2138, (310) 393-0411, extension 6686.

Published in 1993 in the United States of America by Westview Press, Inc., 5500 Central Avenue, Boulder, Colorado 80301-2877, and in the United Kingdom by Westview Press, 36 Lonsdale Road, Summertown, Oxford OX2 7EW

Library of Congress Cataloging-in-Publication Data
Fuller, Graham E., 1939–
    Turkey's new geopolitics : from the Balkans to Western China /
Graham E. Fuller and Ian O. Lesser with Paul B. Henze and J. F.
Brown.
        p. cm.
    "A Rand study."
    Includes bibliographical references and index.
    ISBN 0-8133-8659-4—ISBN 0-8133-8660-8 (pbk.)
    1. Turkey—Foreign relations—1980– 2. Turkey—Politics and
government—1980–   I. Lesser, Ian O., 1957– . II. Henze, Paul
B., 1924– . III. Brown, J. F. (James F.), 1928– . IV. Title.
DR603.F85 1993
327.4961—dc20   93-20402
                                                                                          CIP

Printed and bound in the United States of America

10   9   8   7   6   5   4

Contents

Foreword

Ambassador Morton Abramowitz

The world on Turkey's borders has changed radically in the last three years. To the north old and new states are trying to make the transition from communism to market economies. To the south the Middle East is no longer the stage on which Cold War rivalries are played out, but it still remains a mélange of fundamentalism, authoritarianism, and militarism. And to the east new nations have emerged from the debris of the Soviet Union, each looking for a path into the twenty-first century. Turkey, in the center of it all, is striving to come to grips with these changes.

A fresh look at Turkey in its new surroundings is badly needed. In fact, since Turkey gets little attention from the American media or the American public, one could almost say that any look is a useful one. In 1990 the press incredibly managed to overlook an extraordinary two-day legislative battle between two Senate titans, Robert Dole and Robert Byrd, over a proposed Armenian genocide resolution and its potential impact on American-Turkish relations. This neglect prompts readers hoping to gain a grasp on events in Turkey to rely on such British publications as the *Financial Times* or the *Economist*.

The five essays composing this book are thus a badly needed and much welcomed introduction to the impact of recent upheavals on Turkey and its role in a nascent new world. While Paul Henze provides a broad treatment of such major domestic issues as the role of Islam in Turkish society and Turkey's deepening problems dealing with its Kurdish minority, the book's focus is on geopolitical and foreign policy concerns. The basis for this orientation is RAND's interest in the magnitude and suddenness of the transformation of Turkey's neighborhood.

All of the authors have experience in Turkey and keep in close touch with the current situation; two have lived there. They approach the Turkish scene sympathetically and with the conviction that Turkey can become a regional leader. They stress that the long-term importance of the country, deriving from its geography, must not be overlooked. They argue that Turkey's role in the world has been significantly enlarged by the breakup of the Soviet Union and that in the next decade Turkey's influence will stretch from the Balkans to Chinese Central Asia.

Greater integration into the West tops the list of Turkish priorities, but the authors are skeptical that Turkey will ever gain admittance to the European Community. Moreover, the demise of the Warsaw Pact, the strengthening of the United Nations, and the creation of organizations such as the Western European Union have caused NATO to lose at least some of its cogency. As NATO erodes, so too do Turkey's ties with its NATO allies. The "Southern flank," once an integral component of containment strategy, now resonates with a certain hollowness. While looking to readjust its foreign and defense policies to a changed world, Turkey clings to NATO, less for security than for its psychological value as Turkey's principal institutional tie to the West.

These essays cover much ground, quickly and effectively, providing a useful introduction to the new era emerging in Turkish foreign and defense policy. The threat of the past 400 years—Russia—has been virtually eliminated. Turkey is now more secure than it has been since its birth as a republic after the First World War. Instead of being surrounded by an expansionist empire, Turkey finds itself bordered by a plethora of states that are militarily and economically inferior. Some even look to Turkey for help and support. While Turkey carefully watches its southern neighbors—Iran, Iraq, and Syria—it faces no serious threat from them for at least the next decade, except from their capability to roil Turkey's troubled domestic scene by supporting the PKK (Kurdish Workers Party) insurgency. Despite its own internal weaknesses, Turkey is by far the strongest state in the area.

The book highlights a growing struggle between those who share Ataturk's devotion to keeping Turkey's interests focused on Anatolia and those who envision a more cosmopolitan role for their nation. Such a role, which dates back to the pan-Turkist movements abolished by Ataturk, stems from Turkey's awakened interest in Turkish-speaking populations outside of Turkey, an interest carefully squelched while the Soviet Union existed. Despite Turkey's secularism—another of Ataturk's lasting legacies—Turkey remains an Islamic nation that feels an affinity for some Muslim communities, especially those once ruled by the Ottomans. Bosnia and Herzegovina fit that label because the bulk of their 43 percent Muslim population was converted by the Turks, a tie buttressed through the years by the emigration of Bosnians to Turkey. The populace has been aroused by the atrocities perpetrated against Bosnian Muslims, and, while unilateral action is out of the question, Turkey is willing to contribute troops to an international peace-making force.

Among the book's principal conclusions are the following:

1. Turkish foreign policy will increasingly focus on Central Asia, the Balkans, and the Middle East. In the Central Asian republics, Turkey's role will be critical and of significance to both Turkey and the West. The emerging states will look to Turkey as a model for their development as well as for material help. Turkey will take advantage of these newly opened markets for investment and trade and can serve as a funnel for Western investment.

Destructive nationalism in the Balkans clearly was dormant for the past half century, not dead. As one author suggests, Balkan history is now "making up for lost time." Turkey cannot avoid veering attention "back to the Balkans." Regardless of the outcome in Bosnia, with 2 million Muslims in Kosovo and another 500,000 in Macedonia, Turkey could be drawn into an expansion of the Yugoslav conflict.

Turkey's emerging defense strategy will be driven, in large part, by Turkey's need to protect itself against the threat posed by Arab or Iranian accumulation of advanced weaponry. Because of its prominence in the Gulf War Allied Coalition, Turkey fears an ultimately revived Iraq; it risks conflict with Syria and Iran over their support of the PKK; and it has competing aims with Iran in Azerbaijan. In addition, water is also a major source of conflict with Syria and Iraq. Despite the potential for trouble over these contentious issues, Turkey wants to avoid an alliance that makes it appear as an instrument of Western policy in the region.

2. Turkey's relationship with the United States will increase in importance if Turkey continues to find itself excluded from the new Europe. However, cuts in defense and foreign aid budgets will reduce American resources in the country and accelerate the reappraisal of U.S. strategic interests in Turkey. Although the Gulf War may have increased appreciation in some American quarters for strong defense ties, Turks themselves are ambivalent. Prime Minister Demirel appears reluctant to place the same weight on U.S.-Turkish ties as his predecessor, Turgut Ozal. The post-Cold War relationship between the United States and Turkey is more likely to consist of a reduced defense arrangement and a "more mature" relationship involving economic and political interests.

3. Turkey's most challenging domestic problem is the growth of Kurdish nationalism. For a long time Turkey denied it had a Kurdish problem; successive governments refused to concede that Kurds existed; and use of the Kurdish language in Turkey was strictly prohibited. The bloody war with the PKK in southern Turkey, which has gone on for eight years, has changed that situation and has led the Turks to discuss the Kurdish issue publicly and seriously. However, the Gulf War and the creation of an autonomous Kurdish province next door in Iraq have

heightened fears in Turkey that its own Kurdish population will intensify its demands. Some Turks would actually prefer a revitalized Saddam
atop a solidly centralized state to a federated Iraq without him.

4. The threat of Turkey turning into a fundamentalist state is exaggerated. While the cultural influence of Islam is pervasive, the devotion of
Turkish Muslims varies greatly: some are devout; some practice their
faith like Americans practice Christianity. While new ties to the republics of Central Asia and Western inaction with regard to Bosnia may
increase attention to Islam in Turkey, the nation will remain a secular
state. However, continued rejection by the European Community might
generate some shift in Turkish foreign policy toward opportunities in
the Islamic and Turkic world.

These conclusions touch important matters. All are arguable and
most are being vigorously discussed in Turkey. I agree with many of
them. For example, the Kurdish issue will be around for a long time and
could blight Turkish relations with the West. The issue is immensely
complicated because over half of Turkey's Kurds now live in urban areas outside the southeast. The upsurge of fighting in the southeast has
created some tensions in major Turkish cities and has hampered, at least
temporarily, the continuing and important integration of Kurds into the
Turkish polity. The war is also an increasing economic burden and a
threat to Turkish democracy. Sooner or later, Turkey may learn to live
with a real degree of autonomy for the Iraqi Kurds and to allow Kurds
in Turkey to be both Kurds and Turks.

I also agree that despite the late-1992 local elections in which Islamic
fundamentalists increased their portion of the vote, the danger of a fundamentalist takeover is overblown, often fostered by itinerant Western
journalists. Turkey may be a state of Muslims, but it is far from an
Islamic state and will not become one unless its army disintegrates, its
modernization program totally falters, or its political system deteriorates
badly. Even the EC's closed doors will not alter Turkey's pro-Western
orientation; the Turkish modern sector has no intention of committing
suicide.

Turkey's economic growth can serve as a model for the nascent states
of the former Soviet Union. Turkey's cheap consumer goods will promote economic ties. Turkey can and should play a useful role in central
Asia, contributing educational, technical, and modest financial assistance. However, the area will remain unstable for a long time, and the
resources required by these states vastly exceed Turkey's capabilities.
Turkey will need to decide just what the true strategic significance of
Central Asia is to its interests and how much of their resources they can
afford to invest. Of far more concern are the potential ramifications of
the incessant fighting in the Caucasus between the Armenians and the

Azerbaijanis over Nagorno-Karabakh. This conflict, which shows no signs of going away, could give rise to bitter disagreement with the West and damage relations.

The Balkans also represent a potential quagmire for Turkey depending on how Turkey defines its interests. The most worrisome development—one that might possibly bring a unilateral Turkish military response—is if a fragile and ethnically divided Macedonia were to disintegrate, particularly if Serbia were to add it to the list of areas in need of "ethnic cleansing."

I believe that a security arrangement between Turkey and the West which extends "out of area" to the Middle East would face major domestic opposition in Turkey. Turkey has a deep-rooted dislike of publicly antagonizing Arab neighbors that the Ottomans once ruled; indeed, at times its behavior borders on the obsequious. While the Turkish military welcomes continued Western military aid, they are not anxious to become embroiled in a Western alliance system in the Middle East. In any event, the possibility for such an alliance seems to have passed with George Bush's sidestepping of President Ozal's requests for "strategic cooperation" after the Gulf War.

The domestic issues for Turkey are critical. Turkey has witnessed two revolutions in the last decade: the one outside its borders and an ongoing internal one. Domestic transformation has produced rapid growth, economic liberalization and social progress. Yet despite the extensive modernization, Turkey remains today a country of large pockets of poverty and backwardness, in which a significant portion of the nation stagnates in almost a Third World.

In terms of political and social development, democratization and free expression (made more vigorous by the recent introduction of commercial television) are on the rise. Much has been accomplished in only fifty years, and Turkey's prospects are far brighter than those of its neighbors. Nevertheless, not all the signs are encouraging. Political progress now lags far behind economic. Indeed, the political system is fragmenting amidst major party factionalism and personalism with the "non-political" president forming his own political party after abandoning the one he originally established. Turkey's political parties are still a long way from being institutionalized or popularly based, while politicians are far more obsessed with retaining power than with getting things done. New leaders from a new generation are not even visible on the horizon. And for a country that aspires to EC membership, its human rights practices leave much to be desired. The fact that torture still exists is an obscenity.

The rapid growth of the 1980s has recently been tempered by world recession and the slowing of reform. Turkey's present growth rate of 5 percent may be impressive compared to Western growth, but it is simply not adequate for a country still as poor as Turkey and with a 2.5 percent annual population growth. Inflation hovers stubbornly at 70 percent per year and if not soon corrected could lead to a precipitous decline in popular confidence in the currency. The inflation is fed by a bloated state sector, and talk about privatization—both under Ozal and now Demirel—has far exceeded action.

Despite the significant foreign challenges, I remain optimistic that Turkey's dynamism will continue and deepen—even if it is suffering from occasional lapses in government attention. Turkey is not Taiwan, but it has shown it can grow at 6 to 8 percent a year. Its private sector is notable and expanding, and its human resources are impressive. While serious privatization and other reform would greatly increase foreign investment in Turkey, such investment is nonetheless on the rise. Success is probable but by no means assured. If the past is any guide, progress is likely to be undulant.

This is where the West comes in. The growth and vigor of Turkey hinge on the expansion of Turkey's scientific and technological capabilities, its institutional growth, and its ties with Organization for Economic Cooperation and Development countries for trade and investment. While Turkey may derive modest trade benefits from enhanced relationships with Russia, Central Asia, the Balkans, or the Middle East, Turkey's future lies in its closer cooperation—formal or informal—with Western Europe, the United States, and the other OECD countries.

What of U.S.-Turkish relations? For the last two decades the United States and Turkey have been joined in a military defense guarantee, the United States providing military aid in exchange for the use of Turkish bases. However, since the Americans have opted against pursuing a politically difficult alliance based on Middle East contingencies, that arrangement no longer accords with reality; a new relationship must be forged. Turkey is increasingly aware that its friendships in the world do not run deep and that the United States is indeed its best and most concerned friend. Turkish leaders recognize that a good relationship with the only remaining superpower serves their nation well.

The United States is, and should be, most interested in seeing Turkey continue as a stable, democratic, secular, economically dynamic state in a region that will remain turbulent for a long time to come. If that is indeed an important concern, then the United States must do its part in promoting trade and investment in Turkey, narrowing the economic disparities between Turkey and other Western countries, reducing impediments to EC membership, and generally encouraging Turkish integration into the West. Whatever the limitations, whatever the political and cultural difficulties, and whatever time it takes, the effort will be worth it.

Preface

Turkey is among those countries most profoundly affected by the recent revolutionary changes on the international scene. Throughout the Cold War, Turkey was a distant outpost on the European periphery, a barrier to Soviet ambitions in the Middle East, and a contributor to the security of Europe. For almost forty years, Ankara's geostrategic "reach" was largely limited to its role within the Atlantic Alliance and, more narrowly, its place within NATO's Southern Region. The Gulf War thrust Turkey into the strategic forefront. With the disintegration of the Soviet Union and turmoil in the Balkans, Ankara is now poised to play a leading role across a vast region, from Eastern Europe to western China.

This volume has its origins in a RAND study launched in the fall of 1990, at a time when the transformation of Turkey's regional environment was only just beginning. The impetus for the study came from the identification of internal and external trends that, taken together, suggested a growing role for Turkey and a growing need to understand the implications for regional stability and U.S. policy. The idea of undertaking a sweeping reassessment of Turkey's prospects and orientation grew in equal measure out of ongoing RAND research focused on the Mediterranean, the Balkans, the Middle East, and the Soviet Union. The four authors herein bring to bear an active interest in these areas and, in the case of Graham Fuller and Paul Henze, long experience as observers of the Turkish scene. Since the formal completion of the study in the summer of 1992, developments in and around Turkey, from Bosnia to Central Asia, have only reinforced Turkey's significance. The chapters below have been revised and updated to keep abreast of these changes. Inevitably, events will outpace this discussion. But the focus is on long-term trends, and the basic lines of analysis should hold.

Taking the evolution of Turkish society itself as a starting point, the following chapters explore where Turkey is headed, where its long-term interests will lie in the face of formidable new opportunities and challenges, and the implications for the United States in its bilateral and institutional relations with Turkey. What will be Turkey's orientation between the Islamic East and the West? To what extent have traditional

Ataturkist precepts regarding the dangers of international activism fall-
en away? Will Turkish and American interests in Europe, the Middle
East, and Central Asia converge or diverge? What are the prospects for
Turkish behavior in regional crises?

Turkey's domestic scene is changing almost as rapidly as its external
environment. In Chapter 1, Paul Henze explores political, social, and
economic trends. He suggests that Islamist political elements have not
gained ground, despite the growing prominence of Islam in Turkish society. At the same time, Turkish nationalism has emerged as a more potent force in the wake of the Persian Gulf War. Domestic trends are
likely to support a more assertive foreign and security policy, but the
Kurdish insurgency in southeastern Anatolia and a problematic human
rights record will pose continuing internal and external challenges for
Ankara.

Turkey faces tremendous opportunities and new risks in Central Asia
and the Middle East. In the Turkic regions of the former Soviet Union,
Turkey is emerging as a political, economic, and cultural magnet and an
important secular model for development. In Chapter 2, Graham Fuller
surveys this new environment and its meaning for Turkey, including the
emergence of a potentially dangerous regional competition with Iran.
Looking to the Middle East, the Gulf War has given impetus to a violent
Kurdish separatist movement on Turkish soil, with strong implications
for Ankara's relations with Iran, Iraq, and Syria as well as with the West.
Turkey's pivotal resource position, both as a conduit for Iraqi oil exports
and as a source of water for its Middle Eastern neighbors, will reinforce
Ankara's role in the region.

Ian Lesser treats the evolution of and outlook for Turkey's relations
with the West in Chapter 3. The prospects for Turkey's joining Europe
in the institutional sense, through full membership in the European
Community and the Western European Union, remain poor. The Gulf
War returned Turkey to the strategic front rank even as its Cold War importance waned. But the strategic value of Turkey is now seen largely in
Middle Eastern and Central Asian terms, making its integration into
emerging European security arrangements more difficult. Turks like to
refer to their country's role as a *bridge* between east and west, north and
south. By contrast, Europeans are increasingly inclined to view Turkey
as a *barrier* to turmoil on the European periphery, even a source of instability in its own right. Our analysis suggests that Turkey will remain
broadly pro-Western but will adopt a more reserved approach to regional and security cooperation with Washington.

The proliferation of ethnic conflicts and separatist movements in the
Balkans is of great concern to Ankara. Against the background of the

Ottoman legacy, James Brown examines the prospects for a revival of Turkish involvement in the Balkans in Chapter 4. Beyond the crisis in Yugoslavia (and Turkey has been at the forefront of calls for Western intervention in Bosnia), developments in Albania, Macedonia, Greek Thrace, or Bulgaria could lead to a more direct political, even military, role for Turkey. Concern for the fate of ethnic Turks and the roughly nine million Muslims in the Balkans as a whole is already having a pronounced effect on the Turkish political debate. The analysis supports the conclusion, developed in Chapter 3, that Turkey's isolation from Europe would worsen the prospects for stability in Turkish-Greek relations and the evolution of the Balkans as a whole.

Finally, in the concluding chapter, Graham Fuller looks across the preceding analyses and offers some overall observations on how changes in and around Turkey are shaping the way Turks see themselves and deal with others. He goes on to discuss more specific implications for the United States in its policies toward Turkey and the surrounding regions—policies that will take on added significance as Turkey begins to define and act on its own interests in a new geopolitical setting.

The authors wish to express their thanks to RAND Vice Presidents Lynn Davis and George Donohue and to Jonathan Pollack, RAND corporate research manager for international policy, for their support in bringing together in this volume the results of the joint Arroyo Center–Project AIR FORCE study on Turkey's future strategic orientation. RAND colleagues David Ochmanek, Nanette Gantz, Joseph Kechichian, F. Stephen Larrabee, James Steinberg, Jeremy Azrael, Mary Morris, and Cindy Kumagawa provided valuable comments and assistance. We are also grateful to Heath Lowry of the Institute of Turkish Studies in Washington for his comments on two draft chapters and to William Rau of the Turkish–U.S. Business Council for his assistance with contacts in Istanbul. Finally, we wish to thank the many individuals in Turkey and elsewhere who contributed their views over the course of this research.

Ian O. Lesser

1

Turkey: Toward the Twenty-First Century

Paul B. Henze

Reflecting on the history of the Turkish Republic over the past seventy years and, in particular, on Turkish accomplishments since the military coup of September 12, 1980, my purpose in this essay is to discuss what I consider the most important features of Turkey's development as the country progresses through the 1990s and into the twenty-first century. I use the verb "progress" intentionally, for Turkey as a nation has not only established a record of accelerated net progress during the past decade, but shows every indication of being able to build on that foundation during the decade of the 1990s. In other words, with continued success, it will enter the twenty-first century as one of the world's most successful and promising medium-sized nations.

The main emphasis in this chapter is on internal trends and developments. These must always be the basis for assessing a country's prospects for progress and projecting the course of its relations with the rest of the world. Turkey became much more directly connected with the world during the 1980s. This process will accelerate during the 1990s. As in many other countries, there are elements in Turkey who would like to turn inward, escape into some form of isolationism or political or religious extremism. They would like to restrict the impact of the world on their societies and limit processes of development which they consider adverse to their interests. Such notions are utopian wherever they are found, and especially for a country with Turkey's geography and history. Nevertheless, reactionary forces are so often overdramatized by journalists, superficial researchers, tendentious critics, and apprehensive government officials that they dominate dialogue about Turkey, and important basic facts and trends are obscured. I may be accused of giving too little attention to Islamic extremists, pan-Turkists, sentimental socialists, and political demagogues in the sections which follow. My purpose is to discuss predominant and characteristic trends and probabilities.

Turkey's geography subjects it to influences from all sides which it cannot escape. The great burst of economic, social, and political development which the country experienced during the 1980s has greatly improved its ability to cope successfully with internal and external forces that impact upon it. Even more important, perhaps, is the fact that Turks have increasingly come to realize that their country need no longer be merely a passive element in international political and economic life. It can influence the world around it, not only in its own neighborhood but in more distant regions.

The disintegration of the Soviet Union has had rapid and profound impact on Turkey. For four centuries, the Russian Empire was always a threat, not only to the Ottoman Empire but to the entire world of the Turks stretching from the Balkans deep into China. It absorbed half of them. The Turks have proved more vigorous than the Russians. Can they transform that physical vitality into political and economic dynamism? The Turks and Muslims of the former Soviet Union look to Turkey to help them achieve momentum, consolidate their independence, and gain status and respect in the world. Turkey has done it—why can't they? As they respond to the appeals of their Turkic brothers, Turks show little sign of losing sight of Russia and the rest of the Slavic world.

A favorite question of observers who like to cast speculation on international relations in "either-or" terms—Will Turkey choose Europe or the Middle East?—can be expanded to offer a third alternative: the Turkic/Muslim republics of the former Soviet Union, including many so-called "autonomous" republics within the Russian federation. The answer has never been one or the other and is now not one or two of the three. It is "all of the above." These "choices" are not contradictory or competitive, they are complementary. And, as the London *Economist* argued so effectively in late 1991,[1] it is very much in the interest of a Europe which regards Turkey as an integral component that Turkey maximize its relations with the Middle East and Central Asia. It is also in the interest of the United States.

Social, Economic, and Political Trends

Turks' Expectations

What do Turks want of life? How do they want their country to develop? Where do they expect to be as the twenty-first century begins?

Most Turks want continued modernization, improvements in the quality of life, opportunity to better themselves as a result of education and work. Their aims are those of most Western-oriented societies: more material goods, better educational opportunities for their children, and affordable medical care that will prolong life. Beyond these elementary desires, they want more leisure time to enjoy sports and entertainments, to go to beach and mountain resorts where many are acquiring second homes, and to be able to travel abroad. But few want to emigrate. Many want to work abroad, and most who go to work abroad intend to return. Most do. Those who do not, usually retain ties with relatives and friends and maintain an interest in life at home. By and large, Turks take it for granted that their desires and aspirations can best be satisfied in the framework of an open society and a democratic political system. But they are not purists about democracy. They want close relations with the United States; they want closer integration into Europe; they consider themselves to be part of the Free World and are distressed when Freedom House, as it does in its 1991 assessment of the state of freedom in the world, lists Turkey as only "partly free" along with countries such as Pakistan, Yemen, Ethiopia, Zimbabwe, and the Central African Republic.

Most Turks are patriotic. In contrast to many Western societies, expressions of patriotism in Turkey are not made apologetically and do not attract ridicule except from a few residual Stalinists on the extreme left and a few religious demagogues on the extreme right. Ataturk's principles continue to be accepted by most Turks as the basis for modern life and the existence of the republic. Turks want their country to be strong, successful, and respected in the world. They expect that its rapidly growing population and economic success will give it greater influence in world affairs in the twenty-first century. They have no desire for territorial expansion, but are increasingly inclined to display a direct interest in the life and welfare of Turkic kinsmen in the Balkans and in Asia. Though the exceptionally high status in Turkish life which military men have enjoyed since the founding of the republic has gradually eroded, the prestige of the military profession remains high. For young men to shirk military service is still less than admirable. Turks believe their country must remain militarily powerful, but notions of what constitutes adequate armed forces are now in flux.

The political, economic, and social degeneration they experienced in the 1970s remains a vivid memory with Turks. They do not want to see the country fall into disarray again and will accept some degree of economic stringency and moderate restrictions on their freedoms to avoid disorder. They are not, however, inclined to consider a turn to authoritarianism as a cure for difficulties or a means of avoiding trouble. They have faith in democracy, which, for the most part, they enjoy practicing and understand as a system for reconciling conflict and adjusting to change while society moves forward. They are not awed or easily duped by politicians whom they regard as much less than superhuman. Except for Ataturk and to some degree Inonu, who have been idolized only in retrospect, Turks are not inclined to glorify political leaders or follow them blindly. Nor do they fear or deplore change of leadership— they take it for granted.[2] They have learned, as many newer democracies have not—that politics must be the art of the possible and that successful conduct of government requires bargaining and compromise. If governments do not meet their expectations Turks are always ready (perhaps too ready) to throw them out and try again. Gradually—but still to a much more limited extent than most Europeans and Americans—Turks have come to expect less of government and think more in terms of private initiative, not only in economic matters, but in many aspects of social and intellectual endeavor as well.

There are exceptions to every generalization made above, some of which will be noted in the sections which follow. They should not be permitted to obscure the fact that in terms of basic cohesion and sense of nationhood, Turkey is comparable to the major nations of Europe and far in advance of most Third World states. Turks possess a high degree of consensus about their society and their republic. The Turkish Republic is new and may in some respects be compared to new Third World states. In its early stages, republican Turkey had to grapple with most of the problems of political consolidation and economic development that have confronted the Third World in the middle and late twentieth century. But Turkey no longer wants to be judged by Third World standards. It is not part of the Third World.

Turkey contains no large alienated groups of people who are challenging the existence of the state or working to change the prevailing political and economic order.[3] Social classes in Turkey do not have deep historical roots. Class attitudes are not sharp and are not sharpening. Income differentials, however, have broadened substantially during the economic upsurge of the 1980s, with the result that successful entrepreneurs (some of very modest origin) have indulged in conspicuous consumption and adopted life styles patterned on Western models of affluence. This phenomenon has so far had few political consequences.

Unlike most European countries, Turkey has no significant groups of guest workers or recent immigrants who present an accommodation or assimilation challenge. During the 1990s, Turkey may have to contend with immigration or refugee movements from the Balkans and the southern republics of the former Soviet Union. Turks do not see this possibility as particularly welcome. Therefore, they understand that a good pragmatic reason for helping the newly independent Turkic/Muslim republics is to keep conditions from deteriorating to the point where large numbers of people want to leave.

Turks are not fearful of the future. Political rhetoric and journalistic exaggeration aside, there are few Turks who would not admit that they are better off as individuals and as a nation in 1991 than they were in 1980. With both ups and downs, they expect to continue to gain during the remainder of the 1990s. They face the twenty-first century not with trepidation, but with confidence. All the trends and characteristics outlined above appear more likely than otherwise to persist through the 1990s.

Religion

The great majority of Turks are Muslims in the same way that most Europeans and Americans are Christians. Their religion is an integral part of their culture and significant in an individual's life primarily as a framework for rites of passage. Especially in the countryside and in provincial towns,[4] adherence to Islamic practices is socially important. For most Turks, avoidance or rejection of Islamic behavioral expectations would disrupt the cohesiveness of their social and professional relationships, make daily life uncomfortable, and bring no compensating advantage. So businessmen in Kayseri will leave their shops to join Friday noon prayers in the mosque in much the same spirit that upstanding citizens in American towns attend Sunday morning church services. Intellectuals who have seldom attended a religious service will be buried with religious rites. The inhabitants of a new *gecekondu* (urban settlement) will raise money to build a mosque as soon as the settlement is connected to power and water lines. This is not because they are Islamic fanatics or beset by feelings of alienation but simply because they feel a need for the structure and symbols of stable life they knew in the village. Highway truckers' stops, roadside shopping centers and even filling stations have small *mescits*—prayer chapels. Only Western alarmists unfamiliar with the quality and tempo of Turkish life could regard these as a manifestation of Muslim fundamentalism.

The main characteristic of Islam in Turkey is that it is routine. Islamic traditions are an integral ingredient of Turkish history, but they are not an overwhelming aspect of it, as they are for Arabs. The pre-Islamic Central Asian past has as much appeal to Turks as any period in the Islamic era. Like many peoples worldwide, as education has spread and modern media developed to reach most of the population, Turks have become increasingly interested in their roots. The heroic Turkic element looms larger than Islam in the Turkish past but Turks see little conflict between the two.

In addition to terminating the caliphate, Ataturk carried out reforms that corrected obscurantist and degenerate tendencies in Turkish Islam, e.g., by outlawing the dervish orders.[5] Under the relatively authoritarian governments that prevailed for the better part of the first three decades of the Turkish Republic, Islam enjoyed no official favor and appeared to be on the defensive. Some classic Ataturkists, rationalist reformers who idealized Western secular society in oversimplified fashion, came close at times to disavowing Islam. Intellectuals of this mentality still sound cries of alarm whenever they perceive religious influences penetrating Turkish political and economic life. Such warnings serve to restrain otherwise moderate politicians from the temptation to engage in demagogic exploitation of religion, but the danger of any virulent form of Islamic resurgence in Turkey during the coming decade is not great.

The opening up of Turkish politics and society that came with the turn to multiparty democracy in 1950 brought what appeared to many to be a resurgence of Islam. The dilemma that classic Ataturkists have had to face ever since—and have not solved—is how can a democratic society suppress religion if a sizable portion of the population considers it important? Since the 1950s Islam has gradually become normalized as a basic, but not predominant, element in the pluralist political and social structure. There is no good reason for thinking that it will not continue in this same fashion.

Islam in Turkey is not an emotional phenomenon. Turks are not readily stirred by demagogic religious appeals. *There is no significant hierarchical structure in Turkish Islam.* Ataturk destroyed the *ulema.* No traditions of honoring religious personalities or men thought to be especially holy have survived in Turkish society as a whole. Intellectuals' concerns over the past two decades about the retrogressive influence of religious schools *(imam-hatip okullari)* on young Turks have proven to be exaggerated. Similar concerns about the negative impact of teaching of morals *(ahlak)* as a cover for religious instruction in public schools since 1981 have also been overdrawn. Turkish youth show no evidence of falling victim to religious fanaticism. Most young Turks feel uneasy if complimented for displaying Islamic piety. Young people in Turkey have much the same tastes as European and American youth. Almost any young Turk feels insulted if you tell him he looks, thinks, or behaves like an Arab or an Iranian. Almost all young Turks glow with satisfaction if you tell them they look or act like an American.

Religious extremism in Iran continues to have no significant impact in Turkey, and there is no prospect that it will. There is no pro-Iranian or pro-Arab political party in Turkey and none is likely ever to gain significant strength. In Turkish politics, politicized Islam—and Arab and Iranian money—play a role no greater than the Moral Majority and the Unification Church in American political life.

Perennial Islamic political leaders—e.g., Necmettin Erbakan—have found appeals to religiosity per se inadequate as a basis for seeking followers and votes, and talk in terms of improving the standard of living, creating jobs through expansion of industry, and increasing earnings from trade with Middle Eastern countries. This economic orientation is evident in the name of Erbakan's current party: *Refah Partisi*—the Welfare Party. The 1982 constitution forbids organization of political parties on the basis of religion, ethnicity, or authoritarian political philosophies. There is little reason to believe that if this restriction were lifted (as it may well be in the 1990s), extremist—including Islamic—parties would flourish.

Increased orientation during the 1990s toward the Islamic republics of the former Soviet Union is unlikely to cause Turkey to become more Islamic in any radical sense, for religious and political attitudes in these republics appear likely to evolve along lines parallel to Turkish experience.[6] The appeal of Turkey to the Islamic peoples of the ex-Soviet Union rests in part on shared Turkic blood, language, and traditions, but it gains its most powerful impetus from the example Turkey provides of a successful, prosperous, democratic country where Islam, modernization, and westernization have been successfully reconciled. The fact that Turks are Muslims provides a comfortable context for broadened relations, but of the different factors that combine to make Turkey appealing as a model for Tatars, Azeris, and Uzbeks, Islam by itself is probably in pragmatic terms the least important.

There are significant modern currents in Turkish Islam and a potential for further development of modernism. Most third- and fourth-generation urban Turks can be said to practice a modernist form of the Muslim faith, though almost none would articulate their religious behavior in such terms. A widespread movement, the *Nurcular*—followers of Said Nursi—stresses that science, modern knowledge, and serious modern education are as essential a component of Islamic faith as tradition. The movement is considered clandestine and subversive by many Turkish intellectuals, but their judgment may be superficial.[7] The same may be true of the negative attitude of many Turkish intellectuals toward the Sufi brotherhoods—especially the Naqshbandis—which, as in the former Soviet Union and many other parts of the Islamic world, are influential, especially in the east and in provincial towns. In many respects, they appear to function in much the same way as Freemasons and other similar fraternities in Christian countries. They are not obscurantist or backward-looking. Nevertheless, too little is known about them. They merit dispassionate study.[8]

The Role of the Military in Turkish Government and Society

The Turkish Republic came into being as the result of military-led rebellion against a remnant Ottoman government and military resistance to foreign intervention in both the east and the west of the country. The republic's founder, Mustafa Kemal (Ataturk), was a well-trained and battle-hardened professional military man, as were most of his close associates. They did not govern, however, as a military junta. In contrast to most recent Third World leaders, Ataturk observed a clear distinction between military and civilian government. On becoming president, he took off his uniform, never put it on again, and insisted that all his associates who held civilian government posts do the same. He established the principle that Turkish military leaders act as trustees of parliamentary government but intervene only if parliamentary processes degenerate or become deadlocked.

Ataturk had autocratic tendencies and habits, but these were consciously and effectively moderated by his deep admiration for Western civilization and his firm commitment to the establishment of a European-type parliamentary system of government in Turkey. He did not succeed in establishing a working multiparty system, but he created the groundwork on which Inonu could turn this ideal into reality. Ataturk's reforms, though incompletely implemented in his lifetime, laid the basis for evolution toward an open, pluralist, secular society in which military forces have a clearly defined, limited role. Ataturk's principles have served Turkey well and have ensured a degree of stability unusual among new states.[9]

Six of the Turkish Republic's eight presidents have been former military men. Turks' conviction that a military man as president could best ensure the stability and security of the state and guarantee continuation of Ataturk's principles was reinforced after the civilian-led Bayar-Menderes government deteriorated and was brought to an end with a coup led by colonels in May 1960. Two generals and one admiral followed as presidents during the next twenty years. The last, Admiral Fahri Koruturk, proved to be a weak president, hesitant to invest his prestige and authority in efforts to stem the political and economic deterioration and combat the terrorism that engulfed the country during the 1970s as coalition governments led by quarrelsome politicians succeeded one another.[10] General Kenan Evren, the chief of staff who led the junta that took power on September 12, 1980, was, in effect, president for the next nine years, for he served as interim head of state until he was elected president concurrently with the referendum that approved a new constitution in November 1982.

The military takeover in September 1980 was the third military intervention into the democratic political process in two decades. Each was different in character. In 1960, colonels deposed the Bayar-Menderes government by direct action. In 1971, mounting terrorism led the senior military leaders to mount a "coup by memorandum" that forced Prime Minister Demirel to resign and permit organization of an above-parties government. In 1980, the country's five top military leaders took power after both repeated warnings to politicians and careful planning.

Following the pattern of the two previous interventions, the military leaders maintained the structure of civilian government in 1980 and immediately disavowed any desire to remain in power. They committed themselves to an orderly process of political reform and restoration of representative government. Hoping to do a more thorough job of correcting shortcomings in the political system than had been done in 1960 or 1971, Evren and his colleagues took three years to complete the transition which (quite unexpectedly to them) brought Turgut Ozal to the prime ministry in October 1983.

This three-year process, though systematic, well-intentioned, open, and humane, was less than fully successful in the terms in which it was undertaken. In other respects it succeeded beyond the generals' expectations. The 1982 constitution includes much detail that would better have been left to legislation. Thus, in some respects it has proven too rigid. The commendable desire of the military leadership to create an electoral and political party system which would discourage a multiplicity of small parties and preclude weak coalition governments was amateurishly implemented. Aiming for a two-party system, the generals created a center-right and a center-left party by rather arbitrary procedures. Much of the population regarded both as hollow fronts, and Ozal's Motherland Party, organized over a good deal of obstruction by the military, swept the October 1983 elections. The Ozal era, which continued with his election as Turkey's second civilian president on October 31, 1989, culminated—and may in a sense have come to an end—when his rival, veteran politician Suleyman Demirel, captured the prime ministry in the elections of October 1991. The two now share leadership responsibility, but not, however, in the sense of being equal partners. Constitutionally, real power rests with the prime minister, i.e., Demirel.

Demirel was twice ousted from the prime ministry by the military (1971 and 1980). Until the very eve of the 1983 elections, Evren attempted to discourage voters from choosing Ozal. To their credit, neither afterward let resentment prevail. They cooperated for the benefit of the country during the ensuing six years. Demirel became an increasingly open critic of military influence on politics during the 1980s. In their avoidance of a subservient relationship with the military, both Ozal and Demirel moved in tandem with the evolution of the attitudes of most Turks. Military leaders themselves showed no disposition to interfere in politics during the 1980s. Junior officers in too close relations with political and religious extremists were summarily dismissed from service. When generals have disagreed with government positions, they have not attempted to take their case to the public. As the Iraq-Kuwait crisis mounted in the fall of 1990, General Necip Torumtay, chief of staff, suddenly resigned over apparent policy conflict with President Ozal. The resignation was handled with discretion by both parties and the substance of their disagreement has never been revealed.

The Turkish military services continue to adhere to a rigid up-and/or-out system which ensures a steady flow of new blood into senior military positions. Professional training is of high quality and includes indoctrination in the nature of civilian-military relationships. Turkish military academies are not infected with politics. Close association with the armed forces of other NATO countries as well as participation in NATO headquarters and regional commands—assignments which all Turkish officers experience at some point as they move up the career ladder—helps inculcate understanding of the desirability of subordination of military forces to civilian authority. There is, thus, little likelihood that Turkish military leaders or any significant group of junior officers will develop political ambitions during the 1990s.

A military career used to be considered a lifetime commitment in Turkey. Professional military officers maintained high standards of integrity and in return were assured emoluments and privileges which gave them elite status and compensated for long years of service in isolated locations with substantial sacrifice for their families. During the past twenty-five years, change has set in. Military professionals need, and receive, good technical education. They are required to learn foreign languages, study management, and master the skills of the electronic age. Military service used to offer men of modest background unique career opportunities. As the Turkish economy has expanded, many other career possibilities have opened up, for Turkish society has always been open to talent. More and more Turkish officers and professional enlisted men now regard military service as a stage on the way to a subsequent civilian career. There is much more turnover among military professionals than there used to be. On retirement, senior officials frequently join industry or business. As the Turkish military services have become more open and interrelate with the society in ways that are normal in modern democratic states, they have lost the aura of special status.

For many years now, universal military service has made more manpower available to the Turkish armed services than can be effectively utilized. Continued high population growth and improvements in health have come to make universal military service a burden on the defense establishment rather than an advantage for it. The term of required military service has been steadily reduced. The collapse of the Soviet Union confronts Turkish military leaders with the necessity of reviewing and revising the concepts that have dominated their manpower thinking for decades. Siphoning lower-quality draftees off into service in the national rural police force—the *Jandarma*—is no longer an efficient solution to either the surplus manpower problem or the requirements of rural policing. Turks regret losing the sense of national commitment and pride that comes from putting all young men through military training where they get to know regions of the country with which they were unfamiliar. As in many other countries, the possibility of broadening universal military service into a system of national service for a variety of other purposes will need to be considered and may lead to important changes in the 1990s.

The Turkish defense establishment has maintained a priority claim on a proportionately larger share of the country's budgetary resources longer than in any other NATO country. Other demands on available revenue—as well as declining foreign assistance—have been bringing military planners under increasing pressure for several years. Patriotism as well as a commitment to national defense, unquestioningly supported by most of the public, have enabled the Turkish military to build up modern defense industries—including manufacture of fighter aircraft—that are bound, given the changes that have occurred during the past three years in Eastern Europe and the fragmentation of the Soviet military establishment, to come under scrutiny. Is further development of military industry an effective expenditure of the country's resources? Turkish generals and admirals are going to have increasing difficulty competing with civilian demands for resources not only for defense industries but for maintenance of large, general-purpose armed forces. Adjustment to the changing strategic environment is one of the highest priority tasks for the Turkish military in the 1990s. It will need to be accomplished on the basis of realistic estimates of the purposes Turkey's defense establishment serves.

Cyprus

Preservation of Turkey's position in Cyprus may still rank among Turkish Ministry of Defense priorities, but it is an anachronistic requirement. Politically, though not economically, Cyprus is likely to continue to stagnate during the 1990s and is more deserving of benign neglect from Western governments than priority peacemaking efforts.

In Turkey as well as in Greece, Cyprus has become a politically marginal issue. The status of the island does not affect any vital interest of either country. Nevertheless, the issue is still sufficiently emotionally charged (though the emotional temperature has fallen in both countries) that any national politician can be harmed by appearing to be soft on it. Thus, it is unwise for any Turkish or Greek politician to accede to or advocate concessions toward a permanent settlement on Cyprus that domestic rivals can use against him. There is, unfortunately, every prospect that this situation will continue to prevail throughout the coming decade.

None of the parties involved—neither Greece nor Turkey, neither the Turks nor the Greeks in Cyprus—is sufficiently disadvantaged by the present status of Cyprus to feel compelled to make any serious concessions to bring about a settlement. All wish to exploit whatever international attention the Cyprus issue can attract for parochial advantage. Cyprus costs Greece nothing, since Greek Cyprus is a profitable undertaking and Greek Cypriots enjoy a higher average standard of living than Greeks in Greece. Turkish Cyprus continues to scrape by economically. Without subsidies in various forms from Turkey, some of which come through Turkish occupation forces, the standard of living might fall. But Turkish Cyprus, with a smaller population than all but one or two of Turkey's seventy-one provinces, does not constitute so great a financial burden that Turkey cannot afford to shoulder it indefinitely.[11]

The United States has no strategic interest in Cyprus. U.S. commercial and political interests are not seriously affected by its divided status. The prime U.S. concern about Cyprus has always been derivative of more fundamental U.S. interests, i.e., that the island not be a source of contention and potential armed conflict between Greece and Turkey and attract intervention from the Soviet Union. The latter concern is no longer relevant. It is difficult to conceive, in fact, how either Turkey or Greece could find it in its interest to take military action against the other over Cyprus. The relationship of both countries to the European Community precludes unilateral action.

Turkey had fallen into a passive stance on Cyprus by 1974. The Greek colonels abetted a coup against Archbishop Makarios by Cypriot ultra-conservatives and triggered Turkish intervention which resulted in occupation of the northern third of the island. Ecevit had tried to persuade Britain to exercise its treaty rights to avoid Turkish military action, but was unsuccessful. The Cyprus situation has been essentially frozen ever since.[12]

Deep-seated European and American public attitudes will probably always continue to give Greece and Greek Cypriots the advantage of being seen as injured parties while Turkey and Turkish Cypriots will continue to be regarded as the instigators of the Cyprus problem. Turkey's maintenance of a comparatively large contingent of troops on the island works in its disfavor. Even if European and American pressure on Turkey were successful in bringing about a major reduction or withdrawal of Turkish forces, restoration of a bi-communal system of government in a "united" Cyprus would probably still prove impossible to negotiate—if, indeed, it is actually desirable. Like Kashmir, which has remained a source of contention and periodic conflict between India and Pakistan for more than forty years, Cyprus could continue indefinitely in its present partitioned condition. Unlike Kashmir, its condition has led to no armed clashes or mini-wars. No lives have been lost in Cyprus since 1974.

Population

During the sixty-nine years of the republic, Turkey's population has grown from an estimated 12 million in 1923[13] to almost 58 million at the beginning of 1992. The final results of the October 1990 census revealed a population of 56,664,458, an increase of 5,808,577 in five years and 11,736,078 more than ten years before. Turkey has been adding well over a million people to its population every year and seems likely to go on doing so well into the twenty-first century. The World Bank projects a population of 68 million by the year 2000 and 92 million by 2025. These may prove to be conservative expectations. While birth rates have remained well above 2 percent since 1970, the death rate has been declining slowly and infant mortality has fallen sharply during the past decade. Thus, net growth has remained high. Overall life expectancy reached age 66 in 1990. The urban population grew at an annual rate of 6 percent during the 1980s. Urbanization reached 60 percent in 1990. Rapid urbanization has so far had only limited effect on the national birth rate. No sharp decline is to be expected during the current decade.

High and steady population growth necessitates high rates of economic growth to sustain the demand for expanded education, health, and social services, and to provide employment for an ever-expanding labor force. The economic reforms of the early 1980s improved the capacity of the country to meet these requirements, but return comes slowly to the economy from investment in training a continually growing population for productive labor. Though reduction of the rate of population growth is not a high priority with Turkish governments or with the public, changes in perspective may develop during the 1990s.

Growth rates among Kurds have been much higher than among the basic Turkish population, but as rural Kurds of the southeast adapt to urban conditions in Turkish cities, high rates of reproduction decline. The process takes considerable time, however—perhaps as much as a generation.

The Economy

Turkey's economic performance since 1980 has been impressive, though all aspects of policy have not been uniformly successful.

GNP growth averaged 5 percent per year for the 1980s, with 1990 topping the decade with almost 10 percent. Growth fell almost to zero in 1991, but is expected to top 5 percent in 1992. The 1991 drop resulted in large part from the losses in income and direct and indirect costs to Turkey as a consequence of the Gulf War. Per capita gross national product (GNP), calculated on the basis of the annual import exchange rate of the U.S. dollar, rose from $1,287 to $2,595 during the decade while, calculated according to the Organization for Economic Cooperation and Development (OECD) purchasing power parity formula, it rose from $2,482 to almost $5,000. The share of agriculture in GNP declined steadily from 22.6 percent in 1980 to 16.3 percent in 1991. Industry accounted for 27.7 percent of GNP in 1991 and services 55.9 percent. Turkey has long since ceased to be principally a provider of primary agricultural produce.

Economic policy since 1980 has emphasized decontrol and openness, realistic exchange rates which have brought Turkish currency to practical convertibility, exports and decontrol of imports, competitiveness in world markets—and consequently quality and productivity in industry, and privatization. After a long history of stubborn adherence to unrealistic exchange rates which drove much of the country's most productive economic activity underground during the 1970s, deprived the government of revenue, and distorted economic priorities, a realistic exchange-rate policy, with adjustments often occurring daily, has been in effect since 1980.

Exports totaled only $2,910 million in 1980 with agricultural products constituting 57 percent. Exports rose to $13,598 million in 1991 (an increase of 367 percent in nominal terms), with agriculture's share falling to 19.7 percent. Turkey was strikingly successful in becoming an exporter of industrial goods during the 1980s. The current balance between agricultural and industrial exports may not change sharply during the 1990s, for Turkey retains a potential for increased food exports to hungry neighbors. Turkey essentially meets its own food requirements (not an insignificant accomplishment for a country whose population is increasing by more than a million each year), but Turkish agriculture still has a substantial potential for increased productivity. By far the largest part of steadily increasing exports will continue to be provided by Turkish industry. Turkey can expect to be earning at least $25 billion annually from exports by the year 2000.

Imports rose from $7,909 million in 1980 to $21,032 million in 1991, a rate of increase of 166 percent, well below the rate of increase of exports. Since Turkey imports very little food or other agricultural products (only 4 percent of total imports in 1991), the major portion of Turkish imports consists not of consumption goods but of inputs into Turkish industry and economic infrastructure. Energy imports (petroleum and coal) accounted for 17.8 percent of imports in 1991.

These statistics show a basically healthy economy and positive trends. So do comparisons of invisible earnings for the decade. Tourism has grown from a marginal industry to a major earner of foreign exchange: It earned a net balance of $212 million in 1980; $2,705 million in 1990, and $2,062 million in 1991 because of the effect of the Gulf War. Tourism income is reported to be rising sharply in 1992, and its earning potential is far from realized. Remittances from Turkish workers abroad were all that enabled the country to maintain a precariously positive balance of payments in the 1970s; they continue to be important, but not crucial, having risen from $1,789 million in 1980 to $3,246 million in 1990 and declined to $2,819 million in 1991. Turkish contractors have continued to earn well from construction projects abroad. While Turkish construction projects were concentrated in the Middle East at the beginning of the decade, a substantial diversification occurred by the end of the 1980s, with Turkish contractors building hotels in the USSR as well as German-financed housing for troops returning from the former German Democratic Republic and eastern Europe.

Turkish contractors, traders, and industrialists are now energetically exploring opportunities in the newly independent ex-Soviet republics, including the non-Muslim ones, and new contracts, investment agreements, and trade arrangements are being made weekly. The Turkish Export-Import Bank, organized in 1989 on the American pattern, provides credit and investment guarantees for much of this activity. It is too early to assess how far Turkish economic involvement in the former Soviet republics will go, but it is conceivable that by the year 2000 a substantial share of Turkish trade, business activity, and foreign investment may be taking place in the Caucasus, Central Asia, Ukraine, and Russia itself. Turkey, with its ready access to the new Muslim nations, may also serve as a convenient partner and base for American, European, and Japanese investors interested in these countries. Some exploratory projects are already being undertaken but it is too early to assess prospects.[14]

The downside of Turkey's economic success can be summed up under four headings: persistent high inflation, slowness in privatization, widening budget deficits, and mounting external debt. The first three are closely interrelated, the last not unrelated to the rest but not particularly serious as long as the Turkish economy continues to expand and debts can be serviced.

Inflation has proved intractable during the 1980s. The most convenient measure of it is the exchange rate for the Turkish lira vis-à-vis the U.S. dollar: It rose from less than 100 in 1980 to more than 7,000 in mid-1992. Nevertheless, Turks have learned to live with inflation with surprising ease. Elaborate indexing arrangements have mitigated its effects. The new Demirel-led government which took office at the end of 1991 committed itself to reducing the rate of inflation to 10–15 percent by 1993. As of mid-1992, there is little expectation that Demirel will take the harsh measures required to reduce inflation that no government during the 1980s was ready to resort to. Prospects for the 1990s are perhaps some reduction but continuation of inflation at a rate well above the OECD average.

Inflation was fed by the high priority the government gave to expansion of infrastructure during the 1980s. Highways were extended, other forms of transport improved, communications modernized and expanded, and the countryside electrified. The enormous Southeast Anatolia Project (Turkish initials: *GAP*) was launched in 1981, centered on the construction of the Ataturk Dam on the Euphrates, and is now nearing completion. Though it has had little international publicity, in scope and effect it is more significant than Egypt's Aswan Dam. It has been financed primarily out of Turkey's own resources.

Inflation has also been fed by government subsidies to state economic enterprises, which still represent a major segment of the Turkish economy. If repeated policy declarations, public discussion, and studies by many private groups and official commissions could bring about privatization, Turkey would have disposed of most of its state-owned industrial operations, mines, and transport organizations by now. Very few have been privatized. They continue to skew utilization of budgetary resources and the direction of development in important sectors of the economy. In this area, too, the new Demirel-led coalition has promised rapid progress. Without drastic action provoked by economic crisis, privatization has proved difficult everywhere.

Demirel's promises provoke skepticism, especially in light of his record as a compromiser on difficult political and economic decisions.

Nevertheless, he may be forced to take bold action by budget deficits which have been soaring during the past five years, reaching an all-time high in 1991. Turkey's tax system underwent some modernization during the 1980s, e.g., the introduction of VAT (value-added tax) in the middle of the decade. But tax collection is still far from efficient, VAT is often evaded, and upper income earners pay a proportionately smaller share of their income in taxes than comparable groups in Europe and the United States.

None of Turkey's economic problems has been serious enough to discourage foreign investment, which has risen sharply during the past three years and promises to continue rising during the 1990s. After a disappointing beginning (average of less than $100 million a year until 1988), net foreign investment reached $663 million in 1989, $700 in 1990, and $783 million in 1991. The total for the decade of the 1980s was $2,369 million. Turkey's economic problems have not been adversely affected. In view of its record of accomplishment during recent years, its high economic momentum, and its good debt servicing performance, Turkey has had no serious difficulty borrowing on the international market. Medium- and long-term foreign debt reached $40,003 million in 1991; short-term debt, $9,117 million. Turkey ran a modest positive current account balance of payments in 1991 and appears likely to continue to do so, so it should be able to service its foreign indebtedness without difficulty well into the 1990s.

Politics

The Vital Center. Turks love competitive party politics. The electorate was ready for party competition when the multiparty system was introduced in 1946 and demonstrated a clear understanding of political choice when the long-dominant Republic People's Party was turned out of office in 1950. Politics vies with football as the favorite form of entertainment for the average Turkish male, though women have become increasingly active in politics as well. Voter participation rates are high. Since 1961, they have never fallen below 64 percent in national elections and rose to an all-time high of 93.3 percent in 1987.

To most outsiders and many Turks, Turkish political life looks disorderly, sometimes almost hopelessly so. Multiparty democracy in Turkey means a multiplicity of parties that are continually fragmenting and reforming and large numbers of politicians whose loyalty to their parties is often far less intense than their desire to hold office. Politicians cross party lines, majorities are short-lived, coalitions fragile, and politicians appear to take an opportunistic view of the national interest while extracting maximum personal advantage from their time in office. All this is to some extent true, but it is also too crass and superficial a view. Beneath the surface, remarkably stable characteristics have persisted in Turkish political life.

In reality the Turkish political spectrum has always consisted of a moderate right and a moderate left, represented by two to four parties which occupy most of the center, and a variety of smaller parties, some extremist, some merely maverick. The following table demonstrates the dominance of the major centrist parties from 1950 to the present.

Strength of Turkish Political Parties
(Percentage of Votes Received in National Elections)

Election Year	Major Centrist Parties	Minor Parties
1950	92.6	7.4
1954	91.4	8.5
1957	87.9	12.1
1961	73.0	27.0
1965	81.6	18.4
1969	73.9	26.1
1973	75.0	25.0
1977	80.1	19.9
1983	98.9	1.1
1987	88.7	11.3
1991	83.0	17.0

The center has never been evenly divided. Except in the 1970s, when the Republican People's Party under Bulent Ecevit enjoyed a peak of popularity, the center-right has ordinarily gained a large margin of votes over the center-left. Even at the peak of his popularity, Ecevit was unable to gain a majority, peaking at 41.3 percent of the total vote in the 1977 national elections. Demirel's Justice Party gained a clear majority of the popular vote in 1965 and came close to repeating that accomplishment in 1969. Compared to his popularity in the 1960s, Suleyman Demirel's 27.5 percent of the popular vote in October 1991 was a rather poor showing. Turgut Ozal's first victory was his greatest but did not constitute a majority: 45.2 percent in 1983. His Motherland Party *gained only 36.3 percent* in 1987[15] and, under the leadership of Mesut Yilmaz, fell to 24.0 percent in 1991.

Analysis of votes cast provides a good measure of the attitudes and temper of the Turkish electorate. Popular votes reveal much less about parliamentary composition and parliamentary strength of parties, for the voting system has changed from almost pure proportional representation in the 1960s to proportional representation sharply modified by a barrier system since 1983. Given the tendency of dissident groups to break off of both major center-right and center-left parties, clear parliamentary majorities have been exceptional in Turkey. Demirel was able to form a single-party government after 1965, Ozal after 1983. No party was able to come close to that goal during the 1970s, a period during which coalitions in Turkey reached their nadir of effectiveness. The current decade has begun inauspiciously, but a coalition or unification of the two competing center-right parties—Demirel's True Path and Ozal's Motherland Party, now led by Mesut Yilmaz,—could bring about a return to stable majority government. Together, these parties attracted more than 50 percent of the vote in October 1991. There is very little difference in their platforms, far less than between either and the Social Democrat Populist Party led by Erdal Inonu, Demirel's current junior partner in governing, which gained only 20.5 percent of the vote in the 1991 election. Though inherently precarious, the Demirel-Inonu coalition has proved remarkably durable during its first months in office.

The reforms the military junta oversaw during the early 1980s were designed to prevent a repetition of opportunistic, indecisive, fragile coalition governments. In pursuing this aim, the military leaders had broad public consensus behind them. They saw in the strong center of the Turkish political spectrum a natural basis for a two-party system. They rejected single-member, winner-take-all parliamentary constituencies, but believed that by modifying proportional representation and requiring a party to gain a certain percentage of votes to qualify for parliamentary seats they could achieve the desired result. The generals also hoped to attract a new generation of more responsible leaders by temporarily banning politicians judged responsible for the deterioration in Turkish politics in the 1970s.

Neither aim was achieved in the 1980s. By the beginning of the 1990s, the Turkish political spectrum was even more fragmented than it had been in the 1970s because the dominant center-right was divided in two and the center-left was even more deeply divided. The division between the two center-left parties that competed in the October 1991 elections was less serious, however, because Ecevit's Democratic Left Party attracted so little support in October 1991 (only 11 percent of votes cast) that it could not be taken seriously as a political competitor by either Inonu or the center-right parties. The cleavages within Inonu's Social Democrat Populist Party brought it close to fragmentation on several occasions from 1988 onward, and it has faced reheated internal crises even though it has formed part of the government since the end of 1991. Personal rivalries and fundamental ideological strains will almost certainly cause the Social Democrats—and the center-left in general—to undergo a realignment during the next few years. The center-left in Turkey has never been able to devise an agenda attractive to a majority of the electorate.

The Extremes. Right and left extremist groups have usually attracted only a small proportion of votes cast, and never more than 20 percent combined. The religious and ultra-nationalist rightist parties reached a peak of appeal with 15.3 percent of the vote in 1973 and 14.9 percent in 1977. An electoral coalition of rightist and special-interest parties attracted 16.5 percent of the vote in the 1991 elections but has since broken up.

Though no extremist political movement has ever come close to attaining power in Turkey—and extremist leaders have exercised direct influence on the governing process only when they have been able to exploit their status in weak coalitions—Turkish intellectuals are chronically concerned about the threat of rightist reaction, whether nationalistic or religious or some combination of both. These concerns make good copy for foreign journalists. Intellectuals will continue to fret and journalists will go on writing stories about the threat of political reactionaries through the 1990s. Worries will be fed by fears of contamination from neo-authoritarian, religious, and pan-Turkist[16] movements in the former Soviet republics.[17] Far leftists, out of frustration over the collapse of "socialism" in the Soviet Empire and for lack of other grist, will feed these fears. Massaging of this problem serves at least one positive purpose in Turkey: It helps insulate the public and the political process from susceptibility to even mild forms of demagogic reactionary appeal.

For almost the entire history of the Turkish Republic the communist party has been illegal. It came closest to gaining a very modest measure of intellectual respect during the late 1980s, when the argument that a country required a communist party to demonstrate its commitment to full democracy gained currency, and Turkish communist leaders returned to Turkey to challenge the ban on them directly. However, arguments for tolerance of communism in Turkey have been left hollow and the appeal of communism and leftist authoritarianism to the electorate (never great) has been reduced almost to zero by the collapse of communism in the Soviet Union and a number of other countries; the decline of communist parties in all Western countries where they had strength; the cessation of Soviet subsidies for them; and the revelation of the corruption, dishonesty, prejudice, arrogance, and incompetence which characterized communism in the Soviet workers' paradise, along with its identification with oppressive gerontocracy in China. The Marxist intellectual and erstwhile terrorist, Dogu Perincek, was able *to attract around 3 percent of the vote in the October 1991 elections* with an amusingly anachronistic Stalinist appeal. It is difficult to envision how leftist extremists could become a political force of any consequence in Turkey during the 1990s, for the overwhelming majority of Turks will be further insulated from the fascism of the left by continual awareness of, and close involvement with, developments in the former Soviet Muslim republics where communism is likely to remain in disrepute.

New Challenges and Opportunities

Kurdish Questions

Perhaps the greatest single challenge Turkey must face in the 1990s is to find ways to successfully adjust its policies toward its Kurdish population. The classic Ataturkist position—that only Christians have official minority status while Muslims cannot be regarded as minorities and are not entitled to recognition—has run its course. The republican approach was actually an extension of the Ottoman principle that Islam took precedence over nationality among Muslims, and it has always been contradictory to the basic nationalist emphasis on Turkishness and de-emphasis on religion in the Turkish Republic.

Turks know very little about their Kurds. Neither does anyone else. How many Kurds are there in Turkey? Estimates vary between eight and twenty-five million. How many Kurds speak Kurdish? How many know Turkish? High-quality Turkish censuses, which are taken every five years, provide no information about ethnic identity or language use among the population. Both Turks and foreigners were officially discouraged—often prevented—from studying Kurds from an ethnolinguistic, sociological, economic, or political point of view.[18] While from the late 1950s onward, Turkish and foreign writers and scholars have produced an impressive body of sociopolitical literature about communities in western and central Turkey,[19] there is no comparable literature on Kurds or on sociopolitical and ethnic relations in the eastern part of the country. Foreign writing on Kurds has for the most part been superficial or partisan and the field, not surprisingly, now verges on the propagandistic.

Until recently, Turkish official policy toward Kurds was narrow and rigid. It is true, of course, that Kurds in Turkey have full conventional civil rights and these rights have meaning (which Kurds do not have, for the most part, in Syria, Iran, and Iraq). Large numbers of Kurds have long been active in all aspects of Turkish life, including government and the military services. Kurds have the same rights as all Turkish citizens to travel inside the country or abroad, to reside where they wish and to be active in politics and civic organizations. But not as Kurds.

Until recently, they did not have the right to use their language anywhere but in the home or in small groups. They were forbidden to engage in cultural activities where Kurdish songs or plays were performed or Kurdish customs were identified as Kurdish. Nothing, even linguistic studies, could be published in Kurdish. At the same time, the government encouraged naive, pseudo-scholarly historical studies aimed at proving, variously, that (1) Kurds are really an ancient Turkish people who penetrated into Asia Minor two or three millennia before other Turks arrived; (2) Kurds as such do not really exist; (3) Kurds are Turks who were corrupted by Iranian influences; (4) the Kurdish language is a degenerated hodgepodge which does not deserve recognition as an independent language; or (5) Kurdish is actually an ancient Turkic dialect. This "research" is offensive to Kurdish and Turkish intellectuals alike and provokes an equally irrational and emotional response. Considering the high quality of most Turkish historical and linguistic research, this pseudo-scholarly writing has been an embarrassment to Turkish and Western scholars alike.[20]

Officially, use of the Kurdish language in administration, in courts, or for political campaigning was proscribed. Maintenance of all these restrictions was incompatible with Turkey's desire to be credited with practicing full democracy and measuring up to international standards in human rights. Fortunately, political leaders have reached consensus during the past two years, and many of the restrictions have been lifted. But the lifting has come so late that it is not yet evident that it has produced the positive effect that had been hoped for.

For too long, Turkish governments have been too ready to resort to oppression and force in Kurdish areas. Violence by the Marxist Kurdish Workers' Party (PKK) left little choice and brought out the worst in military and civil officials trying to contain it. The problem has worsened steadily since 1982.

However, there are two sides to every story. The Kurdish issue has suffered in recent years from a great deal of oversimplification by Kurdish activists and their supporters who have replaced a complex and controversial history with a body of oversimplified mythology, and by journalists who are unfamiliar with the social conditions or political past of this part of the world. Kurds are demonstrably one of the more ancient peoples of the Middle East. In comparison to them, Turks are relative newcomers, having entered Anatolia—in political terms—with the Battle of Manzikert in 1071, only five years after the Norman conquest of Britain.[21] Kurds for the last 2,000 years have played off the Persians to their east against the empires to their west—first the Romans and the Byzantines and then their Ottoman successors.

Historically, Kurds played a larger role than ethnic Turks in the tragic ethnic turmoil in the Ottoman-Persian-Caucasian border area during the late nineteenth and first quarter of the twentieth century. The losers were the Armenian and Assyrian (Nestorian) communities that had also existed in this region since ancient times and to whose presence only a few ruins now attest. Late twentieth century Kurdish activists have conveniently forgotten the Assyrians. During the 1980s, Kurds forged alliances of convenience with extremist Armenian exile groups. Such tactics, combined with the espousal of Marxism-Leninism by young Kurdish militants, made dialogue with rational Turks more difficult at the very time when it might have been possible to initiate it. The tactics also deprived them of international respectability.

Several important facts about Turkey's Kurds need to be kept in mind: no more than half of them (perhaps fewer) now live in the traditional Kurdish provinces of the southeast; socially and economically, those who have remained there have maintained the most traditional society in Turkey; they have been extremely conservative politically with politics revolving around tribal and clan leaders. At the same time, Kurds have been among Turkey's most energetic internal migrators. For at least thirty years they have been streaming into the cities in the south, center, and west of the country. Kurdish migration does not differ much from migration from other parts of the country—e.g., the Black Sea region or Central Anatolia. Kurds come to improve their economic status and to obtain better education for their children. Until recently Kurdish migrants in urban areas have seldom been politically active as Kurds. In the *gecekondu* suburbs of cities such as Adana, Ankara, Istanbul, and Izmir their assimilation into modern Turkish life accelerates. Only very recent evidence indicates that the sense of alienation among most Kurds is greater than among other rural groups in Turkey who migrate to cities—which means that it is quite modest.

Like other Turkish citizens, Kurds migrate abroad, too, in search of work and to accumulate capital to improve their status when they come home—perhaps to the southeast, perhaps to the cities. Kurds from the southeast constitute a significant share of Turkish laborers in Germany. Here, a process familiar in the history of development of nineteenth and twentieth century nationalism takes place: small numbers of migrants become increasingly aware of their Kurdishness and susceptible to the appeals of nationalist intellectuals, political activists, and agitators.

Thus, Kurdish self-awareness and self-assertiveness in Turkey has been nurtured by currents from two directions: external and internal. To make this observation is not to say that greater self-awareness among Kurds is not genuine. That is what Turks have come to realize at the opening of the 1990s. The wonder, perhaps, is that manifestations of

Kurdish nationalism in Turkey have until recently been so weak. There was little evidence until recently that the PKK had developed deep roots among the population. Its lack of roots had driven it to use intimidation, violence, and terror as its primary techniques for getting the population to support it. One of the most interesting and important questions for the 1990s is: Will PKK militants succeed in becoming the prime spokes-men for Kurdish aspirations—whatever they may be? Turkish leaders need answers to two sets of questions: (1) How much influence has the PKK gained? Is it based on conviction or intimidation? and (2) What do Kurds in Turkey really want? Is there any consensus?

The situation of Kurds in Iran and Iraq during the 1980s has been incomparably worse than in Turkey. In these two countries, oppression and violence against Kurds at various times during the past decade can justifiably be characterized as genocidal. It cannot in Turkey. Turkey, aspiring to, and in most respects operating, an open political and social system, has been more accessible and therefore an easier target for pro-Kurdish activists in the West. Until the denouement of the Gulf War in early 1991 brought the tragic situation of Kurds in Iraq to international attention, the publicity resulting from the activities of human rights groups in Europe and America created the widespread impression that Kurds were oppressed primarily in Turkey.

It should be noted that the contribution of Soviet and pro-Soviet pro-paganda outlets in fostering a Pro-Kurdish/anti-Turkish view has been substantial. From the 1920s onward, the Soviet Union found the Kurdish issue an attractive entry point for meddling in Middle Eastern politics and at times invested considerable effort in overt and covert activities encouraging Kurdish dissidence throughout the region where Kurds live.[22] This process reached a peak at the end of World War II. Frustrated in 1946 in overt efforts to encourage Kurdish separatism in Iran as a basis for gaining leverage over Kurds throughout the entire region where they live, Moscow in subsequent years made use of the rel-atively small Kurdish minority in the Caucasus to staff a variety of opera-tions fostering Kurdish nationalism and dissent. There is not a great deal of evidence that broadcasts, propaganda, and agent activities had great impact on Kurds in Turkey, but these activities alarmed Turkish govern-ment and military leaders and helped justify maintenance of a highly restrictive policy. Any softening, any concessions, they feared, would be exploited by the Soviets. These were not groundless fears. Publications in Kurdish, which few Turks could read, would spread pro-Soviet propa-ganda, expressions of Kurdish culture would be turned into anti-Turkish agitation, and Soviet money would flow in to support political activists and subsidize any organizations that were permitted to form.

Kurds played a minor role in the great wave of Soviet-supported terror in Turkey in the 1970s. The basic strategy of the supporters of terror was to encourage extreme demands and violent actions by both leftists and rightists throughout Turkey.[23] But both Turkish and Western students of this period share the hypothesis that Moscow shifted its strategy for subversion in Turkey to foster Kurdish militancy after the 1980 military takeover brought terrorism in most parts of the country to low ebb. From the beginning, the PKK was openly Marxist. It was able to use Syria as an operational base during a period when Syria was unabashedly pro-Soviet and was receiving large amounts of Soviet military aid. PKK defectors and captives were providing evidence by the mid-1980s of Soviet links. Turkish requests, demands, and pressure on Syria did not bring restrictions on the PKK. It continued, through 1991, to operate from Syria. A combination of direct diplomatic pressure and more discreet threats of retaliation offer some promise of gaining Syrian cooperation in suppression of the PKK in 1992.

The collapse of the Soviet Union coincides with ever-widening recognition in Turkey that the republic's Kurdish policy needs to be revised. The process is now under way, but the outcome is far from clear. Fresh consideration of the status of the Kurds in Turkish society leads inevitably to questions about the nature of the Turkish state and governmental system. The Turkish Republic has been a highly centralized state. Democratization after 1950 had only limited impact on the centralized state structure. In 1991, for the first time it became possible to discuss federalism openly in Turkey as a possible alternative form of organizing the state.

Kurds are by far the most numerous but by no means the only Muslim ethnic group that has been submerged in the amalgam of modern Turkish society. There are purely Turkic groups such as Turkmen and Yoruks. There are the Laz of the eastern Black Sea coast. They are an ancient Georgian-related subgroup, essentially the same people as the Ajars of Georgia who were given their own "autonomous" republic in the 1920s because the majority of them were Muslim.[24] There are also several hundred thousand Islamicized Georgians in the interior of the northeast, many of whom still speak a dialect close to standard Georgian.[25]

Several million people in Turkey, living in many parts of the country, are descendents of North Caucasians and Abkhaz who came as refugees to Turkey in the great flood that followed the Russian conquest of the North Caucasus in the late 1850s and 1860s. They were augmented periodically by additional refugees from anti-Tsarist and anti-Soviet rebellions. The most numerous element in this Caucasian immigration were the Circassians, and all have tended to be grouped together in Turkey as *Cerkesler*. The opening up of the North Caucasus, which is now occurring in the wake of Soviet collapse, and the resumption of links between Caucasian-origin Turks and their kinsmen in the Caucasus, may result in a reassertion of separate identities in Turkey: Chechens, Kabardans, Karachays, Nogays, Kumyks, Lezgins, Avars, and others.

Sizable groups of Turks are descendants of refugees or returnees from Crimea and the Balkans, the most recent being Turks who fled the Bulgarian forced-assimilation campaign of the late 1980s. During Ottoman times, large numbers of Albanians and Bosnians migrated to what is today northwestern Turkey in search of greater economic opportunity. Modern Turkey may contain two to three million of their descendants. Even this listing does not exhaust all the groups that can still be identified, not far beneath the surface, in the population of the Turkish Republic. The exchange of populations between Greece and Turkey in the 1920s brought hundreds of thousands of Greek-speaking Muslims from Greece and Crete, many of whom settled in the Aegean region but some of whom were reestablished as far east as Cappadocia. Finally, there are the religious minorities within Islam, primarily Shi'ites known in Turkey as *Alevi*.

Recognition of the Kurds as a distinct ethnic group with language, cultural, and political/organizational entitlements confronts Turkey with the likelihood that some, at least, of these other groups will also wish to assert their identity. The thought was an anathema to classic Ataturkists whose ideal was a Turkish population with little or no ethnic or religious differentiation. The Turkish elite, government officials, and the great majority of Turkish politicians accepted this concept until recently. The Demirel-Inonu coalition government, which took office at the end of 1991, has with its initial policy pronouncements on the Kurds brought the country across a watershed that makes turning back to old positions impossible. During the 1990s, Turkey must develop a societal and legal order which recognizes that the country's population consists of many strands that are entitled to some degree of identity if they desire it. The country will emerge stronger if it is successful in this endeavor.

The situation is rich with both opportunities and dangers. The experience of other countries provides lessons for Turks to ponder. Why should Kurds who are scattered all over Turkey and to a significant degree already assimilated into the mainstream of Turkish life and politics not be given appropriate recognition? Why cannot other ethnic groups who wish to do so be permitted to assert themselves—even to the point of functioning as political lobbies—in the same way ethnic and interest groups operate in other democratic systems? The danger to be avoided is ethnic structuralism. The examples of failed communist states such as Yugoslavia and the Soviet Union demonstrate the unwisdom of casting everything having to do with state structure and administration in ethnic terms. Federalism does not necessarily have to take ethnic form. Federalism based on regions is a far more flexible concept, one which permits automatic adjustment as rapidly developing societies change and people move from one region to another.

The idealism with which the Demirel-led government is approaching the Kurdish problem may not bring rapid results, for the coalition is weak and in constant danger of fragmenting. Nevertheless, the problem is on the political agenda and cannot be removed. Basic changes in constitutional systems should be based on broad consensus. Turks need to study other systems objectively and do deeper analysis of the way their own system has been operating. They could weaken their state; they could greatly strengthen it and equip it for steady progress in the twenty-first century. One generalization seems certain: by the year 2000, Turkey is likely to have evolved a different concept of the internal organization of the republic and a different relationship between politics and ethnicity than it has today.

The Black Sea Initiative

One of the most creative initiatives Turkey undertook at the end of the 1980s was to launch a project for bringing all the countries of the Black Sea region together to expand economic relations, develop joint technical and scientific projects, monitor and control pollution, and encourage tourism and cultural exchanges. The collapse of the Soviet Union has increased the urgency of this initiative. In addition to its economic, technical, and cultural objectives, it offers a framework for dealing with political and security problems that may arise among all the states of the region, including Russia. In meetings in Istanbul at the end of June 1992, formal agreements on cooperation among Black Sea states were signed. Armenia, Azerbaijan, and Central Asian leaders were also present.

The Collapse of the Soviet Union

The collapse of the Soviet Union confronts Turkey with far more opportunities than problems. Economic opportunities have already been noted in the section above on the economy, and reduction of the Soviet military threat has also been mentioned. It is too early to judge, however, to what degree military developments in (or tensions between) the successor states will be a problem that Turkish military planners will have to take into account in the 1990s. Turkey has disavowed any intention of intervening militarily in inter-republican clashes in former Soviet territory,[26] but it is conceivable that Turkish forces might be invited by these states to play the role of peacekeepers between or within them. The most basic gain for Turkey from Soviet collapse is that it removes the pervasive "Fear of the Bear" that has overshadowed Turkish foreign policy during the entire existence of the Turkish republic.[27]

Generations of Turkish diplomats operated in a tradition that required almost obsequious correctness toward Moscow and fostered apprehension lest anything more than the most benign and formalistic cultural relations with the Turks and Muslims of the Soviet Empire might provoke Soviet retaliation.[28] Of course, not all Turkish diplomats and relatively few military men adhered to this pattern of behavior. Nevertheless, it often led Turkish governments to tolerate Soviet support of surrogates who sponsored anti-Turkish propaganda, training of terrorists, and subversive activities within Turkey (e.g., Palestinians, Syrians, Bulgarians, Armenian terrorists, and Kurdish Marxists). In the 1970s, it contributed to Turkish willingness to tolerate a high degree of Soviet-sponsored subversion that included the drug trafficking and massive terrorism that came close to undermining the Turks' confidence in themselves.

Republican Turkey continued and formalized the Ottoman policy of giving asylum (and rapid citizenship) to all refugees of Turkish blood from the Caucasus and both Soviet and Chinese Central Asia. These people were permitted to organize only for welfare and cultural purposes. Political organizations, information activities, and agitation of any kind were strictly proscribed. With patience and skill, determined individuals could evade some of the prohibitions, so Caucasian- and Central Asian-origin Turks were able to publish journals and memoirs. A few Turkish historians and other scholars engaged in study of these peoples and their history,[29] but compared to the freedom Soviet and Chinese exile activists and scholars enjoyed in Europe and America, the Turkish position until recently remained highly restrictive.

Turkey aimed to be as neutral as Switzerland when World War II threatened. After war broke out, the country remained officially neutral but tilted gradually toward the Allies. In early 1945, Turkey declared war on Germany and Japan and became a founding member of the United Nations—and thereby also an ally of the USSR. These actions did not deter Stalin from making crude territorial demands both before and after the war ended. These drove Turkey into the Western alliance. Once in, Turkey became a strong and dependable proponent of collective security, sending troops to Korea in 1950 who distinguished themselves, and eagerly joining NATO in 1952.

Since the Truman Doctrine was promulgated in February 1947—more than forty-five years ago—Turkey's highest-priority security relationship has been with the United States. In this context, Turkey has been a consistent and dependable supporter of NATO policies, maintained troops ready for action on both the Balkan and Caucasian fronts, and provided facilities for specialized intelligence collection against Soviet targets. From the 1960s through 1990, Turkey was reticent about cooperation with the West in the Middle East, arguing that NATO obligations did not apply to threats or problems in noncommunist areas. President Ozal reversed this policy as the Kuwait-Iraq crisis mounted in intensity in the autumn of 1990 to the great benefit of Turkey's standing in the United States.

During the summer and autumn of 1991, Turkey was slow (though not so slow as the U.S. Government) to recognize that Gorbachev had failed, and the Soviet system was approaching terminal collapse. Once the decision to change policy was taken, implementation came fast. In September 1991, the Turkish Foreign Ministry sent teams of diplomats to the capital of each Soviet republic to assess political developments and the desirability of closer relations, including establishment of diplomatic posts and granting of formal recognition. Rapid action was recommended when these teams returned. In one of its last foreign-policy acts, the ANAP (Motherland Party)-led government of Mesut Yilmaz recognized Azerbaijan on November 9.

By the end of 1991, Turkey had totally abandoned its Moscow-centered stance and embarked full-force on a program of active relations with the Soviet successor states. In quick succession, the presidents of Uzbekistan, Turkmenistan, and Kyrgyzstan were welcomed by Ozal in Ankara in November and December 1991 and given promises of support and assistance. Turkey has been more cautious in dealing with Muslim nationalities within the Russian republic who also look to her for support and inspiration: e.g., the Tatars and Bashkirs, the many Muslims of the North Caucasus of whom the Chechens are the most numerous, and the Crimean Tatars. All seek closer contacts with Turkey. Even the Gagauz of Moldavia, who are Christian Turks, have displayed a strong interest in relations with Turkey which has in some degree been reciprocated.[30] Public interest in all these peoples has been inspired by extensive press coverage and visits of journalists and academics to their homelands.

Turkey received millions of refugees from the Caucasus and the Crimea in the nineteenth century, and the flow of Turkic and Muslim refugees and escapees from all parts of the USSR never stopped, though it slowed to a trickle from the 1950s onward. Most of these people have assimilated well into Turkish life, but to an extent that has only recently become apparent, many have also retained recollections of their origins. The earlier rationale for restraining them and discouraging attempts to establish contact with their kinsmen has now disappeared. An upsurge of activity of many kinds among these people must now be expected, including a proliferation of private and official contacts with the territories of their origin.

In terms of rewarding economic relationships, the Ukraine and Russia are likely to be as important to Turkey as the Muslim and other Caucasian republics.

Among other gains from the collapse of the Soviet Union will be the collapse of residual subversive and propaganda operations that Moscow continued to support in Turkey until the end of the 1980s—though at a level greatly reduced from the 1970s. As KGB and communist party files continue to be exposed and studied and former operatives tell their stories, revelations embarrassing to Turkish communist party members (groups such as the Marxist-Leninist Armed Propagandists, Revolutionary Youth (Dev Sol), Armenian terrorists, and radical Arabs as well as journalists who functioned as Soviet agents) are likely to come to light.

It is difficult to envision how any of the Soviet successor states other than Russia itself at some future date might find it in its interest to devote resources to resuming subversive political activity or terrorism in Turkey. Among the constructive challenges Turkish foreign policy will face during the 1990s will be to develop a relationship with Russia that overcomes 400 years of antagonism and creates a long-term basis for mutual respect and cooperation. If this is to occur, Turkey will also be well advised to develop at long last a corps of professional academic and governmental Russian specialists comparable to those who exist in most other Western countries.

Turks have watched the collapse of the Soviet Empire with awe approaching disbelief. The liberation of the Muslim republics has generated excitement and curiosity, which is likely to persist. Turks now know that the road to reform and modernization that Ataturk chose for them seventy years ago has stood the test of time far more successfully than Lenin's system. Lenin's statues have been pulled down throughout the former Soviet Empire. Except from an occasional demagogue, Ataturk's monuments are not in danger. Ataturk's sayings retain meaning for Turks. In times of stress, as at the end of the 1970s and the beginning of the 1980s, Ataturkism provided a common denominator on which almost all Turks could agree. Ataturk was, however, never deified. He has emerged from history more human as his life and work have been studied and restudied. In Ataturk, Turks see a mirror image of themselves with both their strengths and their failings.

Only now, as the twentieth century approaches its end, is it becoming clear in the world beyond Turkey that Ataturk would have been a much better model for the developing world than Lenin. If some of the faltering states of the Third World and the newly free ex-Soviet republics have the good fortune to find leaders with some combination of Ataturk's qualities, they will be fortunate indeed.

Notes

1. "Turkey, Star of Islam," *Economist,* Special Section, December 14, 1991.

2. Adnan Menderes, who was ousted in a military coup in 1960 and hanged after a long trial in 1961, has been rehabilitated in recent years and restored to an honorable place in modern Turkish history.

3. Kurds? Not yet, at least. Most of Turkey's Kurds are functioning constructively within the framework of the Turkish political and economic system. This could, but is not necessarily predestined to, change during the coming decade. Kurds nevertheless represent a serious challenge for Turkey. They will be further discussed below.

4. The same is true of the suburbs of most large cities, which are the gateway for passage into urban life and to which people from the villages and country towns transfer their customs and norms.

5. They were driven underground, where they continued to play an important religious role at the popular or folk level. With the lifting of official persecution in the 1950s, they again came to the surface and since then have been officially regarded as cultural phenomena.

6. It may, of course, be premature to judge how political currents that have proliferated among Muslims in the ex-Soviet Union will develop. Religion was a strong component of underground opposition to communism and Russian domination. The fact that a religious leadership in Iran successfully defied outside powers generated sympathy and a desire for emulation among some Soviet Muslims. For others, puritanical Wahhabi doctrines seemed an effective antidote to the materialism and corruption that became pervasive under Soviet rule. Just how much political force these conservative, austere religious attitudes will have in democratic political life in these newly independent republics remains to be seen. The main preoccupations of their rapidly growing populations are almost all economic—how to overcome the effects of Soviet colonial-style exploitation and degradation of the environment and begin rational agricultural and industrial development. Radical Islamic movements are strong on protest but have not advanced credible agendas for coping with the most serious problems that face ex-Soviet Muslims. The Sufi orders, on the other hand, which steadily gained adherents during the Soviet period, are strong among some of the most progressive elements in these societies. Most of them are not notably conservative. Some, in fact, are dynamically modern in their approach to economic and social issues.

7. For a recent study of this movement by a Turkish academic specialist see Serif Mardin, *Religion and Social Change in Modern Turkey: The Case of Bediuzzaman Said Nursi*, Albany: State University of New York Press, 1989.

8. The Naqshbandi order, which includes politicians and businessmen as adherents, provides a natural medium for contacts with the emerging entrepreneurial classes of the newly independent Turkic republics of the ex-Soviet Union.

9. Turkey is both a new and an old state. The Turkish Republic was juridically the successor to the Ottoman Empire but it also represented a sharp break with the principles of governance that prevailed in the Ottoman Empire. The Ottoman Empire was not a national state. It was multi-national and multi-religious with clearly defined provisions for association of non-Muslims and non-Turks with the state. The sultans combined secular and religious authority. The empire was an autocracy which began to develop representative institutions only during its final decades. The Republic of Turkey was launched as, and has remained, a secular national state in which civil authorities have no religious status. In contrast to the United States (but in keeping with the practice of many European countries), the Turkish government takes responsibility for administering portions of the country's religious establishment.

10. Koruturk stepped down when his term expired in April 1980. Adhering to strict legality, he made no effort to influence Turkish government or political life afterward. The deadlock which ensued as parliament proved unable to elect a new president continued until September 1980, when the military leadership, constituting itself a National Security Council, intervened in a bloodless coup to break it.

11. When Ozal recently broke the long-held taboo and stated that the Turkish presence in Cyprus was costing the Turkish taxpayers over $200 million per annum, some commentators did in fact begin to suggest that the price was too high and unnecessarily diverted funds needed elsewhere.

12. For a comprehensive analysis of these events see Paul B. Henze, "Turkey, the Alliance and the Middle East," Working Paper No. 36, Woodrow Wilson Center for Scholars, Smithsonian Institution, Washington, D.C., December 1981.

13. The first republican census in 1927 counted 13,648,000 within borders that did not include the Hatay, ceded by France from its Syrian mandate in 1939.

14. The *Economist's* Special Section, "Turkey, Star of Islam," December 14, 1991, makes a good case for utilization of Turkey as a base for business with the Middle East and the former Soviet areas. It advises, "Look eastward, Europe, and see why you need a successful Turkey."

15. Nevertheless, the features of the 1982 constitution, designed to discourage party fragmentation and reward winners, translated this vote into an absolute majority in parliament. Eventually, the fact that the parliamentary majority did not reflect the distribution of opinion in the electorate worked to the disadvantage of the Motherland Party, as became clear in 1991.

16. Why pan-Turkism should have acquired the reputation in the twentieth century of an evil, "fascist" movement, while pan-Arabism and pan-Africanism have enjoyed wide favor as liberal, "progressive" concepts, deserves more incisive analysis than it has received.

17. Extreme political movements have proved slow to develop in the ex-Soviet republics and they are not widely regarded as an immediate danger. The likelihood that such movements would have feedback influence on Turkey seems fanciful.

18. There has been a veritable flood of publishing about Kurds in Turkey during 1991 and 1992. Little of what has appeared is based on serious anthropological or ethno-linguistic research. A rare exception by a young Turkish scholar, based on extensive field research, is Lale Yalcin-Heckmann, *Tribe and Kinship among the Kurds,* Frankfurt: Verlag Peter Lang, 1991.

19. A sampling of works in English includes: Mahmut Makal, *A Village in Anatolia,* London: Vallentine, Mitchell & Co., 1954; John F. Kolars, *Tradition, Season and Change in a Turkish Village,* Chicago: University of Chicago Press, 1963; Paul J. Magnarella, *Tradition and Change in a Turkish Town,* New York: John Wiley & Sons, 1974; Peter Benedict, *Ula, an Anatolian Town,* Leiden, Holland: E.J. Brill, 1974; Kemal Karpat, *The Gecekondu, Rural Migration and Urbanization,* Cambridge: Cambridge University Press, 1976; Fatma Mansur, *Bodrum, a Town in the Aegean,* Leiden: E.J. Brill, 1972; June Starr, *Dispute and Settlement in Rural Turkey,* Leiden: E.J. Brill, 1978.

20. Examples include Mehmet Eroz, *Dogu Anadolunun Turklugu (The Turkish Character of Eastern Anatolia),* Istanbul: Turk Kultur Yayini, 1975; Sukru Kaya Seferoglu, *Anadolu'nun ilk Turk Sakinleri, Kurtler (The First Turkish Inhabitants of Anatolia, the Kurds),* Ankara: Turkish Cultural Research Institute, 1982; and Aydin Taneri, *Turkistanli bir Turk Boyu, Kurtler (A Turkestani Turkish Clan, the Kurds),* Ankara: Turkish Cultural Research Institute, 1983.

21. Turks penetrated from Central Asia into the area north of the Caucasus and the Black Sea much earlier. From the sixth century onward, Byzantine sources report contacts with Turkic peoples: Khazars, Pechenego, Cumans, and finally Seljuks. These have been extensively investigated by a Hungarian scholar, Gyula Moravcsik who published a two-volume study in 1983, *Byzantinoturcica (Turkish Language Remnants in Byzantine Sources),* Leiden, Holland: E. J. Brill. With the emergence into independence of the Turkic peoples of the former Soviet Union, we can expect a greatly increased interest in this obscure history in Turkey and elsewhere. The Turkish Historical Association has published several major source-works in the past few years.

22. I am not implying that Kurdish aspirations for accelerated economic development, cultural autonomy, and political recognition were exclusively the result of Soviet propaganda and manipulation. The fact remains, however, that Kurds have been the slowest of major Middle Eastern peoples to experience the growth of modern nationalism. Kurdish rebellions in eastern Turkey in the 1920s were manifestations of resistance by tribal leaders to imposition of central

government authority and antipathy to Ataturk's secularizing reforms. The extent to which comprehensive nationalism has superseded tribal loyalties is even now far from clear.

23. Information on Moscow's subversive programs in Turkey is almost certain to emerge as files are opened in Moscow and the Caucasus (Azerbaijan, e.g., which was often said to be a center of operations directed at Turkey) and knowledgeable officials begin to talk in the wake of the collapse of Soviet power.

24. Georgian nationalists now regard them as purely Georgian and maintain that few have continued to be Muslim. Ajaria experienced some political turmoil during the first months of 1991 but has been quiet since. Though people in both Turkey and Georgia have been renewing family ties since the border was opened, there has been no evidence in either country of interest in political links and neither country has advanced irredentist claims. See Paul B. Henze, *Turkey and Georgia*, P-7758, Santa Monica, CA: RAND, 1992.

25. They have shown no interest in being reunited with Georgia, which has not controlled the region since the Middle Ages. In addition they are divided from the Orthodox Christian population of Georgia by religion, having gradually converted to Islam from the sixteenth century onward.

26. Prime Minister Demirel warned Azerbaijan in December 1991 to avoid escalation of tension with Armenia and reminded them that diplomatic recognition should not be interpreted as an indication that Turkey will back Azerbaijan in action against neighbors. This places Turkey in the position of responsible elder brother vis-à-vis the newly independent Turkic republics and could, in effect, establish a policy of support for mediation between quarreling post-Soviet nations. Demirel's remarks brought a constructive response from Azerbaijan and praise from Armenia, but as fighting in Nagorno Karabakh has escalated and spread to Nakhichevan, Turkish leaders have had to face pressure from their own society to intervene. Responsible Turkish leaders, foremost Demirel, have continued to resist this pressure.

27. On the positive side, this fear reinforced Ataturk's dictum against irredentism and developed the habit among Turks of avoiding thinking in terms of territorial expansion. This was, of course, a net gain, for irredentist agitation or continuation of the kind of intervention that occurred in the Caucasus and Central Asia in the years immediately after the Russian revolution would have entangled the new Turkey in unproductive adventurism and diverted energy from the all-important task of consolidating the republic.

28. Turkey's then foreign minister, Ilter Turkmen, in a conversation in his office in Ankara in May 1981, told me that those like myself in the West who speculated that national feelings among the Turks of the Soviet Union might eventually become a problem for Moscow were quite unrealistic. Azeris and Uzbeks and all the rest, he insisted, had been turned into good Soviet citizens, pleased with the economic advantages that the Soviet system had brought them. While national feelings might still motivate some of the older generation, youth

would be content to capitalize on the advantages communism had brought them, since they knew no other political or social system, and would probably be gradually Russianized.

29. There has been almost no scholarship in Turkey on Russian and Soviet history or Russian culture and almost no teaching of Russian or other languages of the Soviet Empire. Until recently, Turkey's foreign broadcast services have had no broadcasts in Russian or other languages used in the Soviet Union except Azeri—where the pretense was that such broadcasts were destined only for Azeris in Iran.

30. The Ministry of Culture, which became active in the 1970s in publication of Turkic literary classics and other writing on Turkic peoples, recently issued a thick paperback on the Gagauz: Harun Gungor and Mustafa Argunsah, *Gagauz Turkleri, Tarih, Dil, Folklor ve Halk Edebiyati (The Gagaus Turks—History, Language, Folklore and Popular Literature)*, Ankara: Kueltuer Bakanligi Yayinlari, 1991.

2

Turkey's New Eastern Orientation

Graham E. Fuller

Turkey now inhabits a new world. Within a few years of Gorbachev's coming to power, Turkey's geopolitical environment began to change in three out of four directions of the compass. To the northwest, truly independent Balkan states have emerged, which are now in the process of creating a new Balkan state system. Directly to the north, Turkey has an opportunity for direct relations by sea with a newly independent Ukraine and a distinct new Russian entity. To the northeast, three independent states have appeared on the scene in the Caucasus with whom Turkey has already established direct relations: Georgia, Armenia, and Azerbaijan. Further to the east, five independent Muslim states have emerged in former Soviet Central Asia. Not only has Turkey acquired a new set of political relations with these entities, but it will be hard put to avoid being drawn into complex new regional quarrels that in a few cases have already moved into armed conflict.

Even to Turkey's south, while no new states have yet emerged, a far more difficult situation has arisen in the Persian Gulf with the Gulf War, Saddam Hussein's bid for regional power and his quest for weapons of mass destruction, and the potential breakup of Iraq. And an Arab-Israeli peace process—far more promising than anything that has emerged in the past before—also may open possibilities of new relations between Turkey and the Arab world.

Turkey is thus surrounded by new opportunities and potential new problems—all of which pose extraordinary and complex challenges. These challenges have come in a decade when Turkey itself has hardly been standing still: The eighties have probably brought sharper change to Turkey than perhaps any time since Ataturk, who founded the new Turkish secular nation-state on the ruins of the Ottoman Empire.

In a period when chaos will predictably be a major feature of political events in the Balkans and among the republics of the former Soviet

Union—not to mention in the Middle East—the international system benefits from a nation whose stability and track record for international prudence is by and large impressive. (In this context, I view the Cyprus issue as a major exception, where Turkey, rightly or wrongly, chose to move unilaterally rather than in conjunction with international instruments.)

The Impact of Turkey's Domestic Change on Its Foreign Policy

If changes in the international climate have been dramatic, so have the rapid developments in Turkey's own domestic situation over the past decade. Potential geopolitical changes in Turkey's foreign policy can only be understood in this context.

Turkish politics had in fact already begun to change well in advance of the Gorbachev revolution. Turgut Ozal, first as minister of state for the Turkish economy, later as prime minister, and finally as president, has arguably been one of the most influential political figures on the Turkish scene since Ataturk; by the time of Gorbachev's ascendance he had already helped bring about a profound reorientation of Turkish domestic policies, particularly in the economic arena. These policies have exerted direct impact on Turkey's foreign policy as well. While these new policy departures evolved primarily under the influence of Ozal, their roots had been forming for a long time. But the primary catalyst was Ozal—a remarkable if controversial and flawed figure.

Change comes first in the rapidly advancing process of democratization within the country. The origins of active democratic politics go back to the opening of the political process by President Inonu, leading to the first open elections in 1955. A more populist government and a more open economy emerged during the Menderes presidency in the late 1950s. The progress toward democracy faltered with the military interventions of 1960, 1970, and 1980, based on the fear of the military's top leadership that the country was drifting away from the principles of Ataturkism and toward anarchy. These political interventions have been very controversial within Turkey, and the military's motives have been both positively and negatively assessed by differing parts of the Turkish politic and social spectrum.

Whatever the wisdom of military intervention on each occasion, Turkish democracy in practice has emerged more vigorously after each intervention, regardless of the laws passed in the immediate aftermath of the coups. Turkey has quite simply been growing more accustomed to the practice of democracy, the competition of political parties, and the steady broadening of the political spectrum. This gradual evolution in the direction of ever greater democratic practice, while far from complete, strengthens Turkey's standing in the West where democracy is perceived as a fundamental value. Today, Turkey is the only Muslim country in the Middle East that has regularly witnessed the defeat of party governments in elections and the smooth passage to power of the new victorious party—surely a fundamental criterion of the viability of democracy. And Ankara is aware that any weakening of democratic practice at home simply makes it harder for the Western world to deal closely with Turkey.

Today, Turkish democracy, while incomplete, is creating a society far more open to discussion of once-forbidden ideological taboos such as communism, Islam, and the Kurdish issue. While these debates are controversial, and even divisive, ultimately they serve to broaden and strengthen the Turkish political system and increase the overall stability of the country.

The second, and perhaps even more radical internal change in Turkey, is in the economic sphere: the abandonment under Ozal's direction of nearly seventy years of statist policies and a reversion to an open market economy. Statism had already begun to be tempered in the Menderes era, but was not seriously challenged until Ozal's stewardship over the economy in the early 1980s. These policies not only brought an extraordinary surge of growth to the Turkish economy, but lent it an international orientation that has a direct effect on Turkish foreign policy. Turkey particularly began to see opportunities for major new markets in the Middle East with the advent of the petrodollar boom in the 1970s. The Iran-Iraq war in the 1980s greatly enhanced Turkey's foreign trade with the Muslim world as both of those countries became deeply dependent upon Turkey for transit access to the West and for Turkish consumer goods. Turkey's growing economic interests in the Middle East inevitably raised Turkish consciousness toward Middle Eastern politics as well.

Turkey's new export-oriented policies sharply increase its interest not only in the Middle East, but in the newly independent economies of the Balkans, the Black Sea, and the emerging independent republics of the Soviet Union. Most of all, new economic interests whetted Turkish interest in western Europe itself, where Ankara views the frustrating quest for integration into the European Community (EC) to be a prime foreign policy goal with immense political implications for Turkey. This opening up of Turkish economic policies—partially akin to the process of perestroika in the Soviet Union, or the *infitah* in Egypt—has still not attained all its goals; the process of Turkish privatization in particular has slowed in recent years.

But Turkey now possesses an international perspective as well in its economic orientation, quite unprecedented in its past. Whereas foreign policy had long been the exclusive preserve of a narrow, highly skilled and educated foreign policy elite, today Turkey's external economic interests serve to widen the base of foreign policy formulation and to interject broader elements of public opinion into the process. This process is still under way, although it is typically resisted by the foreign policy professionals—as in nearly all countries.

The greater popularization of foreign policy does not, of course, automatically lead to stability of the foreign policy process. Public opinion is usually far more fickle and nationalistic than is the foreign policy establishment in most countries; it is quite possible that the sobriety that has so long characterized Turkish foreign policy will be increasingly affected by other domestic interests and emotions. These interests include economic and commercial goals which the business community might urge upon Turkish foreign policy; Islamic groups and sentiments that introduce an "Islamic factor" into Turkish foreign policy; nationalist/neo-pan-Turkist impulses that increase Turkish interest in the Turkic world to the East; and potential emotional resentment toward a western Europe that denies Turkey entry into the EC and otherwise offends the Turks by passing judgment on their internal politics (such as dwelling on human rights issues and the Kurds). Popular opinion now plays a greater role in the republic's foreign policy than ever before.

Finally, in a post-Cold War world in which major reevaluations of national interests are under way in nearly every country—starting in Russia and stretching to the United States—Turkey too may need to reconsider the character of its national interests in new ways. Here the democratic process in Turkey will liberate this process of policy reformulation. Already, much of the revered Ataturkist tradition—so valuable and critical to the national survival in an earlier era of Turkish history—is coming under reexamination.[1] With a lessening of some Ataturkist values—statism, isolationism, elitist paternalism, avoidance of Islamic and pan-Turkic ideological interests—factors such as nationalist/pan-Turkist and Islamic ideologies have greater room for influence. Neither of these ideological tendencies can be described as purely negative or positive in itself: the wisdom and efficacy of such policies depend entirely on the wisdom, moderation, and skill with which they are implemented.

Reemerging Ethnicity in Turkey: Kurds and Turks

Much of the world is undergoing ethnic upheaval as a result of the sweeping political changes of the late 1980s. First, the collapse of communism has brought about the liberation of many countries whose nationalist development was frozen under communism—most notably in eastern Europe and among the Soviet republics. The emergence of neo-nationalist movements in these states is releasing new nationalist aspirations, passions, and rivalries formerly submerged—and inspiring others outside the old communist system. Second, the spread of the values of democracy and human rights is making it both easier to express nationalist and separatist aspirations and more difficult for the West to ignore and deny them. Few countries are likely to remain untouched by this process. Turkey is no exception.

In Turkey's southeast, the Kurdish situation, the country's most prominent ethnic issue, was the first to be reawakened in the new environment. The Kurds had long been suppressed in Turkey whenever they sought the status of a distinct ethnic element. Turkey's ethnic policies have never recognized the existence of a minority. An individual's ethnic origins were traditionally irrelevant to success or failure as long as they were never publicized; as a "Turk," a Kurd could to rise to the highest places within Turkish society and the governing structure.[2]

The Kurdish issue had grown more prominent in Turkey over the past decade, however. The Iran-Iraq war dragged Kurdish guerrilla elements in Iran and Iraq into the conflict, inevitably touching the Kurdish population of Turkey as well. Saddam Hussein's gassing of his own Kurdish population in this war raised further international concern. At the end of the war Saddam Hussein unleashed vast operations of retribution against Kurdish villages and populations, leading to the death and disappearance of tens of thousands of people. The radical liberation organization of Turkish Kurds, the Kurdish Workers Party (PKK), began to gain prominence in this period, particularly due to Baghdad's lack of control over northern Iraq—where the PKK launched operations into Turkey and due to Syrian support for PKK training camps in Lebanon. Kurds from Turkey, Iran, and Iraq have increasingly found greater opportunity to meet each other outside the region, particularly in western Europe, not only exchanging ideas and gaining a greater sense of solidarity among themselves, but also in starting to propagate their ideas and publications. They also began to press their grievances onto the EC, sparking a greater interest among Europeans in the plight of Kurds; Turkey as a fellow NATO member was particularly vulnerable to criticism in this respect.

The Gulf War in 1991 was the ultimate catalyst, highlighting more than ever before the existence and predicament of the Kurds as a whole, especially as Saddam moved once again to crush any Kurdish resistance to his regime. These actions resulted in the U.S.-led international interventionary expedition to carve out a safe haven for Iraqi Kurds in northern Iraq. As many as 500,000 Kurds took refuge over the Turkish border in this period, bringing the problem home to Turkey more than ever before.

Faced with this massive Iraqi Kurdish refugee population and its destabilizing character for Turkish Kurdistan, Western troops under UN command in southeastern Turkey in the spring of 1991 inaugurated Operation Provide Comfort to help feed the refugees. But the presence of these troops and their carving out of a security zone in northern Iraq free of Iraqi control awakened anxieties and even suspicions among Turks themselves, who began to feel particularly vulnerable to Western criticism on Turkey's handling of the whole issue, despite the promptness of Ankara's response.

Many Turks were concerned that the presence of Iraqi Kurdish refugees on Turkish soil would only intensify feelings of Kurdish nationalism and separatism among the Kurds of Turkey. Other Turks wondered whether the foreign troop presence, particularly the British, was not specifically designed to intensify Kurdish separatism in the region. Those of a suspicious turn of mind recalled that the British had allegedly incited a Kurdish uprising against Ankara in 1925 in order to weaken Turkey's bargaining position for the oil-rich territories once part of the Ottoman Empire and then part of British Iraq. Still others suggested that the Europeans, especially the British, do not want Turkey in the EC, are anti-Turkish by nature, and see the Kurdish issue as a way to weaken Turkey and even cause territorial loss; an emerging Kurdish separatist state would then allow the European powers to better control the region and even to gain control over the rich oil resources of Mosul. Some leftists even suggested that the United States provoked the Kurds, then allowed them to suffer defeat and flee into Turkey as a means of weakening Turkish resistance to a Kurdish state and opening the way to a U.S. role as local gendarme.[3]

However dubious some of these arguments are today, there can be little doubt that they are based on part of the British and European imperial experience during the age of colonialism in the Middle East. Today, western Europe, particularly Germany, is still seized with the Kurdish issue; Turkish friction with Bonn has grown over this issue, and Ozal himself has criticized the Germans publicly for their apparent willingness to allow the PKK to operate at will out of Germany.[4] Turkish suspicion of European ulterior motives in this respect—less of American motives—has not yet been laid to rest.

Confronted with the brewing crisis of Kurds inside both Iraq and Turkey, Ozal took a bold policy gamble that has been deeply controversial within Turkish politics. He proposed legislation that would repeal a law forbidding the use of the Kurdish language in Turkey and began to openly address the issue of possible Kurdish autonomy in northern Iraq; these policies were immediately implemented by the new Prime Minister Suleyman Demirel in late 1991. An unprecedented investigation into problems of the "southeast"—a euphemism for the Kurdish question—had also been undertaken by the Socialist People's Party (SHP) in the previous year, serving to legitimize not only recognition of the existence of a huge ethnic minority in Turkey, but also to address the problem of potential Kurdish separatism and the measures which Turkey should undertake in order to ameliorate the root causes of the problem.

The handling of the Kurdish situation in Turkey had impressively shifted by late summer 1991. Whereas once the word "Kurd" could not be found in public print, today the word regularly appears in the Turkish press. Bookstores carry textbooks in Turkish on how to learn Kurdish; other books are available in Kurdish of Kurdish poetry and traditional tales, as well as books on the great Kurdish uprisings during Ataturk's time, lauding the heroic leaders of these movements; and even bilingual left-wing publications are available carrying articles with provocative titles such as "The Turkish State, in Pursuit of Expansionist Goals, Attacks Southern Kurdistan," or "Kurdistan Cannot Advance Under an Exploitative Administration."[5] Newspapers, too, are now available on the streets in Kurdish.

Despite all these developments, Ozal himself took many further substantial steps toward opening up the Kurdish Pandora's box. He permitted the establishment of a de facto autonomous Kurdish region in northern Iraq, opened up direct and regular contacts with the two key Iraqi Kurdish groups who have now openly visited Ankara on several occasions,[6] and, most important, acquiesced to elections in northern Kurdistan that represent a major step toward de facto independence. Prime Minister Demirel, now Ozal's successor as the key policy figure in Ankara, has in effect bargained with the Iraqi Kurdish guerrilla movements to grant them some status and freedom of action in return for an explicit statement—for what it is worth over the longer run—that (1) they do not seek an independent state in Iraq, and (2) they agree to constrict the activities of the PKK—a movement openly dedicated to the liberation of Turkish Kurdistan. He has even permitted the Iraqi Kurds to open an office in Ankara. Many Turks believe that Ozal was extremely foolish in allowing the Kurdish issue to evolve to this extent, perhaps creating the prospects of an eventual autonomous or even separatist movement among the Turkish Kurds themselves.[7]

Ozal has apparently been playing for possibly even greater stakes. In the eyes of some political observers,[8] Ozal might have a geostrategic vision of the future of the Kurdish movement which he will never explicitly articulate because it is simply too volatile. That vision would foresee the ultimate "inevitability" of Kurdish separatism in the region as a whole, beginning most likely in Iraq. If Turkey as of now can play a sympathetic role toward the establishment of an independent or autonomous Kurdish state in Iraq, there is a likelihood that that state would look to Turkey as the "natural center of gravity" of the Kurdish speaking world. Not only do the majority of the world's Kurds live in Turkey—perhaps 12 million out of 20 million scattered throughout Iraq, Iran, Turkey, Syria, and the USSR—but the Turkish Kurds are the most advanced and least tribalized, already playing a major role in Turkish society—especially those Kurds who live in the population centers of western Turkey. Under these circumstances, if there were ever to be a united Kurdish state, or even aspirations toward such an eventual creation, Turkey would have the dominant voice and power over such an entity. Such a creation would give Turkey a great deal of influence in the Kurdish regions of Iraq and Iran. And under any circumstances, so goes the rationale, Turkey is better off getting out ahead of such a movement than it is resisting the inevitable, thereby establishing Turkey as the key enemy of a future Kurdish power. (See "Turkey and Iraq," below, for further discussion of the Kurdish problem in the context of Turkish relations with Iraq.)

Most Turks currently consider the emergence of an autonomous Kurdish region in Turkey—much less an independent state—as extremely undesirable, and probably unacceptable. The Turkish General Staff has historically seen itself as the guarantor of the territorial integrity of Turkey and reportedly is strongly dedicated to the preservation of the unitary Turkish state above all else, regardless of whatever cultural and economic concessions are made to the Kurds. If the Kurdish situation began to spiral out of hand, the military would almost surely find that issue a greater impetus for intervention than almost any other issue in many decades. Ankara's politicians thus have to walk a fine line and keep the potential for violence under control. In the meantime the general staff is likely to exercise its own authority in deciding how to deal with military aspects of the insurrection and guerrilla border-crossings in the southeast.

Under any circumstances, the issue is now out on the table and will undergo more intensive debate in the future. The political lines have not yet been clearly drawn, although the nationalist parties of Alpaslan Turkes and Bulent Ecevit are dedicated to the preservation of the unitary state. Ozal's former party, the Motherland Party, which once supported

Ozal's liberal Kurdish policies, now tends opportunistically to attack Demirel for pursuing those same policies. Demirel's coalition partner, the Social Democratic People's Party, is most liberally of all inclined toward the Kurds and at one time housed within the party the embryo of a Kurdish nationalist party. Islamists are ambivalent: They tend to look tolerantly at the idea of Kurdish autonomy since they oppose in principle the idea that the Turkish state should be founded on the basis of ethnicity; on the other hand they do not support separation on the basis of ethnicity either.[9]

While Ozal's reasoning on the Kurdish problem is imaginative and forward looking, there is no guarantee that he is right that Turkey could hope to have a dominant influence over a Kurdish state in the region over the longer run, or that Turkey's interests might not suffer grievously in the process. His forthright approach to the problem in the eyes of most Turks is premature to say the least, and probably contributed significantly to the downfall of his party in the October 1991 elections. Indeed, Ozal's own liberal policies are partially suspect because of his own Kurdishness. Reasonable alternatives are few, however, which is why the Demirel coalition government, on purely pragmatic grounds, has not been able to pursue significantly different policies, despite its unease.

A New Turkish Nationalism?

A new sense of ethnicity may now be emerging among the Turks themselves. This trend has been provoked by the events around them, most notably the growth of outspoken Kurdish nationalism, and the groundswell of ethnicity and separatism in other countries. A strong sense of clearly defined nationalism has been a distinctive feature of modern Turkey ever since its emergence as a nation-state and the instillation of new nationalist pride by Ataturk.[10] But Ataturk's political vision of the new Turkish state was one based quite narrowly on the Turks within the boundaries of modern Turkey.

Today, as Turks watch the reemergence of Turkish communities from Yugoslavia to Iraq, China, and Siberia, their press notes that, for example, Turkish is the "fifth most widely spoken language in the world," according to UNESCO.[11] It is now commonly repeated in Turkey that the twenty-first century is the "century of the Turks," a phrase repeated by President Nursultan Nazarbaev of Kazakhstan during a visit to Turkey in September 1991.[12] All this contributes to a growing awareness—in a society not very used to talking about such things—of the diversity and richness of the Turkish community in the world.

Because of the strategic danger from the Soviet Union ever since Turkey's founding, Turkish policy traditionally discouraged and even punished any academic or other expression of public interest in the Turks of the rest of the world, especially in the Soviet Union. But in fact the present population of Turkey is made up in part of offspring—sometimes only second generation—of Turks of diverse geographical origins, from settlers in all parts of the Ottoman, Russian, and Chinese empires: the Balkans, the Arab world, the Caucasus, Central Asia, and Chinese Turkestan. The year 1991, for the first time ever, witnessed a new tendency among Turks to start talking about their own various geographical origins as Turks from diverse areas.[13] This phenomenon has strengthened feelings of the diverse character of "Turkishness" and a growing awareness of the richness of legacy of old empire—and a distinct pride in being a Turk. From another point of view, the emergence of Kurdish nationalist—even separatist—views in Turkey is leading to a backlash by Turks that could negatively affect the relatively harmonious ethnic relations that have existed in Turkey in the modern period (apart from the treatment by security forces of those Kurds living in the border areas of southeastern provinces affected by PKK activities).

In short, the Kurdish issue is out on the table; during the fall 1991 election campaign nearly every single political party had to take some kind of a position on the Kurdish problem, sometimes still referred to more delicately as the "southeast issue." Nearly all parties explicitly recognized that the issue could not be solved by force, but only by recognizing the economic needs of the area, and by reforming the present military rule of the region and introducing greater democracy. An avowedly Kurdish party, the Populist Toilers' Party (HEP), actually ran in the elections in association with the Social Democratic People's Party, and gained an unprecedented twenty-two seats in the parliamentary elections. A high proportion of those elected are considered to be radicals, many of whom had spent time in Turkish prisons in an earlier era.[14]

The Turkish authorities are deeply concerned that the PKK may now attempt to spread its revolutionary violence to other parts of the country, particularly the major cities of western Turkey where there are also large Kurdish populations. Incidents have already occurred that serve to whip up ethnic hostility between Kurds and Turks that could grow more serious and affect tensions in the southeast as well. The PKK, which from its inception has spouted a Marxist-Leninist line, is resolved on a serious course of separatism and has not hesitated to use violence to achieve its ends in a mounting cycle of actions. Between fifty and one-hundred die monthly in PKK-related violence; in the last seven years some 3,300 people have died in a guerrilla process with partial overtones of guerrilla action during the Vietnam war: Villagers intimidated by the PKK are forced to cooperate with them to a limited extent, only then to be brutalized by Turkish military forces or unofficial death squads seeking to crush PKK activities and intimidate the population from supporting them.[15] The largest raid to date took place in late October 1991, when a PKK battalion of four-hundred rebels killed seventeen Turkish soldiers near the Iraqi border, sparking Turkish air raids against suspected guerrilla bases inside northern Iraq.[16]

Neo-Ottomanism

The Ottoman period, of course, has always been treated extremely negatively in the Ataturkist vision. To the Ataturkist elite, it represented decline, capitulation to the West, the undue influence of non-Turkish nationalities within the empire, absence of democracy, and the excessive power of state Islam. There has historically been little room for an "objective" view of the Ottoman past in contemporary elitist thinking.

During the eighties, however, some reconsideration of the Ottoman past began on the part of intellectuals of the left and right—but not among those in the mainstream. Rightists, in part influenced by Islamic fundamentalist thinking, found grounds for pride in the accomplishments of the empire, especially in its greatest period of vigorous expansionism. The left was inclined to trace the roots of the struggle against Western imperialism from the late days of the empire and found anti-Western, anti-imperialist heroes among the reformers and nationalists.

A broader reexamination of the Ottoman period seems to be under way today. Apart from Turkey's greater willingness to think objectively about its non-Ataturkist past, the very reemergence of much of the territories of the old empire in the Balkans and the Caucasus now focuses new attention on historical Turkish interests and involvements there.[17]

These newer, more revisionist views—still far from widespread—do not represent a wholesale rejection of Ataturk, but rather a recognition that not every idea and value of Ataturk has to be forever valid in Turkish consideration of the future. The Ataturkist tradition itself is thus undergoing some revisionism, bringing with it a more objective treatment of the past rather than maintenance of an uncritical Ataturkist ideology intact forever.[18]

A reexamination and reevaluation of Ottoman history in no way implies the emergence of a new Turkish irredentism or expansionism. It does suggest, however, a renewed interest in the former territories and people of the empire, which includes Muslims who were part of that empire. It suggests that certain organic geopolitical, cultural, and economic relations that had been absent during the "abnormal" period of Cold War polarization may reemerge in the new "normal" regional environment. It suggests that the Turks may now come to see themselves once again at the center of a world reemerging around them rather than at the tail-end of a European world that is increasingly uncertain about whether or not it sees Turkey as part of itself.

This change in Turkish outlook will come only slowly, especially in formal Turkish foreign policy, for it runs against resistance from seventy years of Turkish history and the foreign policy legacy of Turkey's great founder. Nonetheless, it is unlikely that Turkey will forever spurn a greater regional role—in all directions of the compass—for it provides greater avenue for Turkey to fulfill its role of regional great power.

There has been some discussion in Turkey as to whether Turkey might now bear some special responsibility for an interest in the old areas of empire, at least in the Balkans, now that they are independent, and, more to the point, at war with each other. This view would perhaps justify special concern for the Muslims of the Balkans as victims of Serbian depredations during the Yugoslav civil war. This view would also distinguish between the Balkans, as ex-empire, and Central Asia, which has never been part of the Ottoman Empire. While there is undoubtedly historical interest in the Balkans because it was formerly part of the empire—and hence much more familiar to Turks—an interest in Central Asia is justified on the quite different and legitimate grounds of its Turkish ethnicity. Based on history, Turkish policy treatment of the two areas is unlikely to differ significantly.

The defeat of the Motherland Party in Turkey's elections of October 1991 will, however, partially slow the pace of change that has characterized so much of Turkish policy over the past decade. Indeed, the electorate had many grievances against Ozal—inflation, nepotism, and an often high-handed style—that brought his party down despite the remarkable accomplishments of the past decade and the revolutionary new concepts introduced into Turkish policy, both foreign and domestic. It is almost as if the electorate had grown weary of the pace, and of the controversy, and sought change, even if it meant a return to some of the less imaginative, more traditional thinking of an earlier decade. Turkey, somewhat like Margaret Thatcher's England, seems to have been ready for a breathing space, a respite. But the new concepts introduced into the Turkish body politic are likely to be permanent, even if a slower pace occurs. And the realities of the political changes in the world around Turkey indicate that these new horizons of foreign policy cannot be ignored by any new leader.

Turkey and the Arabs

Any observer of the Middle East cannot help but be struck by the sharp differences between Arabs and Turks in their political orientation on a broad variety of international issues. After the founding of the Turkish republic in the 1920s, Turkey consistently aspired to look West. It has identified itself with Western security institutions and has eschewed any kind of membership in Third World "anti-imperialist fronts" or nonaligned groupings. It has generally set itself sharply apart from the hostile anti-Western character of much of Arab politics.

Differences between Turkey and the Arab states reveal interesting aspects of the problems of the region: Given Turkey's clear Muslim character and culture and good ties with the West, friction between the Muslim world and the West cannot then be laid at the door of "Islam." It is the differences between Turkey and the Arab states that provide insights into the character of Turkey's future political and geopolitical orientation—and why the Arab world, or Iran, differ from Turkey in so many respects.

A discussion of the differences among Turkey, the Arab world, and Iran involve a multitude of cultural, historical, and social factors, but a few of the key elements can be summarized as follows.

- Turkey has had a long history of rule in the region: Turks have been conquerors and administrators of empire in diverse places nearly from their first appearance on the stage of world history. Persians and Arabs, on the other hand, over the last millenium have generally been the ruled, rather than the rulers, dominated either by Turks or by Western imperialist states. This has had an important psychological impact on their sense of "victimization" in history.[19]
- Since attaining its complete independence as a new nation-state in the 1920s, Turkey has no longer been threatened by Western Europe (except for the general danger of fascism to all of Europe before World War II). Most Arab states continued to languish under colonialism and imperialism until well after World War II, and in the Persian Gulf until as late as the 1970s; various Arab states have also suffered from Western armed intervention in one sense or another right down to the Gulf War of 1991. Turkey has not suffered this fate.
- Turkey has been immediately threatened over the centuries by Russian power, both Czarist and Bolshevik. As a result, Turkey joined with the West to protect itself. The direct Soviet threat to the Arab world was always minimal (although there was often a

significant proxy threat from radical Soviet client states).
Indeed, actual armed attack on the Arab states came consistently
and solely from the West itself.

- The creation of Israel, supported fully by the West, was a direct
  threat to the Arab world, both in terms of territory lost and the
  resulting armed conflicts in which the Arabs invariably lost.
  Israel posed no such direct problem to Turkey.
- Whereas the Arab world provided a natural network of alliances
  and alignments among the Arab states, Turkey had no "natural"
  allies in terms of states consistently close to Turkey, or sharing
  close ethnic or other cultural values. Turkey was "on its own"
  and more inclined to look further afield for its political associations, either to the equally isolated Northern Tier states or to the
  West.
- Because Turkey had allied itself with the West, it naturally fell
  afoul of most of its Arab neighbors, who perceived Ankara as
  serving interests directly hostile to many of the general interests
  of the Arabs. This conflict of interests tended to perpetuate and
  reinforce itself over decades.

Thus, Turkey maintained a posture of exceptional aloofness toward
most of the Arab world until the mid-1970s. Other historic reasons supported this aloofness from the Turkish point of view:

- Turkish anger at the Arab populations that had rebelled against
  Ottoman Turkey (traitors to the empire) during World War I.
- A Turkish desire to disassociate itself from the former non-
  Turkish parts of the Ottoman Empire and especially from the
  Arab world, which so powerfully symbolized the Islamic her-
  itage that Ataturk sought to reject.
- Turkish border disputes with Syria in which Syria enjoyed the
  support of most Arab countries.
- Turkish rejection of Arab state radicalism that was implicitly
  anti-Western and often gravitated toward the Soviet Union—
  Turkey's main geostrategic threat.
- A general, negative Turkish reaction towards Arabs. While
  Turkish intellectuals speak knowledgeably and rationally about
  most places, when talk turns to the Arab world, a high proportion of them have recourse to visceral and almost racial deni-
  gration in stereotyping Arabs as "dirty," "lazy," and
  "untrustworthy." This emotionalism is stronger against the
  Arabs than against any other nationality except perhaps the
  Greeks. In part it reflects Turkey's visceral desire not to be

associated in any way with anything Middle Eastern. The researcher who says he is in Turkey because he is interested in Middle Eastern politics is quickly informed that he is in the wrong place.

These ingrained prejudices notwithstanding, Turkish policies toward the Arab world began to be revised somewhat during the seventies as Turkey grew unhappy with many aspects of American policy toward it—especially American criticism of Turkey's Cyprus policy.[20] Politically, the Turks were frustrated by the support that Athens seemed able to regularly draw from the Arab and Muslim countries in the UN on the Cyprus issue, while Turkey, itself a Muslim state, could not. Improved ties with the Arab world, it was hoped, might moderate the Arab states' pro-Greek posture on the Cyprus problem. (The Arabs in turn often opposed Turkey on Cyprus because of Turkish recognition of Israel.) At least as important, Turkey was attracted by the growing petro-wealth of the Arab world and sought to establish new commercial relations with many of those states. Turkey began to export workers to the Persian Gulf and to land major construction contracts in various parts of the Arab world.

Ozal had even greater impact on Turkey's economic and strategic view of the Middle East beginning in the early 1980s. Two factors influenced Ozal's thinking: (1) the emergence of an export-oriented economic policy lent even greater weight to ties with the Arab states; and (2) Ozal's personal interest in restoring a more Islamic emphasis in Turkish life led to an interest in improved relations with other Muslim states, including the Arabs.

Not all elements of the Turkish population have shared an antipathy toward the Arab world. Those of Islamic inclination in Turkey have generally felt shared religious ties with the Muslim world and have consequently been much more forthcoming in their attitudes and policies. Indeed, Necmettin Erbakan, head of the Islamist-oriented Welfare Party, set forth the vision of his own party's policies toward the Arab world during the 1991 elections. He denounced other parties as simply being part of a "Western club" with a "discotheque mentality," urging that Turkey not join the EC. He stated his belief in the importance of Turkey's future relations with the Islamic world, indicating that Turkey should instead be a member of an "Islamic common market and an Islamic defence pact."[21]

Turkish contractors in this period enjoyed extraordinary success in Arab countries such as Libya and Saudi Arabia, where, at a time when the domestic market was weak, Turkey was able to obtain contracts worth $3.5 billion by January 1981. By the end of 1982, the value of

Turkey's contracts with Libya, Saudi Arabia, and Iraq totaled some $10 billion.[22] By the end of 1982, the value had risen to $14.74 billion.[23] By 1983, there were approximately 150,000 Turkish workers employed in the Middle East, who remitted some $500 million in hard currency earnings in 1981. Turkey's exports to the Middle East doubled between 1979 and 1981.[24]

Unquestionably, the Middle East will remain for Turkey an important market deserving continued cultivation. Yet here too, many Turkish businessmen have reservations about the character of longer term trade with the Middle East because of the heavy political component to such trade. Because the politics of the region are so volatile and unpredictable, so the economic relationships can be too. The price of oil, for example, has direct impact on the amount of money in the Arab world available for external contracts, especially those in which Turkey enjoys a competitive edge. Concrete business planning is complex in such a volatile market. Indeed, not all of the Arab oil states have even paid their debts on a regular basis: Libya, in particular, reportedly owes Turkish contractors a considerable amount of money from many years back, and there have been periodic suggestions from Qadhafi that his satisfaction with Turkish policies could affect financial arrangements. Qadhafi was highly outspoken against Turkey during the Gulf War. Turkish businessmen are, of course, uncomfortable with these political linkages.

In much of the Middle East then, trading patterns tend to reflect state trade policy of the countries involved rather than market forces, making market prediction nearly impossible when it may be so closely tied to the political whim of rulers who tomorrow may decide that they are unhappy with Turkey. Commercial arrangements often depend heavily on the role of the single leader as opposed to solidly institutionalized commercial relationships, especially in states like Iraq, Syria, and Libya. As long as political rather than market forces reign, there can be no reliable pattern of commerce with the Middle East on which businessmen can build. These factors complicate the normal kind of market research on which Turkish trade depends in Europe or the United States. Turkish businessmen point out, for example, that Turkey's firm stance on the side of the United States in the Gulf War against Saddam Hussein served to prejudice the Arab world against it (just as Qadhafi had charged), damaging the prospects for a longer term commercial relationship with the Arab world.

These views represent a slightly simplistic formulation of course. Radical states such as Libya are hardly a bellwether for general Arab attitudes, and a majority of Arab states did support operation Desert

Storm against Iraq, however reluctantly. Indeed, Saudi Arabia and Kuwait were highly grateful for Turkey's forthright stand against Iraq, its closing of the Iraqi pipeline, the provision of Incirlik airbase to U.S. forces during the war, and the "second front" which Turkey opened against Baghdad. Indeed, these two Gulf states have gone some way toward rewarding Turkey for its stance, as will be discussed below.

Indeed, it is these very factors that help fuel the internal debate— albeit lopsided—over the relative value of Turkish ties with the Islamic world as opposed to a Western orientation. While the vast preponderance of the country would seem to heartily support Turkey's Western orientation as reflecting both Turkey's aspirations as well as its interests, a minority of more Islamic oriented groups argue that Turkey is losing opportunities in the Arab world for both political and economic influence as a result of its "slavish" ties with the United States. These groups argue that only when Turkey is perceived to be truly a Muslim country with a genuinely independent foreign policy will it enjoy the respect of the Muslim world and be in a position to better profit economically from those relations. Similar views are often reflected in the Arab press as well which advises Turkey to think more carefully about preserving its ties with the Arab world rather than chasing after an elusive relationship with the EC.[25]

While those in Turkey who espouse the Middle East option would seem to be a relatively small group, the message is shared in part by some elements of the left who themselves have long been uncomfortable with what they perceive as Turkey's total commitment—or even subordination—to American policies. These leftists would rather see Turkey pursue a greater "anti-imperialist" or Third World orientation. However "anti-imperialist" most leftists may be, however, in favoring a more internationalist orientation for Turkey, they hold no special brief for the Muslim world per se, and indeed deeply distrust any Islamic orientation.

Ozal's own vision for a Turkish role in the Middle East has adroitly bridged both the "Islamist-leftist" view and the Europeanist view. Ozal is totally committed to a Western orientation, but in no way believes that this position precludes a major Turkish role in the Middle East, especially in the economic field. Ozal has spoken of the need for some kind of Middle East regional fund, a sort of Marshall Plan, that would combine Arab oil money and Western funds for the development of the region as a whole.[26] The Turkish role in this kind of economic cooperation would lie in the provision of water to the region—a "water peace pipeline." (See below.) Ozal sees the free exchange of goods, capital, services, and labor as essential to the new Middle East economic order. Stress on

Turkey's economic involvement would be less provocative to regional neighbors than Turkey's military role, which remains, of course, one of the most powerful in the region.

Turkish Relations with Syria

Turkey's view of the Middle East has been significantly shaped by the close ties that so many Arab states had with the Soviet Union during the Cold War. The continuing Arab-Israeli struggle also tended to radicalize Syria's relations with regional states. Now, the demise of communism and the emergence of new thinking in Soviet foreign policy has already produced significant impact upon Syria, the character of Arab politics, and even upon the Arab-Israeli peace process—these factors will inevitably affect Turkey's relationship with the Arab states in the region. More recently, the chances for a comprehensive Arab-Israeli-Palestinian settlement have probably never been better, with the end of East-West tensions, the convening of Arab-Israeli peace talks in Madrid, and the election of a Labor government in Israel. Resolution of that conflict would have major impact on the Syrian role in the region, including its relationship with Turkey; there is no longer an "enemy camp" or radical camp for Syria to belong to, and hence less grounds for Syrian militancy or hostility to Turkey as a symbol of the West. However, border issues, water-sharing problems, and terrorism will remain as genuine bilateral issues.

Syrian-Turkish relations have long been corroded by dispute over Turkey's Hatay (Iskenderun) province. This province was awarded to Turkey by a Franco-Turkish agreement and a plebiscite in 1939 but is still claimed by Syria as its rightful territory. Syria has long enjoyed the support of other Arab states on the issue; Turks carrying passports listing Hatay as their birthplace have routinely been denied visas to Saudi Arabia for the pilgrimage. With the diminution of the general ideological struggle in the region, however, it is possible this territorial issue may gradually lose its salience in Syrian-Turkish relations over time. Significantly, it does not seem to have come up as a topic at all during March 1991 bilateral meetings between the Syrian and Turkish foreign ministers in Ankara.[27]

Water issues present both potential conflict and opportunity. Turkey's construction of the Ataturk Dam on the Euphrates gives it powerful ability to cut off water badly needed downstream by Syria— and eventually Iraq. Turkey has already demonstrated none too subtly to Syria and Iraq that it has the ability to manipulate water flow to achieve political ends. Improved Turkish-Syrian relations could inaugurate far more forthcoming Turkish water policies toward the region.

Indeed, Ozal, in one of his typically creative departures, has suggested that Turkey eventually construct two water peace pipelines that could carry Anatolian water—of which Turkey has an abundance—down to Syria, Jordan, and Israel, and on down through Iraq to Saudi Arabia and the Gulf. In talks with Syria, Turkey recently suggested that it would be willing to discuss joint projects between Syria and Turkey in both drinking water and electricity generation.[28]

Apart from the impact of these potential pipelines on Turkey's bilateral relations with all of these states, the pipeline also directly affects bilateral relations among those same states: They cannot share in the water if there is no general agreement on water usage among all of them, including Israel. Turkey's "political" use of this water thus serves as another stimulus to the Arab-Israeli reconciliation process. Turkey's possession of this critical commodity—perhaps more important than oil itself—could give it major potential leverage over the other states in the region, assuming the project is really feasible. And unlike the maze of oil-pipelines that now crisscross the region, giving states multiple channels by which to market their oil, a major water supply for these states can really come from only one northern source: Turkey. Ultimate reliance on the benefits of this water source for these states also creates a potentially powerful dependence on Turkey—which these states may not want.

Turkish hostility toward the Arab world, especially Syria, has derived in great part from concern about terrorism. Because of Syria's anti-Western orientation and its specific grievances with Turkey, it has for several decades supported political movements hostile to Ankara, including three of Turkey's most dangerous opponents: the Armenian Marxist terrorist organization ASALA, radical Kurdish groups, and Turkish radicals.[29] All have had operational and training bases in the Syrian-controlled Bekaa Valley in Lebanon from which they have conducted anti-Turkish operations. ASALA long conducted a violent assassination campaign against Turkish diplomats around the world. The radical PKK has maintained bases in the Bekaa, as have other violent Turkish Marxist groups affiliated with the Turkish Communist Party such as the Turkish Liberation Army. In keeping with the PLO's general policies in the 1970s of maintaining cooperative relations with a variety of Third World liberation groups to help ensure its own viability and legitimacy—especially at a time when anti-Western terror figured more prominently in the PLO's thinking—nearly all of these organizations have also been at least in liaison in some way with the PLO, or the PLO's most radical branches, despite PLO disavowal of support for them. Turkey's relations with the PLO have been significantly strained as a result, despite Turkey's diplomatic recognition of the PLO and its long-term commitment to the founding of a Palestinian state. And Israel has naturally not shrunk from providing its own information to Turkey on this score.[30]

Syria has periodically used its support for the PKK in particular as an instrument of pressure against Turkey, its support waxing and waning with the political environment. Following the end of the Gulf War in 1991, Syria reportedly set certain limitations once again on the activities of the PKK operating out of Syrian-controlled territory, including cross-border operations into Turkey from Syria.[31] By spring of 1992, the Syrians had asked the PKK to vacate the Bekaa in a gesture to Turkish and U.S. pressure. Even so, typically Syria will continue to gauge the positive and negative values of maintaining this instrument of pressure against Turkey—including the broader costs or enhancements to its image, interests, and relations with the United States and Turkey. It can always resuscitate support to the PKK if its interests so dictate in the future.

Turkey's relations with Syria will continue to depend to a considerable extent on the broader evolution of the Kurdish problem. Basically, the Kurdish issue between Syria and Turkey is a symptom, rather than the cause, of bad relations. The Kurds represent an instrument and not a goal for Damascus. The Kurdish population of Syria is vastly smaller than that of Turkey, Iran, or Iraq, and Kurdish separatism in Syria has never been a potential problem. If the tensions between Turkey and Syria— primarily ideological in character, representing conflict between a pro-Western state and a pro-Soviet state—can be resolved, then the Kurdish issue will lose salience for Syria as one of its weapons of choice against Turkey. Water, too, is more an instrument of pressure between Ankara and Damascus than the source of conflict in itself.

The key question for the future relationship lies in the degree to which Syria may continue to see Turkey as a hostile, anti-Syrian Western presence. Resolution of this confrontation is largely up to Syria in distancing itself from its earlier Cold War-driven policies. If the Arab-Israeli issue can be resolved, Syria may feel less reason to fear Western influences in the region. We cannot now, of course, know what shape future alliances and alignments may take in the region. Syria might easily find itself in search of a permanent counterweight to Iraq, much as it has been long aligned with Iran against Baghdad. One report during the Gulf War stated that Damascus had secretly asked Turkey to host its air force in the event that Saddam sought to attack it during hostilities.[32] Ankara could represent another counterweight to Baghdad, or even to Cairo if an Egyptian-Syrian rivalry should emerge in the future. In trade issues as well, Turkey could be important to Syria as a key transit point to European markets. Syria, too, could be a valuable market to Turkey, especially as Syria's oil resources continue to develop. In short, there is no reason to believe that Ankara and Damascus must always remain at daggers drawn, but Syria must continue to move in the direction of moderation if we are to see a reorientation of this relationship.

A hostile, radical Syria would unquestionably continue to clash with Turkey over Hatay, the Kurds, and water, and over Turkey's pro-Western orientation and its strategic assistance to the United States. Under such circumstances, Syria would opt to remain in its classic role of radical leader in the Arab world, and would refuse to reach any kind of reconciliation with Israel. The continuing existence of radical forces in the Arab world would then suggest that Turkey will be facing hostility not only from Syria, but also from Iran and/or Iraq, depending on the kind of new alignments that might emerge. Turkey will then continue to place particular emphasis on security relations with the West, and particularly with the United States to maintain its military capabilities against such a radical challenge from the Arab world.

A radical, anti-Turkish Syria is unlikely to challenge Turkey in any direct military sense; military confrontation has never been its chosen instrument in the past. Deniable subversion, and support for Turkey's internal enemies such as radical leftists or separatist Kurds would be the mainstay of Syrian instruments against Turkey. If such a negative course of action does in fact materialize, armed conflict between Turkey and Syria could not be ruled out. Syria would be highly vulnerable, given its need to focus its forces primarily on the Israeli front. Such a scenario also presupposes very tense Syrian-Israeli relations in which Israel had refused to negotiate a land-for-peace agreement on the Golan Heights and Syria had reverted to its classical anti-Israeli radicalism. Turkey might also shrink less from undertaking punitive military action against Syria now that the Cold War is over, Russia no longer supports Syrian ambitions, and Syria's anti-Israeli posture would be largely of its own volition. A Turkey determined to play a greater role in the region would also be less tolerant of egregious anti-Turkish subversive activities supported by Syria.

Turkey Between the Arabs and Israel

Turkey has always been intensely ambivalent about Israel. Turkey broke ranks with the Muslim world in recognizing Israel in 1949, an action it justified in pragmatic terms of recognizing reality. Trade between the two states was extensive during the 1950s.[33] Turkey has also shared a de facto security interest with Israel stemming from mutual distrust of radical forces in the Middle East. In addition, Turkey has been well aware of Israel's strong support in the United States, particularly in Congress, where Turkey too has sought support. Israel itself has always been somewhat sympathetic toward Turkey, starting with the highly tolerant attitude of the Ottoman Empire toward its Jewish subjects. Turkey has always been one of the few Muslim countries Israelis could visit— busloads of Israeli tourists can be found in Turkey at any time; indeed, good ties with Turkey have been psychologically significant to Israel, in that they strengthen Israel's hope and belief that its problems are more with the Arab world than with the Muslim world in general.

Turkey established an early and fairly close working relationship with Israel that even included extensive intelligence exchanges on issues of terrorism and Arab subversive movements beginning after the fall of the monarchy in Iraq in 1958. Exchange of intelligence information on Lebanon has likewise always been in Turkey's interests due to the use of the Bekaa Valley by anti-Turkish radical groups; the collapse of central authority in Lebanon since the late 1970s was a source of anxiety to Ankara almost as much as to Jerusalem.[34]

On the other hand, Turkey has always understood that significant costs are needed to maintain formal ties with Israel. Turkey has always wanted the support of the Third World, and especially the Muslim World, for its position on Cyprus. And it has long supported the Palestinian quest for an independent state.[35] In addition, Turkey has sought to share in the bounty of the Arab oil states, especially during the boom of the mid-1970s. Saudi Arabia was not beneath attempting to weaken Turkey's ties with Israel in return for a $250 million loan to Turkey; in the event, Turkey did downgrade its relations with Jerusalem, at least in part due to its interest in economic relations with the Saudis.[36] Turkey's relations with the rest of the Muslim and Arab world have thus continued to expand, partly at the expense of its ties with Jerusalem.

Turkey will always be mindful of its position as a Muslim state; even if Ankara's Foreign Ministry gives scant recognition or importance to any "Muslim solidarity," Islamic sentiment among the general public will always play some role in Turkey's future foreign policy—to be balanced off against other interests. Turkey's relations with Israel are nonetheless likely to significantly improve in the longer run if major progress can be made on the Arab-Israeli peace issue. A significant general deterioration in Arab-Israeli ties, particularly if it emerges from strongly intransigent policies from Jerusalem that reject land-for-peace, will cause Turkey to distance itself from Israel. As noted above, Turkey's potential use of a water peace pipeline to the Arab world and

Israel could have significant impact on Turkey's future role in the area, and lessen the complicating factors of closer ties with an Israel that is reaching accommodation with the Arabs. Israel's technology could be a major attraction to Turkey in its future industrial and technological development.

Turkey and Iraq

The Iran-Iraq War brought war to Turkey's doorstep for the first time since World War II. That seven-year conflict in the Gulf, combined with the Islamic Revolution in Iran, immensely raised the levels of tension in the states just south and east of Turkey, forcing Ankara to devote far greater attention to "Eastern policies" than ever before. In keeping with Turkey's usual pattern of foreign policy in the Third World, it maintained a scrupulous neutrality during the conflict.

Neutrality not only kept Turkey out of the conflict, but served Turkey's economic interests well. The Iran-Iraq War in fact further transformed Turkey's pattern of foreign trade, accounting for a nearly five-fold growth in trade with the Middle East from 1982 to 1987, mostly with Iran and Iraq. Racked by war, both Iran and Iraq needed Turkey as an overland economic lifeline and transportation link to the West as well as a source of products.

But the Iran-Iraq War also raised two other troubling ethnic and territorial questions about Kurdistan and the oil-rich region of Mosul. The Iraqi Kurds, as always, took advantage of the conflict to establish a greater degree of autonomy from the highly repressive regime in Baghdad; in the course of the war they were able to establish a much greater degree of freedom of action in traditional Kurdish areas and resuscitated their ongoing guerrilla war with Iraqi forces. The Iranians supported the Iraqi Kurdish guerrilla movement as a means of weakening Baghdad and creating diversions against the Iraqi army. The Iraqi Kurds, with Iranian support, sought to cut Iraq's oil pipeline that passes through Turkey to the Mediterranean.

Ankara, not wishing to lose the revenues of the pipeline and being hostile to any expression of Kurdish insurgency in the region, responded with a tough line toward the insurgency in Iraq. With Iraq's agreement, Turkish forces made several air raids across the border in 1986 and 1987, into the camps of Kurdish guerrilla insurgents operating against Turkey[37]—thereby establishing a new pattern of involvement in northern Iraqi Kurdish affairs that has since continued and increased. For the first time in decades, the Turkish press—in part unquestionably inspired by the government—began to make references to Turkey's old claims to the Mosul region of Iraq, relinquished in 1926 under pressure from the British. The press repeatedly suggested Turkey might have to enter Iraq and even take over the oil regions in order to protect the pipeline from Kurdish insurgents as long as the Iraqi government was unable to protect it. Turkey reportedly notified Iran and the United States officially in 1986, when Iraq was faring badly in the war, that it would demand the return of Mosul and Kirkuk in the event of the collapse of Iraq.[38] The warning to Iran in this regard was explicit.

Turkish claims—officially renounced in 1926—to the territory of Mosul were based not only on earlier Ottoman control over the region, but was buttressed by the important ethnic presence of 300,000 to 500,000 "Turks," or Turkmen, who live in the region—constituting perhaps 2 to 3 percent of the overall Iraqi population.[39]

These Turkmen feel themselves harshly oppressed by Baghdad and the Kurds, but consider themselves abandoned even by Turkey over the years. Not without significance, the oil resources of this Kirkuk region produced 1.5 million barrels per day in 1990, a very important factor to be considered in any future Kurdish-Iraqi negotiations over the status of Kurdistan.[40]

The Gulf War against Iraq, however, and the defeat of Saddam Hussein, created vastly greater tensions between Ankara and Baghdad. Unlike its posture of neutrality in the Iran-Iraq War, this time Ankara was allied with the United States directly against Iraq in the war; any Iraqi threat of military action against Turkey could have sparked a potential Turkish incursion into the Mosul region. Ankara also explicitly warned both Syria and Iran that in the event of the collapse of Baghdad and general chaos in Iraq, Turkey would not sit by and allow either of those countries to entertain notions of territorial aggrandizement at Iraq's expense.[41]

Geopolitical relationships between Turkey and Iran will remain dominated by numerous contentious issues:

- The accelerating evolution of the Kurdish situation.
- Turkish concern for the welfare of the Turkish/Turkmen population in northern Iraq.
- Turkish concern for Iraqi expansionism and search for hegemony in the region.
- The Iraqi quest for weapons of mass destruction.
- Iraq's potential to serve as a geopolitical counterweight to either Iran or Syria should Turkish relations with those states ever deteriorate; conversely, those two states are counterweights to Iraq in the event of hostile Turkish-Iraqi relations.

- Potential friction over Turkish control of the sources of the Tigris and the Euphrates waters which flow into Iraq.
- Turkish control of the Iraqi oil pipeline to the Mediterranean.

The latter two issues do not represent points of friction in themselves, but could become instruments of hostile action in the event of deterioration of bilateral relations on other grounds—as during and after the Gulf War.

The Kurdish issue is almost certainly destined to create intense friction between Turkey and Iraq. In principle, both states share a common interest in limiting the emergence of any kind of Kurdish autonomy or independence; that shared interest has been revealed periodically in the past few decades. Even during the Iran-Iraq War, Baghdad gave Ankara the green light to help repress Kurdish guerrilla activities in northern Iraq when the Iraqi army was otherwise engaged on the Iranian front. But Ankara and Baghdad have each always viewed their Kurdish problems differently. While the Kurds in Iraq have enjoyed some minor degree of cultural autonomy as an ethnic minority, they have been harshly repressed, subject to massive military onslaught—albeit partially in reaction to their efforts to gain greater autonomy and their periodic service to Iran—and have had no effective voice as a community in Iraqi political life. Until recently, in Turkey, Kurds have never even existed officially, thus could not be a "minority" or suffer from minority status as long as they did not insist on being so.

As Ozal intimated in his remarkable willingness to open up the Kurdish issue in Turkey and to actually meet with Iraqi Kurdish opposition leaders, some elements in Turkey may be willing to reconsider the future of the Kurdish movement. If Turkey is willing to consider the prospect that some time down the road a Kurdish independence movement will inevitably emerge, then Turkey will be facing a whole new political equation. Ankara would be taking the gamble of making a bid for a dominant voice and influence over a future Kurdish state. If a unified Kurdish state were ever to emerge in the future, Turkish Kurds would not only have the overwhelming preponderance in terms of numbers, but also in terms of culture and development. A high proportion of Turkish Kurds do not even live in the underdeveloped southeastern provinces of Turkey, but are scattered around and participating in the urban life of western Turkey. These Kurds will always have intimate linguistic, cultural and societal ties with Turkey that will have decisive impact on the nature of any independent Kurdish state. In short, the question could be posed to Turkey thus: To what extent do you wish to anticipate the future movement of Kurdish nationalism and seek to place your mark on it through positive interaction with it? Or do you prefer to act repressively, perhaps in conjunction with Iraq or Iran, in a desperate attempt to stop the process?

No one can say whether the emergence of an independent Kurdistan is in any sense "inevitable." Turkish policies toward the Kurdish population will have a major, but perhaps not decisive, impact on the process. The nature of interrelationships among Kurds from Iran, Iraq, and Turkey will influence the process as well. Sharp differences exist among them in traditions, clans and tribes, local history, outlook, lifestyle, and even dialect. As one Turk pointed out, if Turkey were to grant the Kurds the right to broadcast in Kurdish from eastern Turkey, the Kurds would rapidly encounter disagreement as to which of two quite different dialects just within Turkey itself—Zaza or Kirmanji—would be the language of communication. But the chances are good that differing Turkish and Iraqi policies on the issue will lead to friction between the two states. Those frictions will be more intense if Baghdad continues to operate as a highly repressive dictatorship, as compared to the functioning democracy in Turkey. In crudest terms, Turkey historically gains when Baghdad is able to control its own Kurds; any development in Iraq that ends up giving the Kurds greater freedom of action only frees them up to broaden their political quest for autonomy everywhere. That is the situation in Iraq today, only perhaps this time it has moved decisively into a new stage. It would appear far harder today for Turkey to cooperate with Baghdad against the Kurds.

Iran, too, is a player in the Kurdish politics of the region. An alternative dynamic is at work here. As long as Iran and Iraq remain hostile, Iran will almost inevitably seek to destabilize Iraq through inciting the Iraqi Kurds. Put bluntly, what is in Tehran's interests vis-à-vis the Iraqi Kurds is contrary to Turkish interests. Should Turkey and Iran come to loggerheads on other issues in the future (see below) then Iran could also seek to support insurgencies among the Turkish Kurds as well. Here is where Turkey will need to decide the degree to which it will "democratize" the Kurdish issue inside Turkey and let events follow their "natural" course.

Increased airing and debate in Turkey of all these issues in the end can only help in softening their impact. Initially, of course, it will be heady for Turkish Kurds to discuss the concept of separatism, and increased friction will inevitably emerge from open discussion of this long repressed volatile issue. In the end, however, as Kurds look at the sober realities of the issue, separatism may lose some of its attraction, and the issue will come to be a major object of debate and disagreement among Kurds themselves.

Iraqi quest for power in the region brings it inevitably into conflict with Turkey, especially now that Iraq views regional power in terms of possession of weapons of mass destruction—chemical, biological, and nuclear. The presence of such weapons in Iraq is fundamentally intolerable to Turkey's own interests. If Iraq is successfully able to move toward acquisition of such weapons, without challenge from the international community, then certainly Turkey too will be driven to seek comparable weapons, if only on a defensive basis. Iran has also long viewed the establishment of its own nuclear program as a necessity in facing Iraq. The prospect thus remains that the Iran-Iraq-Turkey triangle may take on a much more ominous character in the decades ahead, given the conflicting ambitions of three significant powers that share radically different strategic goals.

Perhaps the major question mark for future Turkish politics lies in the degree to which Turkey will seek to actively involve itself at all in Arab politics. As we noted earlier, Turks have traditionally held an intrinsic distaste for the Arab world, and have generally seen the Arab world as lying in part under the influence of the enemy camp, i.e., the Soviet Union. As Arab politics now move toward an era free of the Cold War global polarization of forces, Arab politics will seem less directly ideologically hostile to Turkey. Turkish involvement in Arab politics may then come to be seen as more "normal," particularly if pan-Arab ideologies come to play a lesser role.

Will Turkey, for example, interest itself in the future security policies in the Persian Gulf? The larger Arab states basically are cool toward the idea of any non-Arab states—even Iran—having any say in Gulf security policy. A good argument can be made, however, that it would be quite desirable for Gulf security to be secured by the regional states themselves, instead of requiring the regular intervention of Western forces. But precisely what states are "regional"? This definition would wisely include more than just the Arab states but also Iran at a minimum, and probably Turkey and Pakistan as well. When Arabs alone determine the politics of the Gulf, there has historically been a tendency for the more radical pan-Arab governments to end up defining just what constitutes "Arab legitimacy" of governments in the region. The purpose of including three non-Arab states in a regional security grouping would be to avoid the pitfall of permitting those pan-Arab sentiments from dominating the security discussion in the region. A mixture of Arab and non-Arab states would keep the region's politics from being defined in a specifically Arab vocabulary.

Turkey would be reluctant to interject itself into such a role, unless its participation was sought by others, or was specifically urged by the

United States, who itself would be a key participant. Turkey's former ambassador to NATO stated that Turkey must be very careful in taking part in any such pact and that most Arab countries "do not have a warm feeling" toward Turkey and could have misgivings about its participation.[42] Turkish Islamic fundamentalists, too, are distinctly unhappy with any kind of Turkish "security role" in the region linked with the West, and indeed, opposed Ozal's support of the anti-Iraqi coalition in the Gulf War.[43] On the other hand, Turkey reportedly had indirectly displayed some disappointment that, despite its significant role in the Gulf War, it was not included in the postwar Damascus meeting where the six Arab Gulf states, Syria, and Egypt set forth new future peacekeeping forces in the region in the "Damascus Declaration."[44]

Ozal nonetheless foresaw some role for Turkey in the Gulf when he announced in March 1991 that "Turkey will have a definite role in any security system for the Middle East, but the United States should also be present, or else this force will not be able to keep the peace."[45] Turkish policy has traditionally and instinctively sought to avoid any perception of playing the role of U.S. catspaw in the region. But here again, it was Ozal who specifically broke significant new policy ground in openly articulating the view that Turkish interests were intimately linked with American interests in the recent Gulf War. Ozal's position was not based simply on support of any American regional policy, but also on the participation of broader Western and UN involvement as a whole; Ozal wished to have Turkey perceived as an independent and indispensable actor in its own right. Ozal significantly commented after the Gulf War that this was the "first time in 200 years that Turkey had managed to be on the winning side of a war" and therefore hoped to reap some benefits from it.[46]

For these gains too, then, Turkey might have some interest in a greater security role in the Gulf. As noted above, a major Turkish water peace pipeline would automatically invest it with a greater say in regional affairs. Gulf politics are likely to grow more rather than less complex in the future as well: A predictable degree of instability in the Gulf will emerge over the next decade as existing monarchies move toward their inevitable end. The fall of the old monarchies will not only throw the orientation of the new regimes up for grabs, but might in many cases even raise questions about the longer range viability and legitimacy of some of the earlier sheikhdoms as independent states. Larger regional states may well compete for new influence. Under these circumstances, a strong regional grouping—including Turkey—concerned with regional security would appear desirable.

Turkey and Iran

In the sixteenth century, the Shi'ite religion, newly established in Iran, helped to poise Iran in a massive ideological struggle against the Ottoman Empire, whose Sultan and Caliph came to be the leader of the Sunni Muslim world. Hostile relations of one degree or another continued down to the end of World War I. At that point, two quite remarkable new nationalist leaders came to power in each country: Reza Shah in Iran and Mustafa Kemal Ataturk in Turkey. For the first time each leader saw his own national interests lying in the internal development of his own country, forswearing foreign adventures. Both men sought to establish true national sovereignty free of European imperialist pressures, enabling them to exercise genuine national power for the first time in centuries. Both states promptly signed a series of agreements with each other, and shared a concern for the power of the new Bolshevik empire to the north. Both states joined in various Northern Tier security arrangements such as the Baghdad Pact and CENTO against the Soviet Union. And until the Islamic Revolution in Iran, bilateral relations between the two states had been excellent, despite little admiration of Turk or Persian for each other.

But the Iranian revolution had a major impact on Turkey's basically smooth relations with Iran over the past half century, creating strains resulting from Iran's efforts to "export the Islamic revolution." Turkey was instinctively antipathetic both to the radicalism and the fundamentalist Islamic character of the regime of Ayatollah Khomeini. Tehran declared Turkey's founding father Mustafa Kemal Ataturk to be an enemy of Islam, and flirted with trying to enlist the sympathies of Turkey's own quasi-Shi'ite Alevi population. The Iranian regime also blatantly lent both moral and financial support to Turkey's own fundamentalist Sunni groups, seeking to bolster their anti-Western tendencies. As noted above, Tehran also played in Kurdish politics in Iraq, thereby threatening the Iraqi pipeline into Turkey. Ankara, on the other hand, felt it was important to try to moderate Iranian policies and to treat Tehran's revolutionary stance with as much tolerance as possible, particularly since the Soviet Union in the early 1980s sought opportunities for significant inroads into Iran. Yet more pragmatic tendencies in Tehran in the end have gradually come to the fore, as Tehran has been forced to recognize the importance of good relations with Ankara, in particular in the course of the Iran-Iraq war. Indeed, in 1988 Iran joined Turkey and Pakistan in yet a new incarnation of the old Northern Tier groupings, this time the Economic Cooperation Organization.[47]

Nonetheless, the turmoil of the Gulf War in 1991 caused Iran, too, to explicitly signal to Turkey its concern that Turkey might take advantage of any Iraqi collapse to seize the oil zones of northern Iraq.[48] Iranian concerns were also heightened by the UN's creation of enclaves at the end of the war along the northern Iraqi border with Turkey for the protection of Kurdish refugees. Iran feared that this action might presage Turkish designs against Iraqi Kurdish territory or lead to the occupation of parts of northern Iraq by U.S. or other Western powers.

In short, while neither Iran nor Turkey fear direct aggression from each other, both have become suspicious of each other's intentions toward Iraq since the Gulf War. Neither is willing to allow the other to take unilateral advantage of weakness or turmoil in Iraq. These issues will not go away; they will in fact be exacerbated as Iraq struggles to put together some new political order with greater democratic participation. Any change in the Iraqi political system is likely to involve considerable instability as Shi'ites seek the dominant political position that their demographic plurality should accord them. Turkey and Iran are both likely to seek to influence those developments and to perceive each other as rivals for influence in Iraqi affairs.

But, after long decades of quite harmonious relations, future Turkish-Iranian relations now look very bleak indeed. This strategic sea-change has been unleashed by the collapse of the Soviet Union and the resultant shifts in geopolitical relationships all through the region. Turkey faces sharp conflict and even potential hostilities with Iran due to the following issues:

- The Kurdish situation.
- Potential conflict over efforts by Iran to export concepts of "political Islam" in the region—if in fact the current regime in Tehran should persist in pursuing them.
- Competition for influence in Central Asia.
- Most seriously of all, the evolution of nationalism in Azerbaijan, drawing both Turkey and Iran into competition and threatening the very territorial integrity of Iran. (These latter two issues are discussed below in "Turkey and Central Asia" and "Turkey and the Caucasus: Azerbaijan.")

Turkey and Central Asia

The Central Asian republics of the USSR, while having a less developed sense of national identity than many other republics, have joined the others in declaring independence—perhaps faster than they themselves would have sought. Armed for the first time with the freedom to express their own ethnic and national interests, they are in the process of returning to a clearer sense of their own Turkic character. Indeed, in the past century, the entire region was referred to as "Turkestan" and recognized as a cultural unit. In Central Asia (or Turkestan) today, except for the republic of Tajikistan which is Persian-speaking, all the republics are Turkic in language and culture. Their languages are basically mutually comprehensible (despite sometimes considerable dialectic differences); even the Turkish of Turkey is roughly comprehensible. For these reasons, Turkey has long been the cultural magnet for traditional Turkestan, even in the nineteenth century.

The Turkic republics of Central Asia have growing interests again today in contacts with Turkey, and seek investment and closer cultural ties. The response of the Turkish government was initially somewhat cautious, especially at the outset when the status of the "new republics" was far from clear, and Turkey sought to avoid any perception of seeking to undermine the existing USSR. The Ataturkist legacy had clearly warned against any kind of pan-Turkist adventures such as had characterized the policies of the last days of the Ottoman Empire; then Enver Pasha had attempted to stir up the Turks of the newly founded Soviet state to create a breakaway, independent pan-Turkist state. Ataturk recognized that pan-Turkist policies could only provoke the formidable power of the Soviet state against Turkey, and that the new Turkish Republic should focus its energies on the establishment of a smaller, nationalist, ethnically homogeneous state within realistic borders.

Turkish foreign policy demonstrated rapid change after the formal breakup of the USSR in December 1991. This change was stimulated by Turkish public opinion and the press—which exhibited fascination for Turkey's long-lost "brothers" in the Soviet Union—by international commentary speculating on the future relationship between Turkey and these republics,[49] by the growing interest in ties with Turkey expressed by Central Asians themselves seeking outside "patrons," and by the growing interest of Turkish politicians, who proved bolder than the traditionally-minded Turkish Foreign Ministry and a great portion of the Turkish establishment who adhered fairly closely to isolationist Ataturkist policies.

There is new pride in Turkey in the fact that many geopoliticians discuss the emergence of new Turkic power and have, as noted earlier, dubbed the next century the "century of the Turks," a phrase often repeated in the Turkish press. As "Turkic power" grows in the world—from the Balkans to western China's Xinjiang Province—it will likely exert ever greater impact on nationalism in Turkey itself, spark a more activist Turkish foreign policy, and perhaps a new quest for influence. As Turkish State Minister Kamran Inan stated, "The international environment has changed. The bloc system is ended. Turkey has to accept, against her will, that she is a regional power."[50]

By the fall of 1991, the Turkish Foreign Ministry had put together a special team to visit Central Asia to make recommendations on the formulation of policies toward the newly emerging Turkic Central Asian states.[51] Subsequently, the Foreign Ministry revamped its organizational lines to include a new section on Central Asian affairs (while the U.S. State Department has not yet resolved whether the Muslim states of the old USSR should still be part of the Office of European Affairs).

Typically, it was Ozal himself who was at the forefront of encouraging new relations with Central Asia. He pointedly included Alma Ata on his itinerary during a trip to the Soviet Union in March 1991. In that same month, the Kazakh minister of health visited Ankara and signed an agreement for cooperation with Turkey in the fields of health and medicine in general, and in the production of medicine and medical equipment in particular. Turkey had already signed similar agreements with Azerbaijan and Georgia.[52] By spring of 1992, the leaders of all six ex-Soviet Muslim states had paid state visits to Ankara. The new government under Suleyman Demirel lost no time in building on and expanding these relations, symbolized most dramatically by his week-long visit to Central Asia in May 1992 with a massive contingent of Turkish businessmen and political, cultural, and economic specialists— the greatest attention yet paid to these new republics by a foreign state. During his visit, in a direct and unprecedented challenge to Russian interests in the region, Demirel spoke of the possibility of establishing a Union of Turkish States, and suggested that Central Asia might be better off out from under the ruble zone. Several months prior to that, Turkey had discussed the possibility of providing military training to Central Asia, actively advocated the adoption of the Turkish (Latin) alphabet for all the Turkic languages of Central Asia, and established plans for a satellite link to Central Asia that would carry Turkish broadcasts. Thus, by mid-1992 Turkey had made a bold bid for leadership and influence in the region in the political, financial, cultural, military, and economic areas.

Today, the nationalist and religious press in Turkey carry fairly detailed coverage of events in Central Asia and Azerbaijan. The newspapers of the nationalist party of Alpaslan Turkes, *Yeni Dusunce* ("New Thought"), the nationalist *Turkiye* ("Turkey"), and the Islamic newspapers *Zaman* ("Time") and *Milli Gazete* ("The National Newspaper") have the heaviest coverage and an editorial policy strongly in support of the closest Turkish ties with these republics and general support for all Turks everywhere. The mainstream press also provides considerable coverage of these regions, often on a page dedicated to the *dis Turkler* (external Turks). It is interesting to note that there is no de facto difference between the nationalist and the Islamic papers in terms of their support for the external Turks. Indeed, the extremist nationalist party of Turkes, long a distinct minority party, has claimed that the long-standing nationalist views of its founder have now been utterly vindicated by the new emergence of Central Asia, demonstrating the long-term wisdom of his pan-Turkist policy. Even the heavily circulated non-nationalist papers recognize the popularity of articles about Turks outside the country, including those of the Balkans. The left-of-center papers such as *Cumhuriyet* devote less space to the issue.

Public interest in the Turks living outside Turkey is one thing. The willingness to devote resources to new policies is something else. Public opinion in Turkey is not universally in favor of a nationalist Turkish foreign policy. The left has always opposed any support to the Turks of the Soviet Union, based on several rationales. It sought good relations with the USSR and correctly understood that any policy with a hint of pan-Turkism would be waving an anti-communist red flag before a communist bull. The left also feared that any policies that smacked of resuscitating Turkic nationalism in the Soviet Union was stamped with a CIA label that sought to use Turkey as an instrument in the Cold War struggle against the Soviet Union. And even the "anti-imperialist" left has looked largely to Europe for its leftist political ideology; for Turkey to look back to the East with new nationalist policies could only be reactionary, especially when such policies also contain hints of some kind of "Islamic solidarity" that the left despises.

Today, left-of-center circles point out that Turkey has enough problems at home, making it a waste of resources to focus on Central Asia.[53] They point out that these republics are poor and backward, have little to offer Turkey, and can only be a drain on Turkish resources. How will the republics ever be able to pay for goods from Turkey? They point out that some 300,000 Bulgarian Turks fled to Turkey in the mid-1980s, which only created difficulties for Turkey in the areas of housing and employment, and in the end many of them returned to Bulgaria anyway. Many Turks feel they have far more in common with Europeans than they do with the Turks of Central Asia. Some even associate Central Asian Turks with the ruder, less Europeanized peasant strains of Anatolia who now overflow the streets of Istanbul and Ankara. But for all of these feelings, Turkey cannot remain indifferent to developments in Central Asia and their interest will likely grow over time. As one Turkish intellectual remarked, "It has been a great thrill for Turks to realize that they are no longer alone in the world."

Yet these objections are not groundless. The Turkish economic situation is somewhat stretched with a large deficit and high inflation. Turkey's commitments to Central Asia now reach some $52 million over the next several years. It is questionable whether Turkey will be able to meet these obligations without slighting other necessary sectors of the economy. Turkey may either find itself unable to meet its promises to the Central Asian states or may find itself overreaching the limits of its capabilities. This from a Demirel government which is business oriented and sharing power with a left-of-center party— hardly a strongly nationalist combination. It remains to be seen how a more nationalist government might commit itself to a pan-Turkist policy.

The longer range future of Turkish politics cannot be predicted with any certainty, especially under the remarkable new and rapidly evolving conditions of the post-Cold War world. The emergence of the Turks of the world, from China to the Balkans—and perhaps the distantly related Mongols in China—may yet stir Turkish nationalist feelings, particularly if it is accompanied by a European rejection of Turkey for any kind of close association with the EC. The emergence of a new Turkish nationalist leadership could thus come to devote far greater attention to the external Turks than any policies since the founding of the republic. A rediscovery of the Ottoman Empire, and the recognition that not everything was bad about it, also serves to stimulate interest in former areas of the empire (although Central Asia was never part of it despite the cultural influence there).

These new relationships, of course, are not solely dependent upon Turkey. The Turks of Central Asia themselves will have considerable impact on how Turkey views the region. At this stage, the Central Asian Turks are still deep in a process of self-identification. Although the boundaries of the five republics are utterly arbitrary, established by the Bolsheviks with an eye to "divide and rule," they have been in existence for nearly seventy years. The regional languages/dialects have to some degree now taken on the quality of official languages. Pressures of life in the Soviet Empire created rivalries and even suspicions among themselves, often deliberately exacerbated by the policies of Moscow to prevent the emergence of any kind of pan-Turkist thinking.

Despite a clearly emerging nationalist agenda in all of the Central Asian republics prior to the abortive August 1991 coup in Moscow—that brought down the Soviet Union by the end of that year—the republics were hardly ready for independence, which came faster than they might have desired, leaving them with massive new problems and decisions that would have much better been dealt with over a long transitional period. The former communist leaders of all the republics preferred to maintain at least some form of the old order to receive the benefits of a loose economic union. As the putative benefits of any kind of formal economic union grow smaller with every passing day, and as Yeltsin's

Russia increasingly reverts to a "Russia first" policy, these republics are left increasingly on their own and required to build their own economic relationships for the future.

But should they each be separate, or unite among themselves into some form of the old Turkestan construct? As of now, thinking is in flux. Most of the republics are still under the control of the old communist party structures, now newly refurbished as "nationalist" leadership, which are decidedly nationalist in that they seek the best interests of their own republics. But they are sharply challenged by more fervently nationalist parties that are vying for power, usually pushing a broader reform agenda, and usually more anti-Moscow. If and when the nationalist parties eventually do come to power in the various republics, they will have to determine the degree to which they seek a Turkestan type of federation, if at all, and whether to commit themselves more fully to Turkey.

To date, the old nationalist-communist leaderships that remain in power in all Central Asian republics except Kirgizia are focused primarily—and correctly—on the very pragmatic questions of the future economic relations of the republics, both with the former republics of the Soviet Union as well as the outside world. Turkey is of course a key object of interest to the Central Asian Turks, and a model of much attraction, economically as well as culturally.[54]

But Turkey is not the only focus of their interests. They are also interested in ties with the economic boom states of East Asia, especially Korea and Japan. They have had economic ties in the past with India which could also be of use, and seek new ties with Pakistan, formerly a state out of favor with the old USSR. A key goal is completion of new rail lines linking Beijing, Xinjiang Province, and the Central Asian capitals, running down into Iran with access to the Persian Gulf, and then moving overland to Istanbul and Europe.[55]

The future orientation of the republics' foreign policies is still evolving. While they maintain strong cultural, emotional, and psychological links with Turkey, they also realize that they should not foreclose any of their options. They are aware of the limitations of Turkey's resources. They also recognize that geopolitics at a minimum dictate the crucial importance of Iran as the sole land route to the Persian Gulf and to Turkey itself. Despite Washington's clearly articulated preferences for Turkey over Iran as the model for Central Asian development, no Central Asian republic can afford to dispense with ties to Iran.

Elites in the republics also recognize that Europe is of critical economic importance to them; yet if Turkey itself is denied entry into the EC, then how could Turkey facilitate their ties with Europe? Other states such as India are also cautioning the republics not to commit themselves ideologically—either ethnically or religiously—to any bloc as opposed to keeping close ties with all states in the region. China is also seen as a critically important trading partner, especially for consumer goods, while the rest of East Asia is the world model par excellence for successful development. Close identification with Turkey is recognized to carry the American imprimatur—not undesirable, but, in the eyes of many Central Asians, complicating other options if the commitment becomes too intense. In other words, at this point they would like to keep all options open rather than commit themselves too exclusively to the Turkish connection.

Under these circumstances, Turkey does not yet enjoy a position of monopoly or special privilege in Central Asia, despite its prominence. Indeed, the leadership of Central Asia will continue to be interested in any ties that will be most effective in advancing its economic development. For example, despite their Muslim orientation, both Azerbaijan and Kyrgyzstan have already established some ties with Israel, falling short of full diplomatic recognition. A senior adviser to President Karimov of Uzbekistan even grew annoyed during an interview in May 1991 when this author referred to Uzbekistan as a "Muslim state"; he responded that Uzbekistan was no more a Muslim state than the United States can be called a "Christian state," and he did not think such appellations were helpful to Uzbekistan's relations with the West. Yet these same Muslim connections can be helpful when the region solicits assistance from the Gulf oil states and Saudi Arabia.

Still, Turkish businessmen themselves are interested in new economic ties in Central Asia. It is important to note that Turkey's population contains Turks from diverse parts of the old empire who then migrated back to Turkey when the new republic was established. In many cases, these Turks of "external background" represent both an elite and a skilled class of former Ottoman administrators. There are also perhaps some 75,000 citizens of Turkey today who fled earlier from Russian and Soviet Turkestan.[56] These citizens, many of whom still retain knowledge of Central Asian Turkish languages, are well positioned to play the role of middleman in opening up trade ties with Central Asia. They seek Turkish government support in guaranteeing certain kinds of new trade ties with Central Asia. New publications and organizations also support a new interest in Turkestan. In the summer of 1991, enterprising businessmen, including those associated with *Turkiye* newspaper (which maintains a major commercial and business branch), put together a large and impressive full-color catalog of Turkish products, presented in both Turkish and Russian, that surely must give some kind of edge in Central

Asia to Turkish products that are both of good quality and relatively inexpensive. The Turkish government also recognizes that if it does not offer Turkish businessmen any particular incentives, then Turkey may be at no particular advantage in pressing their case in the region unless the Central Asian states themselves decide on a nationalist basis that they wish to give preferential treatment to Turkey. For this reason, Demirel has also spoken of establishing a Turkish Development Bank in Ankara designed to facilitate Turkish trade with the region.

Generally, Turkish policy toward Central Asia will need to be alert to these republics' sensitivities. Some Turks in Turkey early on started referring to themselves as the "older brother" (*agabey*) to the Central Asian Turks, perhaps unaware that the Russians from the outset of the Bolshevik period used to refer to themselves as the "elder brother" (*starshyi brat*) to all other nationalities in the USSR. Thus the term is hated and redolent of the worst days of Russian domination; the Central Asian Turks are decidedly not looking to find a new "elder brother." Even the term "guide" (*rehber*) as applied to the role of Turkey does not sit well, although nearly everyone can accept the term "model" (*ornek*). Turkey will need to avoid any hint of latter day domination in either the political or the economic realm.

But over the longer run, Turkey might indeed find a natural market, not only in Central Asia, but in Russia itself. And Turkey has already attracted Russian interest in the character of its own economic "perestroika" under Ozal in the early 1980s, involving establishment of a freely exchangeable currency, the lessening of state controls, a process of privatization, and a new export-oriented economy. Other Turkish businessmen, however, point out that just as trade with the Middle Eastern states is highly fickle, trade in Central Asia is still a very iffy proposition given the rampant economic chaos there, the relative poverty of the republics, and the uncertainty of their own new economic associations. Any Turkish success in the former Soviet Union can really only come when companies band together to try to force open new commercial niches in the rapidly evolving former communist states.

Turkish interest in Central Asia will also extend beyond the former states of Soviet Central Asia into former Chinese Turkestan, or Xinjiang Province, in China. That population, primarily Uighur Turks who are some six million strong, is strongly oriented toward Turkey and other ethnic Turks in the region, and feels under greater ethnographic pressure from the Chinese than most of the Central Asian Turks ever felt from Russian power. The Chinese authorities not only are quite capable of absorbing and entirely assimilating the Uighurs, but are actively engaged in the process; Beijing has long been moving vast numbers of Han Chinese to the region to decisively shift the demographic balance, and creating sharp reaction from the Uighurs. The Uighurs are particularly anxious to find external sources of support to help stave off this serious demographic threat, and Turkey is one of the most obvious candidates. But will Turkey wish to pursue this line of policy, or will it value its ties with Beijing more?

Turkish interest goes yet further east. Mongolia, which is enjoying its first true independence in several hundred years, is also interested in finding allies to help ameliorate its very exposed position between two major powers, Russia and China, both of which have heavily dominated Mongolia at various times. Turkey has always considered the Mongols ethnically close to Turks; Mongol names are popular among Turks even today. Mongolia views Turkey as one of several distant powers that can potentially help create a broader network of contacts to assist in asserting Mongolia's independence. This kind of geopolitical thinking is still untested, and Turkey has so far barely accommodated itself to the new realities in Central Asia, much less in Mongolia. But Mongolia would be a natural extension of the "Turkic continuum" that extends unbroken between the two countries.[57]

Turkey's new relationship with Central Asia will not go unchallenged by Iran. Iran has had profound political and cultural influence over Central Asia for over a thousand years. If the administrative language of Central Asia has basically been Turkish, the cultural language was Persian until the Soviet period. Most educated Central Asians have traditionally been bilingual in Turkish and Persian. It is Iran, and not Turkey, that physically borders on Central Asia. Iran believes that it is the "natural" dominant culture in Central Asia. Under the Ayatollah Khomeini, Iran began broadcasts to Central Asia propagating the Islamic Revolution. Today it has keen interest in establishing political, economic, and cultural influence there. It is most influential in Tajikistan, where the language is very closely akin to Persian; most Tajiks seek to emphasize their Iranian roots to distinguish themselves from the sea of Turks around them.

Despite Iran's commitment to political Islam, it has actually undertaken a rather cautious approach to Central Asia in recent years. It has avoided open support of Islamic politics in the region, its press has been highly restrained on the subject, and there seems to be little evidence of Iranian activism in supporting any kind of Islamic subversion. Iran seems more intent on pursuing state-to-state ties and economic relationships. That is not to say that Iran might not in the future be tempted to support Islamic opposition groups in future political showdowns, but "exporting the revolution" has almost ceased since Khomeini's death and the emergence of an independent Central Asia. Russian specialists in Central Asia say they find little evidence of a negative Iranian role in the region these days, and in fact comment that Iran seems to be more restrained than Turkey in pursuing its interests in Central Asia.

Iran's competition with Turkey in Central Asia could become more ideological in the future if its relations with Turkey deteriorate elsewhere, especially over Azerbaijan. In that case, Islamic politics might be one of the Iranian instruments used to oppose Turkish ("Western" or "Washington's") influence in the region.

Iran will need to be cautious about pursuing an ideological approach in any case because of great concern on the part of all Central Asian leaderships for potential Islamic opposition. Although Iran clearly is perceived as a Shi'ite power, and Central Asia is basically Sunni, Iran believes that its vision of a politicized Islam is of relevance to all Muslims. Iran is furthermore in serious competition with Saudi Arabia—its chief ideological rival—in exerting influence in Central Asia. Although Central Asia—with the exception of Tajikistan—has so far shown little sign of Islamic strength in politics, the prospects for Islamic fundamentalist movements in the area cannot yet be dismissed. The attraction and power of fundamentalism will be considerably dependent upon the degree of social, economic, and political tensions that evolve in the region—especially if the tensions are between Russians and Central Asians. Islam is one of the powerful symbols of the cultural differences between the former Russian overlords and the Muslims of the region. It will inevitably play a role if the politics between Russians and Muslims in the area grow ugly, if the economic situation should deteriorate, or if widespread opposition appears against new authoritarian rule in the republics.

Turkey prides itself as a model of successful secularism in the Middle East. It will undoubtedly view its role in Central Asia as contributing, among other things, to a measured view of Islam in society and politics and for a secular approach to government. Iran will be in a difficult position if Turkey is perceived to be promoting pan-Turkism as its ideological banner against Iran; Iran might then respond with an Islamic banner. Iran is also uncomfortable with the idea that Turkey should leapfrog Iran for influence in Central Asia, and seek to extend its influence so aggressively. For these reasons, Iran is already competing with Turkey, whether it wants to or not, for a position of influence in the region. If Islamic politics—in either its state form as urged by the Saudis, or its unofficial political form as supported by the Iranians—have any chance of prevailing in the area, Turkey in turn will have even greater interest in promoting secular pan-Turkism as a balancing factor there. If Iran can sell Islam, Turkey can sell its secular pan-Turkism. Which will the buyer prefer?

Russia, historically nervous about Muslims to its south, was acutely sensitive to any pan-Turkist or Islamic trends in the Bolshevik period. That concern, while reduced, still continues, even if the Central Asian states are completely independent. While initially Russia had grounds for the first time to look benignly upon Turkish influence in Central Asia, those views are now shifting as Turkey moves more aggressively to supplant Russian influence in the economic, commercial, political, and even military spheres.

Some Russians privately express concern that maybe Ankara has become Washington's chosen instrument for influence in Central Asia or to dislodge and displace Russian influence. To balance this Turkish factor, Russia has been looking more favorably upon Iran, and has even embarked on further arms sales to Iran. While Russia has good commercial reasons to make these sales, the sales also serve as a quiet reminder to Turkey that Russia does not completely welcome aggressive Turkish inroads into Central Asia, even if the Cold War is over.

On the other hand, Russia fears the extension of fundamentalism into Central Asia as being deleterious to its own position in the region. If Turkey can serve as a stabilizing force and support a secular approach to politics, then its presence is not unwelcome. But in Russian eyes, aggressive pan-Turkist policies are not much better than Islamic inroads if the net effect is to dislodge Russian influence on ethnic if not religious grounds.

Turkey and the Caucasus

The Caucasus is another region driven today by volatile politics that had been almost totally quiescent—indeed irrelevant—to Turkish interests and concerns ever since the establishment of the Bolshevik Empire. Today it has emerged with the full force of its conflicting national movements among three new independent states: Armenia, Georgia, and Azerbaijan. Each of these states is in search of some external ally: Only Turkey and Iran are available to play this role. Only Turkey can serve as an overland lifeline to the West. The greatest single import of these developments is to bring Turkey into conflict with Iran—even if Ankara itself exercises restraint.

Armenia

Independence has quickly brought Armenia into a serious strategic impasse. Armenians for at least two centuries have looked to Russia as their protector, specifically against the Turks. Now independent, Armenia confronts the reality that it is faced by a hostile Turkic Azerbaijan on one side and Turkey, its traditional nemesis, on the other. Armenia also perceives Moscow to be unsympathetic to Armenian interests in the struggle with Azerbaijan over the autonomous Armenian region of Nagorno-Karabakh, which is located within the neighboring republic of Azerbaijan. It believes Gorbachev to have been angry at Armenia's 1987 irredentist interest in Nagorno-Karabakh in 1987—challenging the Azerbaijanis in the process—and thereby taking the first major step toward the eventual breakup of the Union along ethnic lines. Armenia was one of the first republics after the Baltics to declare its firm intention of independence from the Union, albeit carefully framed within the procedures set forth then by the Soviet constitution. Armenia has consistently been moving to the conclusion that Russia is no longer a reliable protection against the Turkish threat. While Armenia's conflict with Azerbaijan over Karabakh was not foreordained, it was virtually inevitable given Armenia's determination to unite Armenian-speaking territory under its own aegis—even where physically separated.

But early in the independence process, the new Armenian leadership under President Levon Ter Petrosyan came to recognize that it really had little alternative to normalizing its relations with Turkey. Impressive bilateral steps of rapprochement were under way between the two countries until intensified violence in Karabakh halted—and perhaps fatally damaged—the process. In April 1991, the Turkish ambassador to Moscow, Volkan Vural, made the first visit ever of a senior Turkish official to Armenia to discuss the improvement of bilateral relations.[58] Drafts of a good neighbor agreement were drawn up, as well as an agreement to initiate direct cross border trade and the opening of a highway between the two countries.[59] Both sides recognized the need to overcome psychological barriers between the two peoples that stem from the massacre of Armenians in eastern Turkey during World War I. These emotions of hostility are even stronger among the Armenian diaspora than they are in Armenia itself, where some degree of realism about Turkey will require putting aside past grievances to deal with future realities.

Even in early 1991, it was still conceivable that Armenia could actually ask Turkey's good offices to mediate between Armenia and Azerbaijan on the Karabakh dispute. Such a request would have put Turkey in a difficult position: Turkish nationalists might demand that Turkey support the Azerbaijanis fully in any dispute. On the other hand, for Turkey to demonstrate some even-handedness in the region would have strongly reinforced the overall Turkish role in the Caucasus region, and the extreme nationalists in Turkey could have been largely excluded from voice in the issue. Indeed, in late 1991, Turkey had reportedly urged the government of Azerbaijan to reconsider its decision to abrogate the autonomous status of Karabakh, as a step toward defusing the crisis. But the Armenian-Turkish rapprochement was not to be. Azerbaijan moved to strengthen its own (very weak) military position around Karabagh. Armenia itself, in the spring of 1992, moved to expel all Azerbaijanis from inside Karabakh which included the massacre of an Azerbaijani village; to secure a corridor by military means through Azerbaijani territory to Karabakh; and to militarily threaten the Azerbaijani autonomous region (within Armenia) of Nakhichevan for which Turkey statutorily has some defensive responsibilities in an old treaty with the USSR. Turkish public opinion overwhelmingly pressed Ankara to speak out firmly against Armenian actions.

At present, Turkey is very hard put to stay neutral in the conflict, but has not yet crossed the line of actual alliance with Armenia. Turkey has made agreements with Azerbaijan to supply military training and is otherwise engaged in tightening its relations with Baku. The seizure of power by the nationalist, anti-communist Azerbaijani Popular Front in late spring 1992 has brought an even more nationalistically inclined government to power and rendered the Karabakh conflict even harder to resolve. Russian Army Chief of Staff General Shaposhnikov has warned that if Turkey entered in militarily, the conflict could risk turning into World War III. Despite the massive hyperbole of such a remark, it reflects Russian concern for the intractability of this conflict and the possibility of both Turkey and Iran entering into it.

The Turko-Armenian border may also be a subject of dispute, since Armenian independence opens up at least the possibility of Armenian claims to Turkish soil. Historically, any such claims seemed to have been put to rest when Turkey signed a peace agreement with the short-lived independent Armenian Republic in 1921 recognizing existing borders, and later when the Soviet-Turkish treaty of 1921 firmly established all borders between the Soviet Union and Turkey. In this treaty, the USSR implicitly spoke for Armenia, overriding any possible independent Armenian position on the border issue. With the collapse of the Soviet Union, of course, Turkey no longer borders on Russia or the Soviet Union; the validity of that treaty and its provisions for local borders with other former Soviet republics have fallen open to question.[60] Turkey cannot hope that any new federal/confederal/commonwealth authorities in Moscow will be able speak for the republics at all; Ankara must deal directly with the concerned republics themselves. The problem was exacerbated when the Armenian Parliament announced that it did not recognize those borders established by Moscow between Armenia and Turkey.[61] Thus, in spring 1992, Turkey stipulated that it would not proceed to formalize diplomatic relations with Armenia until Armenia provides formal written recognition of existing borders.

Any realistic government in Armenia is hardly likely to open up old border issues with Turkey in any case, given the extreme importance of a road link to Turkey and the West—especially when Armenia's sole rail links with Russia are permanently subject to closure by Azerbaijan. Armenia will also have interest in access to the Black Sea, which can come only through transit rights into Turkey or through Georgia. Turkey has included Armenia in its Black Sea Consortium, an organization that will provide a regular forum for Armenian-Turkish consultation apart from any other bilateral relations. Indeed, in late 1991 Turkey had reached tentative agreement with Armenia on building port facilities for Armenian use in the Black Sea port of Trabzon linked by a road into Armenia. This enlightened policy would have improved Turkish relations with Armenia, as well as subtly increasing Armenian dependency upon Turkey in the process. The dominance of Turkey in any new Black Sea arrangements also suggests to the Armenians that quarrels with Turkey, which they cannot in any case hope to win, are hardly in the best interests of the fledgling independent state over the longer run. During that same period, President Ter Petrosyan had reportedly requested the American-Armenian community to moderate its anti-Turkish agitation in the American Congress.[62] All these promising arrangements fell by the wayside with the intensification of Armenian-Azerbaijani military action in late 1991 and early 1992.

Future Turkish relations with Armenia could be advantageous to Turkey as well as Armenia if it can help bring to a close the virulent anti-Turkish campaigns supported by most Armenians in the diaspora based on their historical grievances. The Armenian community is obviously well placed in both the Middle East and the West, especially in commerce, to assist Turkey. Turkey likewise might wish to avoid complete identification with the Azerbaijani side of the Karabakh issue so as not to further exacerbate its relations with the significant worldwide Armenian community.

Turkish relations with Iran have also been complicated by the Karabakh crisis, since both countries seek a intermediary role between Armenia and Azerbaijan. This facet of the problem will be discussed in the section on Azerbaijan below.

The Karabakh problem, therefore, has major implications for the future of the Caucasus. Both Armenia and Azerbaijan have the full weight of ethnic emotion invested in the issue—redoubled because both are only now emerging from seventy years of incarceration in the Soviet Empire in which nearly all nationalist impulses were stifled. Armenia (1) is vividly aware of the vast expanse—now lost—of classical Armenia in Roman and Byzantine times that extended over large portions of Anatolia, (2) still suffers from living memory of the more than a million Armenians massacred in eastern Turkey at the end of World War I and the flight of vast numbers of others, and (3) is intent on preserving and strengthening its now shrunken demographic power in the Caucasus. Thus, the Karabakh issue commands powerful emotions. To the Azerbaijanis, the loss of the territory of Karabakh from within its borders would be an affront to its national dignity; would be a cancer implanted by Stalin in his redrawing of the Soviet ethnic map in the 1920s; and would represent a capitulation to the Armenians, who once were a minority in Baku, which dominated the economic life of Azerbaijan at the turn of the century. It is hard to see how the issue will be resolved, given the complete zero-sum mentality of both sides.

The only possible hope of compromise might involve exchange of mutual corridors to the Armenian enclave of Karabakh and the Azeri enclave of Nakhichevan, each inaccessible and hostage within the geographical confines to the other state. More pessimistically, perhaps only further bloodletting will bring each party to its senses. However, if decisive military action "permanently" resolves the crisis, that action will remain a psychic wound embittering and poisoning the politics of the Caucasus for years, a tempting issue for nationalist adventurists of either side to reopen at any time in the future.

The seriousness of the problem has been recognized now even in the West where CSCE (Conference for Security and Cooperation in Europe) mechanisms and even NATO are engaged in trying to establish a cease-fire and find some kind of resolution lest the problem spread. From Turkey's point of view, the conflict is a no-win situation. Turkish public opinion sides heavily with Azerbaijan, and any Turkish government is under pressure not to sit on the sidelines as the fighting develops.[63] Nonintervention by Turkey only stirs up public opinion and gives Iran an opportunity to steal the lead from Turkey and play protector to Azerbaijan. Intervention will be extremely costly for Turkey in its future relations in the Caucasus, and in its relations with Russia, NATO, and the United States. Hopefully, the problem can be contained by external forces before Turkey might be compelled, probably fatefully, to move. Much is at stake.

Georgia

Turkish ties will need to be renegotiated with Georgia now that that republic has attained independence. Like Armenia, independent Georgia remains highly vulnerable economically; its land links with Turkey are already of importance in a burgeoning border trade based on private enterprise—including Georgian prostitutes now coming across the border to ply their trade in eastern Turkish towns. Georgian purchases of goods bought privately in Turkey have now reached $15 million per year, and Turkey is increasing the amount of electricity exported to Georgia.[64] Turkey will be very important to Georgia as an alternative to the Russian land link to Europe. Georgia's relations in the Black Sea Consortium will also predispose it to good relations with Turkey given Turkey's immense importance in Black Sea maritime affairs.

Ethnic strife within Georgia itself, however, can have a negative effect on its relations with Turkey. The Abkhazians, primarily Muslims, are seeking independence from Georgia (which is Christian) and look in part to Turkey for support. The Muslim Ajars, who also have their own autonomous republic on the Georgian-Turkish border, also look to Turkey in their demands for greater autonomy, especially as Ajars live on the Turkish side as well. Turkey will probably avoid involvement in these ethnic separatist conflicts, however, and there is little public interest in the fate of these non-Turkic minorities. Turks perhaps have greater sympathy for the Chechens in the northern Caucasus, who are struggling for independence from the Russian republic and who have a small population in Turkey, much of which fled over a hundred years ago during the great Chechen uprising against Russia.[65] Turkey will need to establish how "Muslim" its policies will be in the Caucasus and to determine the extent of its willingness to provide good offices as a mediator. Given the volatile nature of Caucasian politics, it is impossible to foresee what kind of strategic relations will exist among the various states and the degree to which Turkey may or may not be drawn into some kind of alliance. If the past is any indicator, Turkey will seek to avoid any entanglements in the highly localized, passionate, and irreconcilable micro-ethnic conflicts in the Caucasian region.

Since Caucasian politics are only beginning to emerge after seventy years of enforced quiescence, the shape of future Caucasian politics and regional alignments is extremely difficult to predict. Some degree of conflict is the only certitude. Iran and Turkey are the only logical major powers in the area to arbitrate regional conflict, apart from Russia itself. Here again, Turkey and Iran may come into rivalry if Caucasian states should seek to play off Ankara against Tehran as they pursue their regional aspirations.

Azerbaijan

If Turkey and Iran are engaged in a rivalry for influence in Iraq and Central Asia, the potential for conflict between Ankara and Tehran is far more serious in the emerging situation in Azerbaijan. Azerbaijan has been historically divided into two parts since the early nineteenth century, when Russia invaded the Caucasus and took away from Persia the northern half of Azerbaijan. The southern half of Azerbaijan has remained part of Iran with its capital in Tabriz. Yet Iranian Azeris, who speak a Turkic language virtually identical to that of Soviet Azerbaijan and very close to the Turkish of Turkey, have long been considerably integrated into Iranian life. Despite their ethnic and religious ties with the Azeris in the USSR, the Azeris of Iran for seventy years have had very limited interest in any kind of union with the north due to the undesirable and threatening character of the communist regime in Baku, and its prominence in all aspects of Iranian society.

But northern Azerbaijan is now on its way to eventual independence. For the first time in nearly 200 years (with the exception of a brief three-year period between the collapse of Tsarist Russia and the reassertion of Bolshevik power in the Caucasus), Azerbaijan now conducts an independent foreign policy with a new nationalist government in charge since June 1992. For the first time in nearly two centuries, northern and southern Azerbaijan are in a position to broadly increase contacts between themselves. While many Iranian Azeris consider themselves to be first and foremost Iranians, i.e., part of the political and cultural system of Iran, they nonetheless demonstrate an ambivalence about their ethnic identity that, over time, will complicate further their position in the country.

Indeed, the Iranian Azeris are in fact perhaps the only Turks in the world uncertain about their ethnic identity. Some Azeris believe that they are Persians who happen to speak Turkish as a result of a historical accident of occupation by Turks nearly 1,000 years ago. They insist that they are fundamentally Iranian in their overall cultural orientation and that Persian, not Azeri, is their language of education, culture, and communication within the country. Others believe that they are in fact Turks who have long been socialized into Persian culture and politics. They wish to express this identity far more openly, even though they do not choose to break away from Iran. Turkish diplomats who have spent time in Tabriz are full of tales of how Azeris consider themselves Turks and feel distinct or even alienated from Persian culture. There is no doubt that the Azeris play a prominent part in Iranian culture. They represent close to 25 percent of Iran's population.[66] At the turn of the century, their capital city Tabriz was more advanced than Tehran; it was also the cradle of liberal politics in Iran during the same period. Azeris are represented at the highest levels among the clergy; they reportedly make up nearly 75 percent of the bazaar in Tehran.

The continued evolution of the Iranian Azeris' sense of ethnic identity will depend in part on the policies that Tehran maintains toward

Azerbaijan, particularly on the degree of cultural autonomy that Tehran will permit. Iranian Azeris have rarely been accorded the right to publish or to be educated in their own language. They wish to enjoy linguistic and cultural autonomy in education and other fields, and greater independence from Tehran in these matters.

The evolution and policies of an independent Azerbaijan to the north will have great impact upon Iranian Azeris. Members of the Azerbaijan National Front, the leading opposition party over the past several years in Baku and now in power, claim that their ultimate aim is union with the south. They state that they seek to maximize person-to-person contacts with Iranian Azeris, to invite them to the north for visits, family contacts, education, and so forth, in order to raise their Azeri consciousness. When informed that the union of the two Azerbaijan's entails the partition of Iran and the almost certain spin-off of the Iranian Kurds, one nationalist remarked, "Well, Iran is an empire anyway and the days of empire are numbered."[67] Northern Azerbaijan is especially interested in the immense demographic impact that union of the two Azerbaijans would have on Azerbaijan's stature in the Caucasus: The population of the south is probably nearly twice that of the north, giving vastly greater clout to a united state and its position in regional politics.

The new nationalist president of Azerbaijan, Ebulfaz Elchibey, pursues an openly pan-Turkist policy. He champions close ties with Turkey and the adoption of the Latin alphabet for Azerbaijani Turkish.[68] Elchibey is provocatively scornful of the "regime of mullahs" in Iran and predicts the breakup of Iran and the union of the two independent Azerbaijans.

The presence of Turkey in the region exacerbates the dilemma for Iran. If the Iranian Azeris are in some doubt about their Turkishness, the Soviet Azeris are not, despite the Shi'ite religious link with Iran that most Azerbaijanis share. The press in Soviet Azerbaijan is filled with articles about Turkey and the ethnic ties between the two countries. Here Persian does not compete with Azeri Turkish; only Russian competes as the major vehicle of international contact. Books in Turkish are beginning to flow into Azerbaijan from Turkey. There is no doubt that the northern Azeris are growing closer to Turkey every day than to Iran. And Iran, sensing the danger of this cultural pull, is seeking to limit contacts over the border, and believes that Ankara is secretly encouraging these developments.

Even in the Ataturk era, Turkey had distinct interest in Azerbaijan. When the Turkish-Iranian borders were set in 1932, Turkey made sure that it maintained a tiny piece of land contiguous to the Armenian-controlled but Azeri-populated Autonomous Republic of Nakhichevan. It was only in March 1991 that the significance of this contiguous land border was realized when political change in the USSR made it possible for Turkey to build a railroad bridge between the two countries. In that same month, Turkey also inaugurated weekly flights from Ankara to Baku.[69] Turkey was the first state to recognize Azerbaijan's declaration of independence in November 1991. Apart from its ethnic sympathies for Azerbaijan, the Turkish government was also reportedly concerned that it get the jump on Iran in any rivalry for close relations with Baku. (An Armenian business delegation to Turkey, however, told President Demirel that it considered Turkish recognition of Azerbaijan to be "ill-timed," especially because it might encourage Azerbaijan to more aggressive tactics on the Karabakh question.)[70]

This growing sense of Turkishness with time is bound to spill over into Iranian Azerbaijan and possibly "infect" it with a desire for closer ties with Baku. In short, Iran has nothing to gain and everything to lose from the independence of northern Azerbaijan. Even if Turkey does nothing at all to encourage any separatism in Iranian Azerbaijan, Tehran is already suspicious of Ankara's intentions toward the Turkic populations and will inevitably view Ankara as the gainer in these evolving relationships that so directly affect Iran's territorial integrity.

Indeed, nationalist elements in Turkey do support Azerbaijan's efforts to increase a sense of Turkishness among the Iranian Azeris and to seek union with them, and they generally support pan-Turkist policies designed to bring Turkey and the two Azerbaijans closer together. But there is almost no likelihood that Azerbaijan would ever seek union with Turkey—indeed, it views itself as more advanced than Turkey in education and technical fields, and it would not give up its own independence and sense of cultural distinctiveness, which includes considerable cultural and historical influence from Iran. But should a strongly nationalist government come to power in Turkey at some point, the Turkish government could wield a more official pan-Turkist policy that would further threaten Iran, which also has Qashqai and Turkmen minorities within its borders who are Turkic. The Azerbaijan issue thus seems destined to increase conflict between Turkey and Iran, regardless of what either country does.

If Iran comes to believe that Turkey either directly or indirectly is working to increase a sense of Turkishness in southern Azerbaijan, thereby contributing to the partition of Iran, it will surely use every means at its disposal to prevent that eventuality. Iran could seek to strike back at Turkey by inciting the Kurds there to greater separatism. It could also attempt to incite the Turkish Alevi population as a warning marker to Ankara. Ankara in any case has no power to stop the development of Turkish consciousness in southern Azerbaijan even if it wished to. The issue will remain one of the most explosive ones in the region.

These factors also complicate Iran's approach to the Karabakh conflict. Iran wants to maintain good ties with Baku and hence finds it useful to offer itself as a mediator between Armenia and Azerbaijan. Iran also has a large Armenian minority, however, which gives it a special relationship with Armenia. Iranian good offices thus have greater credibility for Armenia than do Turkish good offices, and Iran is anxious to maintain good ties with Armenia. Tehran's dilemma is to decide how far it can go in sympathizing with Armenia before it loses all leverage in Baku, which is already drifting toward Turkey. If in the end Tehran should find Baku implacably hostile in its advocacy of the separation of Iranian Azerbaijan from Iran, then Iran will probably lend full support to Armenia in the Karabakh crisis, placing itself on a further collision course with Turkey.

Iran of course has the geographic advantage of contiguous borders with both Armenia and Azerbaijan, offering it more strategic options than Turkey has. This fact has not gone unnoticed in Turkey, where some nationalist commentators have noted that Armenia and Iran stand in the way of a contiguous land-belt of Turkic peoples right across Asia. Whether this observation would serve as a basis for pan-Turkist expansionism in Turkey is doubtful, but the ingredients are there for jockeying for position and thus for potential future conflict.

The United States will of course have some interest in the evolution of Turkish policies in the Caucasus and the potential for conflict there, which so far surpasses embryonic conflict in Central Asia. It is nonetheless important to recognize that nearly all of these issues are of far greater importance to Ankara than they are to Washington. Whereas during the Cold War Washington worked with Ankara on vital American interests in the region, today Turkish interests and influence far surpass American. Washington simply has less clout with Ankara on regional affairs than before.

Key policy positions for the United States include:

- Discouraging major military build-up or armed conflict in the Caucasus.
- Discouraging extreme nationalist or Islamic fundamentalist trends in the region.
- Supporting Turkish willingness and ability to serve as an honest broker in Caucasian or Central Asian political conflict.
- Discouraging Iranian-Turkish conflict over the Caucasus and Central Asia.

Turkey and Russia

The modern Turkish state came into existence at about the same time as the Soviet Union; until 1991, Turkey's outlook on the world was thus powerfully and continuously molded by the Soviet colossus to the north. Today, Turkey's relationship with the Soviet Union has shattered into a number of constituent parts: where once bilateral relations covered all fronts, Turkey now requires fifteen or more new sets of bilateral relations to cover the newly emerging republics. Significantly, Turkey now no longer even borders on Russia.

Because Russia is still the only truly great power in the region, Turkey will need to focus a great deal of attention upon it. However, Turkey is gradually shifting its priorities away from Russia in its focus on the new Turkic republics of the old Soviet Union. Deciding if and when to give priority to Russian concerns in these areas, over Turkey's own interests, will be critical for Ankara. Moscow itself is still in the process of sorting out its foreign policy interests and has no clear view yet of what Turkish relations should or should not be with the Caucasus and the Turkic republics.

As "new thinking" emerged in the USSR under Gorbachev and Shevardnadze, Russian reactions to Turkish policies were fairly positive.[71] Moscow noted the caution and moderation with which Turkey moved—in sharp distinction to the (mutually rival) policies of Iran and Saudi Arabia, each of which sought to strengthen its position in the Muslim republics through Islamic policies starting with the Afghan War.

Turkey's influence in the former USSR is not, of course, limited strictly to the Caucasus and Central Asia. A major Turkic group, the Crimean Tatars, live in the Crimea (and more of them are continuously returning from former exile in Central Asia), a peninsula that today constitutes part of Ukraine but is an object of struggle for influence between a Russian majority and Ukrainian and Tatar minorities. Similarly, the autonomous Tatar and Bashkir area of the Volga region has proclaimed independence from within the republic of Russia. And the autonomous area of Yakutia in Siberia, rich in minerals, is populated by the Turkic Yakuts, although they are not Muslim and their sense of Turkishness is still only weakly developed. All three of these Turkic areas can look to Turkey as a source of at least cultural, if not economic and political, support.

Turkey will need to think very carefully about how to construct its relations with these former USSR regions, especially those within Russia proper—the issue of their separatism is a highly sensitive one for Moscow. The Demirel government has already chosen to avoid involvement in the quest of the Gagauz[72] for independence in Moldova, whatever the fate of that republic and despite Turkish popular interest. The Turkish role in the region could still be viewed as somewhat constructive from the Russian viewpoint if Turkey would discourage Turkic separatist movements in Russia. Turkish public opinion, of course, remains a major question mark for the future; will it compel the government to express sympathy for these Turkic peoples inside Russia? Will an extreme nationalist leadership arise in Turkey that will consider the cause of the "external Turks" as a leading foreign policy goal?

With the collapse and breakup of the Soviet Union, and—at least as important—the death of communism as a hostile ideology, Turkey now obviously has less to fear from Russia. As the Soviet threat to Turkey fades, Turkey's strategic threat to Russia as a base of NATO operations also sharply fades. Both states can afford to be considerably more relaxed about each other.

Russia, of course, must now calculate its own new national interests. Clouded by seventy years of Marxist-Leninist policies which dictated that the whole world constituted a field of ideological struggle, Russia now needs to think more seriously about a narrow range of national interests. In effect, one of the worst imaginable disasters has already struck with the collapse of the Soviet Empire and the threat of breakaway movements even within Russia itself. Among the powerful states on Russia's periphery that could pose a potential theoretical threat are China, Japan, and Germany.

But despite the more relaxed character of Russian-Turkish relations today, Russia is uneasy with the growing Turkish eagerness to assume a new strategic role in the old areas of Russian domination. As noted above, Demirel's call for a possible Union of Turkic States and questions about the wisdom of Central Asia's remaining within the ruble zone represents a direct challenge to Russian interests and influence. While global strategic struggle is no longer the issue, classical spheres of influence still are, and Russia is not ready to cede to Turkey all the Muslim regions of the former empire. Russia may well overtly pursue more open ties with Iran as a balance to Turkish activities in the Caucasus and Central Asia. And suggestions that the United States may be using Turkey as its vehicle for regional influence also worry the Russians. The Russian-Turkish relationship is, therefore, still in the process of finding a new equilibrium as both states determine the nature and depth of their interests in these regions and the price they are willing to pay for them.

Turkey, whether it wishes to or not, will be involved in Russia's future relations with China. As world empires break up, China, too, is hardly immune. The breakaway of the Central Asian states from the

Soviet Union exerts direct impact on China's minorities. In all probability, the Turkic peoples of western China, most notably the Uighurs and Kazakhs, will firmly reassert their long-time quest for independence. They will likely seek union or a federal relationship with their co-ethnics on the Soviet side of the border. Tibet will surely never give up its goal of independence; the more heavily Mongol counties of Inner Mongolia will surely seek to join independent Outer Mongolia. Even Manchuria's ethnic Manchus could seek some kind of cultural autonomy. Russia and Turkey will both have possible intermediary roles to play in the event of such developments given the Turkic nature of the Uighurs and Kazakhs and the more distant Turco-Mongol relationship. Increased Sino-Russian hostility could well emerge from this process if China believes that Russia might be encouraging parallel breakup of the Chinese Empire. Indeed, Russia almost surely will welcome a diminution of China's geographical spread and the resurrection of buffer states between them.

Russian-German relations, too, will involve Turkey indirectly in the Balkans. Relations between those two powers in the Balkans in the past have historically played themselves in a triangular relationship with Ottoman Turkey as well. While Turkey no longer has any territorial role in the Balkans, it will likely constitute part of a triangular relationship of political influence in the Balkans in the future, especially if there is renascent Russo-German rivalry there.

How would Turkey align itself in such a situation? The evolution of post-Cold War Balkan politics is, of course, still far too new to make any meaningful determinations. At the moment it is history that provides the only clue—and possibly an unreliable one. Slovenia and Croatia would historically seem to be inclined toward a German orientation, with Serbia and Romania (whose populations are Eastern Orthodox) possibly looking more toward Russia. If a Serbian-Romanian and possibly Greek grouping might emerge that looks more toward Russia, Turkey might find itself at odds with it, and drift toward a de facto convergence of interests with Germany. On the other hand, if Turkey's relationships with Germany tend toward friction over Turkish guest workers in Germany and the Kurdish issue, then Turkey might be more sympathetic to a pro-Russian alignment in the Balkans. These potential alignments can only be speculated about for now.

A key new wild card is Ukraine, that has never in modern times been an independent player in the Balkans. If Ukraine will be inclined to view Russia as its key security threat, it might thus find itself drifting either toward Germany and/or Turkey, as counterweights. Turkey will now have more intimate relations with the Ukraine through the Black Sea Consortium. Finally, Turkey might find itself champion of a Muslim bloc in the Balkans which would include Bosnia, Albania, and the Muslims of Macedonia and Greek Thrace. Turkey might support Macedonia in general as an anti-Greek, anti-Serbian element.

Various combinations are possible and have not yet worked themselves out. They will inevitably affect Turkey's relations with Russia, which on the one hand shares a desire to limit the growth of fundamentalist Islam, but on the other could move toward classic rivalry from the days of the Ottoman and Tsarist empires.

In short, the character of Turkish-Russian relations from a geopolitical point of view will have to be reassessed in light of the major changes that are overtaking both countries. Indeed, Turkey now has newly constituted buffer states between itself and Russian military power in the Caucasus. From a military standpoint, however, Russia of course remains the main regional threat. The reduction of strategic weapons in eastern Europe has diminished the security threat to western Europe, but not for Turkey. In fact, the withdrawal of many Soviet strategic weapons and forces beyond the Urals has, if anything, technically brought these forces closer to Turkey. It also means that Turkey can no longer look to NATO to absorb part of a first thrust in the highly unlikely event that the Russian military were to move against Turkey. Indeed, potential conflict today between Turkey and Russia has nothing to do with NATO, but most likely with Caucasian or Central Asian politics.

If NATO has benefited from Turkey's presence, Turkey in turn has certainly strongly benefited from that same membership; few other associations could have as quickly brought Turkey into the "European club" as NATO. With the Soviet threat receding, Turkey nonetheless feels that it is left exposed to security problems in its southeast region: from Iran, Iraq, Syria, and the Kurdish problem. The prospects of realistic hostilities with some of these states are far greater than they ever were with the USSR. Turkey is increasingly concerned about what the nature of NATO obligations to Turkey will be in the next decade vis-à-vis threats from the southeast. Russia as a security consideration is significantly fading from the picture. And western Europe will be increasingly shy of any commitments to Turkey involving Turkish policies in the East.

In fact, Turkey is now much more interested in the potential new economic relations it can establish with Russia/Soviet Union. After a long-standing total annual volume of trade over the years of some $600 million, Russian-Turkish trade tripled to $1.8 billion in 1990 and is expected to reach $2.3 billion in 1991. Turkey hopes to attain a total annual volume of trade of $15 billion by the end of the decade.[73]

The heart of the new trade relationship is an offset gas agreement by which Turkey imports Soviet natural gas for hard currency, "in return for which the USSR is obliged to import Turkish goods and contracting services up to a minimum of 70 percent of the payments for gas." The remaining 30 percent goes to repay Turkish loans to the USSR. This arrangement will involve $700 million annually by 1993. Turkish contracting in the USSR has boomed with a total value of $1.5 billion to be reached by mid-1992, some of it involving high-profile buildings in Moscow. Turkey is also involved in providing the USSR with turnkey factories, construction materials, pipes, and up to 20 percent of Soviet communications lines via Turkey's telecommunications industries. Ship-building is growing, as is the sale of products from multinational corporations based in Turkey in such areas as processed food, pharmaceuticals, packing material, cleaning products, and buses. Joint ventures in tourism, transportation, and other areas are under way. To date Turkey has provided $1.35 billion in loans to the USSR.[74]

Turkey is additionally seeking to present itself to the West as a partner for other countries in arranging trade and investment with the former Soviet republics, especially the Muslim republics. Turkey advertises its geographic proximity, its major Black Sea port facilities, its linguistic and cultural familiarity with those regions, as well as its own experience undergoing a "perestroika" in the last decade—a process of privatization and opening up to international markets in which Turkey has greatly developed its own entrepreneurial expertise.[75]

Apart from direct trade with the USSR, the proposed creation of a Black Sea Economic Cooperation Zone has been among the various creative ideas that Ozal has developed for the economic future of the region. This zone includes all the riparian countries of the Black Sea—at least six countries, including the newly established Ukraine and Georgian independent republics and even the possibility of some kind of new Tatar entity in the Crimea.[76] Trade with Ukraine would seem to be particularly promising in the development of Black Sea trading patterns. Gorbachev has explicitly mentioned the Black Sea project in positive terms.[77]

In sum, Turkey's relationship with the Soviet Union has been utterly transformed in the last five years with the elimination of mutual hostility, the transfiguration of Turkey/USSR relations into individual relations with Russia and the various republics, and the formation of new trade relations in a rapidly evolving market system in the former USSR. Turkey should loom large in the future economic patterns of Russia and the southern republics, including Ukraine.

Turkish foreign policy thus must find a new balance in its relations with Russia. If Turkey pursues its traditionally sober and measured foreign policies (Cyprus being the major exception, in which Turkey opted for unilateral action as opposed to international due process), then it can be expected to avoid involvement in internal disputes in the former Soviet Union. Indeed, Turkish diplomats might expect to be busy with a multiplicity of mediation roles in the region in the coming decades, especially if Turkey can maintain the image and role of an objective and balanced party. At this point, Turkey is undergoing a dramatic shift away from its traditional Ataturk-style isolationism. It is now in the process of becoming a potential competitor in the region, adding to, rather than tempering, regional nationalist sentiments. Given the swirl of rising nationalisms worldwide, it is not impossible that some future Turkish leader might benefit from playing a pan-Turkist card down the road. Nationalist tendencies do exist in Turkey, but they have not become part of mainstream politics. As long as Turkey continues to enjoy economic progress and is integrated into Western trade patterns (even if not a formal member of the EC), then the emergence of nationalist-chauvinist patterns does not seem very likely, even as Turkey's regional role grows.

Conclusion

World events, as well as the evolution of Turkish domestic policies, conspire to give Turkey a new prominence in international politics and a higher profile in the Middle East and the Muslim areas of the Soviet Union and China. While Turkey has traditionally avoided this kind of involvement, it will come under pressure for change, for economic reasons and because other Turkic areas will seek Turkish ties and support. As a major power in the region, Turkey will inevitably need to concern itself more with events in the Arab world, Iran, and Israel as well.

Turkey, then, will almost surely turn greater attention to the politics of the Middle East in the decade ahead. This change will be determined by many factors: economic need, the need for alternative spheres of influence after EC rejection, new opportunities for ties with the Caucasian and Central Asian republics of the Soviet Union, increased turmoil in the Persian Gulf, and the gradual withering of Ataturkist isolationism.

The world itself continues to undergo profound change. It is a world in which we see simultaneous tendencies of breakup and unification. This period of confusion and turmoil promises to be a long one. Hopefully, it will not be exploited by any single new ideological state or force which would serve to polarize these trends.

Turkey itself may go through a breakup phase if a Kurdish national movement comes into being that redraws the regional map. On the other hand, Turkey may also go through a unification phase if the newly emerging Turkic world brings it power and influence over a broad stretch of the globe. One can only hope that Turkey will continue to bring to its foreign policy the sobriety and responsibility that have largely marked its policies since the establishment of the Turkish Republic after World War I.

Notes

1. Hugh Pope, "Legacy of Turkey's 'Immortal' Ataturk Slowly Starts to Fade," *Los Angeles Times*, January 15, 1991.

2. Turkish presidents Cevdet Sunay and Turgut Ozal are only two prominent examples; Turkey's current Foreign Minister Hikmet Cetin is also a Kurd. Large numbers of Turkey's intellectuals, artists, and writers are also ethnic Kurds—the internationally known writer Yasar Kemal being the most famous— although not all have openly identified themselves as such; many more Turks have mixed Turkish-Kurdish blood.

3. See the journal *Briefing*, April 24, 1991, and May 6, 1991, published in Ankara. The author also heard numerous arguments to this effect raised during a research trip to Turkey in September 1991. See also Mehmet Arif Demirer, "British Desire to Resurrect the Sevres," *The Turkish Times*, November 15, 1991, for a discussion of serious distortions in the British media of the facts about the Kurdish case before the League of Nations. For a typical leftist interpretation, see the analysis of Dogu Perincek in Metin Sever, ed., *Kurt Sorunu: Aydinlarimiz Ne Dusunuyor (How Our Intellectuals Look at the Kurdish Issue)*, Cem Yayinevi, Istanbul, 1992, p. 213.

4. "Ozal: 'Germany Protects Marxist PKK Terrorists'," *Turkish Times*, November 15, 1991.

5. *Denge (Turkish journal)*, August 1991, pp. 2, 18. The other books were noted by the author in Turkish bookstores in September 1991.

6. See *Briefing*, March 18, 1991.

7. See, for example, Aydin Yalcin, "Turkiye'yi ve Turklugu Dusunuyorsak" (Thinking about Turkey and Turkishness), Yeni Forum, April 1991; and "Ozal's Links with Kurdish Rebels Come Under Press Fire," *Turkish Times*, October 10, 1991.

8. These conclusions are based in part on the author's interviews with numerous Turkish journalists, academics, and politicians in September 1991 and June 1992.

9. Sever, *Kurt Sorunu*.

10. Prior to the emergence of the modern Turkish state, the very word "Turk" in the Ottoman Empire was frequently used pejoratively and tended to denote a rude peasant or Asiatic Turk.

11. Ali Fuat Ulay, "Turkish fifth most widely spoken language," *Turkish Times*, October 1, 1991. This figure lumps all Turkic languages of the world into one group.

12. See Murat Arvas, "Istikbal Turklerin" (The Future Belongs to the Turks), *Turkiye*, September 25, 1991.

13. Interviews with sociologists in Istanbul, September 1991.

14. William D. Montalbano, "Surge in Kurdish Nationalism Poses Tough Test for New Turkish Regime," *Los Angeles Times*, October 26, 1991.

15. Montalbano, *"Surge in Kurdish Nationalism."*

16. Hugh Pope, "17 Turkish Troops Die in Kurds' Biggest Raid," *Los Angeles Times*, October 26, 1991.

17. See, for example, Osman Okyar, "Tarihe Bakislarimiz Yumusuyor Mu?" (Are Our Views on History Softening?) *Yeni Forum*, August 1991. Also see Murat Belge, *Tarihten Guncellige (From History to Contemporaneity)*, Alan Yayincilligi, Istanbul, 1983, for an original and provocative left-wing view of Ottoman history and its contribution.

18. In his time, of course, Ataturk had good reason to denigrate the old multinational empire and to focus on creating a new nation-state in Turkey that would find fulfillment within new national borders and in a new ethnic, secularist, nationalist tradition. But now that the nation-state is a firm reality, there may be greater freedom to examine the past with less anxiety and greater self-confidence and objectivity.

19. Interestingly, even Turkey, for all its centuries of wielding power, has tended to think of itself as a "loser" vis-à-vis the West for the last several centuries, as the Ottoman Empire fell apart and Western imperialist powers attempted to truncate modern Turkey in its early days. Ozal recently commented (and revealingly) about Turkey's great economic successes and increased stature in the world over the last decade: "Turkey is marching towards becoming a regional superpower. Thank God, the inferiority complex we have suffered before the Western world for 300 years has ended." *Turkish Times*, November 15, 1991.

20. Ali L. Karaosmanoglu, "Turkey's Security and the Middle East," *Foreign Policy*, Fall 1983.

21. "Erbakan's vision: Islamic harmony and a cleansed society," *Briefing*, October 14, 1991, p. 6.

22. Karaosmanoglu, *"Turkey's Security,"* pp. 165–166.

23. George E. Gruen; "Turkey's Relations with Israel and Its Arab Neighbors," *Middle East Review*, Spring 1985, p. 42.

24. See Karaosmanoglu, *"Turkey's Security,"* pp. 165–166.

25. See, for example, the article by Raghib al-Sulh in the pan-Arab daily *al-Hayat*, October 18, 1991, arguing that Turkey should pursue neither a pro-Western nor a pan-Turkic policy, but a "third, Middle Eastern option." Typically, Libya's Mu'ammar al-Qadhafi stated during the Gulf War that he had "lost hope in Turkey" as a result of Turkey's support for the United States against Iraq; he said that Turkey must stop permitting the United States to use Incirlik airbase if "a Third World War is to be avoided." "Qaddafi Threatens: 'Opening of Second Front by Turkey Will Be World War III,'" *Turkish Times*, March 15, 1991.

26. See *Briefing*, February 11, 1991, pp. 3–4.

27. "Shara visit marks new phase in Turkish-Syrian relations," *Briefing*, March 25, 1991, pp. 9–10.

28. *Briefing*, March 25, 1991. Turkish thinking on the water pipeline may be overly optimistic, both in terms of the amount of water Turkey has for export, and the costs of shipping the water south.

29. Neil C. Livingstone and David Halevy, *Inside the PLO*, William Morrow and Company, New York, 1990, p. 82.

30. Gruen, "Turkey's Relations with Israel," p. 34.

31. Ismet G. Imset, "Syria suspends support to PKK," *Turkish Times*, March 15, 1991.

32. "U.S. Asks Ankara to Accept Autonomous Kurdistan," *Turkish Times*, February 1, 1991.

33. Gruen, "Turkey's Relations with Israel," p. 41.

34. Gruen, "Turkey's Relations with Israel," p. 35.

35. Turgut Ozal, "An Unavoidable War," *The Washington Post*, January 21, 1991.

36. Gruen, "Turkey's Relations with Israel," p. 38.

37. Ali Fuat Borovali, "Kurdish Insurgencies, the Gulf War, and Turkey's Changing Role," *Conflict Quarterly*, Fall 1987, pp. 39–40.

38. Richard C. Hottelet, "Mideast Wild Card: Kurds in Iraq, Turkey," *Christian Science Monitor*, October 24, 1990.

39. The percentage figure is from Marr, *A History of Modern Iraq*, Boulder: Westview Press, 1989, p. 9, quoting Richard Nyrop, *Iraq: A Country Study*, U.S. Government Printing Office, Washington, D.C., 1979. A bulletin from "The Iraqi National Turkman Party: Dunya Kamuoyuna Duyuru" (Bulletin to World Public Opinion)(undated), from the Turkmen themselves in 1990 speaks of the Turkmen population as "reaching two million people." This figure is vastly inflated, but reliable figures are not available; Turkey inflates them, the Iraqis and Kurds deflate them.

40. *Foreign Reports Bulletin* (newsletter), Washington, D.C., March 14, 1991.

41. "President Turgut Ozal Warns Syria and Iran to Stay out of Iraq," *Turkish Times*, March 15, 1991.

42. "Ankara Cautious on Defense Pact," *Turkish Times*, March 15, 1991.

43. Clyde Haberman, "Turkish Fundamentalists Call for Withdrawal from Coalition," *The New York Times*, January 30, 1991.

44. *Briefing*, March 25, 1991, p. 10.

45. William D. Montalbano, "Ozal Seeks to Translate Role as Gulf War Ally into Power for Turkey," *Los Angeles Times*, March 16, 1991.

46. "Ozal Upbeat on Gulf Policy and Future," *Turkish Times*, April 1, 1991.

47. Mushahid Hussain, "Iran Forges New Links," *Middle East International*, February 17, 1989, p. 17.

48. See Sheherezade Daneshkhu, "Iran: New Force of Stability?" *The Middle East*, March 1991, p. 8; see also *The Tehran Times*, January 20, 1991, where an editorial explicitly warns of Turkey's long-standing ambitions to take control of northern Iraq.

49. Among others the author's early article in *Foreign Policy* in Spring 1990, "The Emergence of Central Asia," on potential regional impact of change in Central Asia.

50. Montalbano, "Ozal Seeks to Translate Role as Gulf War Ally."

51. It is interesting to note that no Turkic language has a separate word distinguishing a Turk in Turkey from a Turk in Central Asia. While English distinguishes between "Turkish" and "Turkic" and Russian (identically) between "Turetski" and "Tyurkski," only in the middle of 1991 have some Turkish newspapers, especially those more to the left, coined the new Turkish adjective "Turki" to distinguish the Turks of Central Asia from the adjective "Turk," which they now use to refer only to the Turks of Turkey. But this usage is artificial and far from in common parlance today. "Turk" is still the word to describe all Turks from Yugoslavia to Xinjiang.

52. "Kazakhstan Minister Signs Accord," *Turkish Times*, March 15, 1991.

53. These observations are based on interviews with a number of left-of-center Turkish intellectuals in September 1991.

54. James Critchlow, "Ties with Turkey: A Lifeline for the Central Asians?" *Report on the USSR* (Radio Free Liberty Bulletin), February 8, 1991, p. 19.

55. These views are based on the author's research trips to Central Asia in the summer of 1991 and spring of 1992 to examine the geopolitical orientation of the newly emerged republics.

56. This figure is the estimate of the Turkestan Research Trust (Turkistan Arastirmalari Vakfi) of Istanbul.

57. Based on discussions with a Mongol official at the Mongolian Center for Strategic Studies, August 1991.

58. See *Newspot*, English language edition, Ankara, April 11, 1991.

59. See *Hurriyet*, April 12, 1991.

60. See *Briefing*, March 18, 1991, Ankara, p. 3.

61. Coskun Kirca, "The Only Hope for Armenia," *Turkish Times*, February 12, 1991.

62. From an American journalist recently examining Turkish-Armenian relations, December 1991.

63. Over the short term Armenia enjoys far better military skills and superior equipment; over long run however, if Azerbaijan focuses on the long-term improvement of its military capabilities (with Turkish assistance?), Azerbaijan's vastly greater population and its physical encirclement of Karabakh gives it the edge in military resolution.

64. See Paul B. Henze, *Turkey and Georgia: Expanding Relations*, P-7758, Santa Monica, CA: RAND, 1992.

65. Henze, *Turkey and Georgia*, p. 15.

66. Patricia J. Higgins, "Minority-State Relations in Contemporary Iran," in Ali Banuazizi and Myron Weiner, eds., *The State, Religion, and Ethnic Politics: Afghanistan, Iran, and Pakistan*, Syracuse: Syracuse University Press, 1986, p. 178. While figures are unreliable, Higgins estimated Azeris to make up 9 million people out of a total population of some 34 million in 1986. Azeris themselves consider this figure to be extremely low and speak of 12–15 million.

67. Personal interview with a senior member of the Azerbaijani National Front, September 1991.

68. Azerbaijan currently uses a modified Cyrillic alphabet, but will return to its original Latin alphabet from the early 1920s (before even the Turks adopted the Latin alphabet). This is in distinction to the use of the Persian-Arabic alphabet for writing Azerbaijani in Iran.

69. "Azerbaijan Bridge Begins in March," *Turkish Times*, March 15, 1991.

70. "Armenian Special Envoy Brings Message to Demirel," *Turkish Times*, December 1, 1991. Also see "Recognition of Azerbaijan will set a model for other republics," *Turkish Times*, December 1, 1991.

71. Bruce Kuniholm, "Turkey and the West," *Foreign Affairs*, Spring 1991.

72. Christian Turkish minority in Moldova, *Gok Oguz* in Turkish—a name highly redolent of the Turkish atavistic past.

73. The data in this paragraph and most of the next are taken from "Economic Relations Between Turkey and the Soviet Union," by Nihat Gokyigit, cochairman of the Turkish-Soviet Business Council, presented in a report to the Turkish–U.S. Business Council in New York on October 31, 1991.

74. Gokyigit, "Economic Relations Between Turkey and the Soviet Union."

75. This experience in developing a newfound entrepreneurial expertise is very significant not only for Turkey but for other Third World states that were long viewed as having no "entrepreneurial tradition." Commerce in the Ottoman Empire and the early Turkish Republic was very much in the hands of minorities, usually Christian. Turkey's newer generations are now completely at home in the world of commerce.

76. "'Black Sea Prosperity Zone' Agreement to be Signed in April," *Turkish Times*, January 15, 1991.

77. *Economist Foreign Report*, April 11, 1991, p. 6.

3

Bridge or Barrier?
Turkey and the West After
the Cold War

Ian O. Lesser

With the revolutionary developments in eastern Europe and the former Soviet Union, and the transformation of East-West relations, many observers in Turkey and the West anticipated that Turkey would be a leading casualty of strategic neglect after the Cold War. Events in the Persian Gulf have returned Turkey to the strategic front rank, but the longer-term implications of developments in Europe, Central Asia, and the Middle East for Turkey's interests and geopolitical orientation are less clear. The reassertion of Turkey's importance in terms of Middle Eastern rather than European security, in particular, will challenge established images of Turkey's role in Washington, Brussels, and Ankara.

Turks inside and outside the government are increasingly resigned to Turkey's exclusion—at least in the near to mid-term—from the formal process of European integration, including the development of a European defense identity. But Turkey retains a strong interest in the European connection for political, economic, and security reasons. Beyond this, the Turkish elite remains firmly committed to the Western-looking Ataturkist tradition in cultural and intellectual terms. On a more practical level, frustration with Turkey's limited role in Europe has encouraged Turks to turn to alternative outlets for international activism in the republics of the former Soviet Union, the Balkans, and (perhaps with greater reservation in the wake of the Gulf War) the Middle East. The extraordinary flux in the strategic environment as a whole is encouraging the most active reassessment of Turkey's external interests and policies since the establishment of the Turkish Republic. Longstanding assumptions, including the Ataturkist dictates concerning nonintervention and the primacy of relations with Europe are subject to increasingly critical examination.

The elections of October 1991 swept President Turgut Ozal's Motherland Party from power, leaving doubt as to Ozal's own political future. The successor coalition of nationalists and social democrats led by Suleyman Demirel's conservative True Path Party is unlikely to result in a radical reorientation of Turkish foreign and security policy. But certain trends already evident prior to the elections, notably a growing sensitivity to issues of sovereignty, a tougher approach to the Kurdish insurgency (accompanied by a surprisingly flexible attitude on Kurdish cultural and social questions), and renewed rigidity on the Cyprus question, can be expected to solidify.[1] The coalition government has already surprised many observers with its active overtures in the Caucasus, Central Asia, and around the Black Sea. Developments in the Balkans are creating the conditions for a similar assertion of Turkish interests in that region. An activist stance toward any or all of these areas could have important implications for the character of Turkey's relations with Europe and the United States. The character and substance of Turkey's Western orientation, although not in doubt, will be influenced by changing Turkish perceptions of risk and opportunity. Moreover, Demirel and other mainstream politicians are likely to adopt a more conservative approach to relations with the United States on security matters in the wake of the Gulf experience.[2]

The following analysis explores the longer-term prospects for Turkey and the West. Specific issues to be addressed include the relevance of traditional notions regarding Turkey as a bridge between East and West; the prospects for Turkey in Europe, including relations in the Aegean; Turkey's strategic position and alliance relations; and the outlook for bilateral relations with the United States. Finally, some conclusions and implications for U.S. policy are offered. A central theme throughout is that Turkey's future external orientation will not be developed in a vacuum. It will emerge, at least in part, in response to U.S. and European policy. As many Turks will readily admit, strategy toward Turkey is too important to be left to Turkey alone.

Bridge or Barrier Between East and West?

The notion of Turkey as a bridge between East and West is a pervasive theme among the political and economic elite in Turkey and sympathetic observers elsewhere. Geographically, of course, Turkey straddles Europe and Asia. In cultural terms as well, modern Turkey is very much a product of both Eastern and Western influences. As Turks are quick to point out, Westernization in Turkey is not simply a product of Ataturkism. It is much older, and can be observed, for example, in the Byzantine influences on Ottoman society.

In political, economic, and strategic terms, Turkey will continue to be a potentially important actor in Europe, the Middle East, and Central Asia. But does this make Turkey a natural bridge between Europe and the Middle East, and does it give Turkey a special role and status? Physically and philosophically, Turkey has the potential to act as a bridge between these regions, but this role is not automatic and requires critical examination.[3] The history of Ottoman rule, and the more recent experience of Turkish cooperation with Western aims in the Middle East, encourage an arm's length relationship between Turkey and its Middle Eastern neighbors. Economic and resource interests (food, water, and oil) might favor the development of closer relations, as they did prior to the Gulf crisis, but these issues could just as easily emerge as causes of friction. Turkey is clearly linked to the Arab world through Islam, but even here Turkey's secular orientation sets it apart. A growing role for Islam in Turkish society and politics—and Turkey has become more overtly "religious" over the past two decades—might reinvigorate these ties, but would risk an equivalent estrangement from the West.[4]

The Turkish elite's keen awareness of Turkey's long involvement in European affairs, indeed its role as part of the European system, is only dimly reflected in prevailing European attitudes. The Europeans with the most highly developed sense of Turkey's historical involvement in Europe are to be found in the Balkans, and here the experience has left a negative legacy. With the very significant exception of Turkey's role in blocking Russian and later Soviet ambitions in the Balkans and the Caucasus, Europe has traditionally been far more concerned with constructing barriers to Turkish power and influence on the continent than with engaging Turkey as a strategic bridge between East and West. Yet, Turkey has been an active participant in European alliance systems: with France in the sixteenth century; with Britain, France, and Italy during the Crimean War; and with the central powers during World War I. Turkish participation in NATO may be considered an extension of this experience. The Turkish elite's view of this history is clearly framed in European terms.[5] An alternative interpretation would view much of this experience, certainly that of the fifteenth through eighteenth centuries, in terms of Turkish participation in a Mediterranean rather than European security system.[6]

As the half-century imperative of containing Soviet power wanes, Europe has lost a great deal of its interest in the strategic engagement of

Turkey. Indeed, as Europe looks to the creation of its own defense identity, there is a risk that Turkey will be seen as a strategic and political liability: a strategic liability because of its complex and immediate security concerns; a political liability because of its position outside the European Community (EC) and its close bilateral relationship with the United States.[7]

With regard to contemporary security problems in the Middle East, Turkey is again more likely to be seen as a barrier to extra-European turmoil and military threats than as an agent for dialogue. Only in the more limited sense of Turkey's role as a model for political and economic development in the Middle East and the former Soviet Union does the notion of Turkey as a bridge have significant resonance in Europe. Even here, European perceptions are not entirely to Turkey's advantage, as observers are just as likely to identify "Middle Eastern" elements in Turkey's own political situation. In this context, the deepening problem of the Kurdish insurgency in southeast Turkey is likely to exacerbate longstanding European human-rights concerns. Western opinion may find it difficult to reconcile the growing openness on Kurdish cultural issues (a trend begun by Ozal and continuing under Demirel) with Ankara's increasingly aggressive response to Kurdish separatism.

A related argument finds the concept of a bridge unconvincing because the Turks themselves are not in a position to fully understand both Europe and the Middle East as a result of their ambiguous history of involvement in both regions.[8] Although there is undoubtedly some truth in this assertion, it ignores the equally important question of whether Turkey's European and Middle Eastern neighbors are interested in having Turkey as an interlocutor. In addition to being a NATO member, Turkey is a full participant in both the Islamic Conference Organization (ICO) and the Council of Europe.[9] The character of these memberships is often used to support the argument that Turkey plays a unique bridging role between Europe and the Arab world. In truth, membership in these organizations has not greatly enhanced the understanding of Turkey in Europe or the Middle East.[10] The importance of these associations may rest, above all, on their ability to reassure Turkish elites and, in the case of NATO and the Council of Europe, lend an international imprimatur to the process of democratization in Turkey. Finally, the notion of a bridge suggests a country balanced between East and West. In fact, Turkish attitudes remain heavily weighted toward the Western political and economic system, to the extent that alternative opportunities in the Middle East and around the Black Sea are often promoted as vehicles for increasing Turkey's value to Europe and the United States.[11]

The Black Sea Initiative as a Political and Economic Bridge

The pursuit of regional cooperation initiatives has emerged as an important foreign policy trend across southern Europe. Turkey has made a substantial contribution to this trend through its Black Sea Economic Cooperation Project, aimed at the gradual establishment of a free trade zone among the states surrounding the Black Sea. The idea for a Black Sea initiative had been discussed by leading figures outside the government for some time, but was taken up with considerable vigor by President Ozal early in 1990, and given prominence in his discussions with President Bush and President Gorbachev over the course of 1991. Initial priorities include the establishment of more favorable conditions for trade and investment among the littoral states, improvements in communications and infrastructure, and administrative reforms aimed at encouraging commercial contacts. A Black Sea development bank is also under consideration.[12] The first meeting to discuss the Black Sea project was held in Ankara in December 1990, with the participation of Soviet, Turkish, Romanian, and Bulgarian representatives. Subsequent meetings were held in Bucharest and Sofia, and principles of cooperation were finalized in Moscow in July 1991, and initialed in Istanbul on January 3, 1992.[13] Six republics of the former Soviet Union have joined the initiative.[14]

The Black Sea project builds on a rapidly expanding volume of Turkish trade and investment across the Black Sea, embracing Moscow and the republics. Turkish enterprises, led by the construction and pharmaceutical industries, have been particularly active in developing commercial ties in those republics with large Turkic populations, but their activities have not been confined to these areas.[15] The expansion of Turkish involvement in the southern republics has occurred with the support of Moscow, where it has emerged as an attractive secular alternative to the Islamist model offered by Iran.[16]

In strategic terms, the initiative, together with economic and political overtures to Central Asia, has emerged as the centerpiece of Ankara's efforts to develop a more active external policy after the Cold War. The project is not dependent on relations in Europe or across the Atlantic, although, if successful, it could raise the value of Turkey to its Western partners. A leading architect of the Black Sea project regards it as perhaps Turkey's first independent regional initiative in fifty years, and one with potentially important security, as well as economic and political, consequences.[17] Turkish officials have also stressed the ability of the project to improve Turkey's longer-term prospects for EC membership. At a practical level, and after some hesitation, the initiative has been welcomed in Washington and Brussels as an attractive way of engaging the Black Sea states without obviously undercutting Moscow. With its relatively good infrastructure, Turkey could prove a most effective conduit for direct U.S. and EC aid to the southern republics of the former Soviet Union.[18] In some quarters, the Black Sea project has also been seen as welcome evidence that Ankara is developing interests beyond the difficult issue of EC membership. Finally, active cooperation around the Black Sea centered on Ankara could serve as a counterweight to Greek influence in the Balkans and enhance Turkey's position as a regional economic power.[19] Potential impediments to progress in Black Sea cooperation along the lines proposed by Turkey could arise from more serious turmoil in the former Soviet Union affecting the Black Sea republics, or political paralysis in Turkey itself which might inhibit an active policy toward the region.

Turkey and Europe

The prospects for Turkey's joining Europe in the institutional sense, that is, becoming a full member of the EC and the Western European Union (WEU), remain poor. Ironically, the prospects for Turkish membership in both organizations are probably worse today than before the Gulf crisis. Events in the Gulf, and Turkey's essential role in the allied coalition, have reinforced the belief, widespread among European policy elites, that Turkey is indeed an important and dependable Middle Eastern ally. As the EC explores the development of a common foreign and security policy, it will be increasingly unwilling to accept the additional burden of a direct exposure in the Middle East—particularly in the wake of the Gulf experience. Many Turkish observers are aware of these new obstacles, but preserve the belief that Turkey will nonetheless be a participant in the general process of European integration short of full membership.[20]

Turkey and the European Community

In December 1989, the European Commission, in a move endorsed by the European Council of Ministers, declined to open negotiations on Turkey's 1987 application for full membership. In deferring the Turkish application until 1993 at the earliest, the commission pointed to the extent of the challenges facing both parties: Turkey's low level of economic development by EC standards (almost half the per capita GDP of the EC's poorest countries, despite growth rates averaging over 5 percent throughout the 1980s, well above EC norms); its high rate of population growth (roughly 2.5 percent annually, ten times the EC average) and the prospect of 70 million Turks by the end of the century, compared to some 330 million in an EC of its current size; long-term foreign debt of $38 billion, the world's seventh highest; low tax revenue and high state expenditure (over twice the EC average); and a state-owned sector accounting for 40 percent of manufacturing output, despite Ozal's privatization campaign. To this daunting catalog, one might add an inflation rate of roughly 70 percent in 1992. Turkey is, however, one of the world's most favored agricultural producers. Turkish membership would increase the community's usable agricultural area by 22 percent and double European output in a variety of important products. In short, even the positive sides of the Turkish situation would pose considerable problems of adjustment for the community, not least the prospect of the free movement of Turkish labor at a time when immigration policy has emerged as a pressing issue across Europe.[21]

But the issue of EC membership is only partly about the economic consequences of extension for Turkey and Europe. Far more significant in the current debate are the political and strategic implications of full membership, and the awkward cultural questions of how Europe should be defined, and whether it should be defined at all. The fundamental issue for many Europeans is whether Europe can or should embrace an Islamic country of 57 million. Significantly, the issue is being posed at a time of mounting intolerance and xenophobia in western Europe, much of it directed against Muslim immigrants from the Maghreb and Turkey. Even on strict geographic grounds, the Turkish foot on the European continent is outweighed in European perception by the sheer size and political and economic weight of Anatolian Turkey. Former Foreign Minister Mesut Yilmaz's comment that "Europe is a state of mind, not an arbitrary line drawn down the Bosporus" is a very accurate reflection of elite attitudes in Turkey; most Europeans would agree, but would return to the question of cultural differences.[22]

Historically, Turkey has been part of the European and Mediterranean economic systems. The main trading partners of the Ottoman Empire were European, whether Venetian, Ragusan, Genoese, or English.[23] After the nineteenth century, these were dependent relationships, but prior to that point they were conducted essentially on an equal footing. However, within the current European economic system, Turkey is not in the European mainstream, a situation reinforced by the marked westward drift of the European economic center since 1945. Its position on the European periphery hinders communication with the rest of Europe, although this is undoubtedly a declining bar to economic relations in many areas (e.g., access to financial markets). Moreover, being outside the European mainstream is not unique to Turkey.

Portugal, Ireland, Greece, and, to an even greater extent, the Balkan countries, confront the same situation. In this context, it is worth speculating on the long term consequences of the reintegration of the eastern European countries, and perhaps the emergence of some of the republics of the former Soviet Union as significant economic actors, for the economic balance of Europe and Turkey's position in relation to it.[24] The notion of Turkey as a bridge between East and West may well be more convincing in the economic than the political context. Turkish initiatives in the former Soviet Union and the Balkans, including the ambitious plan for a Black Sea Economic Zone, could make Turkey a more promising economic partner for Europe, regardless of EC status.

From a strictly practical point of view, the essential economic objective for Turkey is not EC membership per se, but assured access to the European market. Less tangible, but critical from the Turkish perspective, are the symbolic value of EC membership and its domestic and external political consequences. Full membership would confirm and reinvigorate the Western-looking Ataturkist tradition, and give a valuable external imprimatur to the democratic process in Turkey. It would also provide a strong context for Turkish foreign and security policy at a time of strategic flux. The incentives for Turkey are elegantly summarized in Professor Seyfi Tashan's observation that "NATO is our legal foot in the Western camp, but the EC is the real one."[25]

The European Commission's 1989 decision rules out the possibility of full membership in the near term. The longer-term prospects for membership will be shaped not only by economic and political developments in Turkey, but by the evolution of the EC itself. An EC of roughly the current size and composition, giving priority to the deepening of existing institutions and arrangements, is unlikely to encourage the formal integration of Turkey. On the other hand, an expanded EC, having embraced the EFTA (European Free Trade Area) countries and perhaps some of the countries of eastern Europe, may be more amenable to Turkish membership. In October 1991, Turkey concluded a free trade and cooperation agreement with EFTA. Together with the EC's recent decision to include the EFTA countries in its conception of the post-1992 European economic space, the new agreement will contribute significantly to Turkey's integration in the European economic system.[26] If formal expansion of the EC into eastern Europe, particularly the Balkans, does not lead to more active consideration of the Turkish application, Turkish frustration and resentment are bound to increase.

From the Turkish perspective, the EC Commission's assessment of Turkey's economic position reflects an overly "static" approach. Critics of the commission's opinion charge that it fails to reflect the dynamic quality of Turkey's economic, industrial and social evolution, and neglects the rapidly narrowing gap between the EC and Turkey. Moreover, it is argued that similar disparities existed at the start of accession negotiations with Greece, Spain, and Portugal. The EC's failure to establish even an approximate date for the opening of accession negotiations is seen as a particularly discouraging indication of the community's intentions.[27]

Indefinite postponement of the Turkish application has, however, been accompanied by a commitment from Brussels to revitalize economic cooperation under the existing Association Agreement, including completion of the customs union between the EC and Turkey by 1995, release of assistance funds earmarked for Turkey (distribution of which continues to be blocked by Greece pending progress on the withdrawal of Turkish forces from Cyprus), and the expansion of joint programs in the areas of science and technology and education.[28] To the extent that Turkey's application is taken seriously in Brussels, there has been considerable confusion over the meaning and implications of recent Turkish trade initiatives. The notion of a free-trade agreement with the United States, however unlikely, and elements of the Black Sea program are regarded as incompatible with full Turkish membership in the community. Indeed, these initiatives might conflict with arrangements to which Turkey has already committed itself under the Association Agreement, not least the establishment of a full customs union.[29]

Prospects for Participation in New European Security Arrangements

The likelihood that Turkey will be excluded from efforts to construct a European defense identity (with an operational dimension) around the WEU, has emerged as a more disturbing prospect for Ankara than the broader problem of exclusion from the EC.[30] President Ozal expressed his dissatisfaction with Turkey's observer status in the WEU, asserting that Turkey cannot be expected to play its traditionally strong role in defense of the continent if it is unable to "participate fully in the making of the new Europe."[31] Similar reservations exist with regard to Ankara's current, non-voting, associate status in the organizaton. Uncertainty about the future role and significance of NATO will reinforce Turkish interests in emerging European defense arrangements. Turkish exclusion from full participation in these arrangements, regardless of their precise form, would be understood in Ankara as a demonstration of Europe's unwillingness to grant Turkey a legitimate security role on the continent.

The denial of a formal role would, in the Turkish view, ignore centuries of involvement in European security affairs. The fact that the Turkish role has more often been that of an adversary than an ally does not change the fact that Turkey's involvement has been of great importance to the European balance in the past (does the history of Franco-German enmity argue against the participation of either country in the WEU?). The reemergence of the Balkans as a center of European security concerns reinforces the relevance of this history.[32]

Turkey's concerns about its role in future European defense arrangements have been of two sorts: The broader fear of a security future cast largely in extra-European terms; and the narrower concern that the European security umbrella would be extended to Greece but exclude Turkey, with serious implications for stability in the Aegean. In this context, former Foreign Minister Safa Giray declared that "EC efforts to add a military dimension to the goal of geopolitical union should not undermine the balances among the countries that play a role in this."[33] Clearly, the WEU's concern about the risks involved in embracing Turkey have also affected debate on the Greek application, but not to the extent of excluding Greece from full participation as the Maastricht decision to offer full WEU membership to Athens made clear.[34] Those European countries that wish to move quickly toward a common foreign and security policy will wish to defer difficult membership decisions. The recent Franco-German proposal for European defense cooperation, in calling for the expansion of the WEU to include Denmark, Ireland, and Greece, and the adoption of this approach at Maastricht, will reinforce Turkish concerns about exclusion from the emerging European security order.[35] If, as seems likely, the EC embraces the WEU as its security arm, or co-opts it altogether, the prospects for formal Turkish participation in European defense arrangements will almost certainly evaporate. On the other hand, a more confident WEU might well seek to bolster existing arrangements with Ankara. The decision to offer Turkey associate status in the WEU, while far from ideal from Ankara's perspective, is evidence of this. Broader cooperation between Turkey and the EC on foreign policy matters might also be encouraged by giving Turkey a role in European Political Cooperation (EPC) mechanisms.

In the wake of Turkey's strong pro-Western stance during the Gulf crisis, the outlook for Turkish participation in the security dimension of European integration, like the outlook for formal participation in the process of economic integration, is no brighter than before. The reassertion of Turkey's strategic importance for Western interests in the Middle East has given new momentum to Turkey's transatlantic relations, but has failed to produce a similar effect in Turkey's relations with the EC and the WEU.[36]

Bilateral Relations with Europe

Turkey's institutional difficulties in Europe are exacerbated by, and to an extent derive from, a lack of solid bilateral support. Not all of the friction between Turkey and Europe at the bilateral level stems from the Greek-Turkish dispute and the unresolved problem of Cyprus. Indeed, many Turkish observers will agree that Greece does not represent the only or even the most important opponent to Turkey in Europe.

Turkish-German relations provide the leading example of the difficulty of relations with Europe at the bilateral level. Germany is Turkey's largest trading partner. Both countries share a history of active economic, political, and strategic cooperation dating to the nineteenth century.[37] This background, together with the presence of roughly 1.5 million Turkish workers in Germany, complicates Turkish-German relations, raising expectations but also producing a certain wariness on both sides. The reluctant German response to Turkish requests for assistance and reinforcement from NATO during the Gulf crisis has left a negative impression on Turkish opinion, an impression that has not been erased by subsequent contributions. Eighteen German Alpha Jets were eventually deployed to Erhac and Diyarbakir as part of the AMF-A (Allied Mobile Force-Air) reinforcements.[38] The swiftness of German assistance to Kurdish refugees in Iran only reinforced the impression in Ankara that the German problem was less the propriety of action outside NATO's Central Region than a reluctance to commit forces in Turkey's defense. German behavior is particularly troubling for Turks as it calls into question the solidity of the NATO security guarantee to Turkey in the wake of the Gulf experience. Ozal's pointed remarks on the German response may contain an element of crisis-induced exaggeration and rhetoric, but there can be little doubt that they reflect an acute and continuing sense of frustration over German policy and attitudes.[39]

German public and official opinion has been among the most sensitive in Europe on the issue of Ankara's human rights record in general, and the Kurdish problem in particular. As the insurgency in the southeast has intensified, criticism of Turkish policy, and especially the cross border operations against the Kurdish Worker's Party (PKK), has increased. In the winter of 1991–1992, a portion of German military credits to Turkey was placed on hold pending the resolution of questions concerning the use of German-financed equipment in raids against Kurdish separatists.[40] Turkish officials, for their part, have been highly critical of Bonn's tolerant attitude toward the activities of Kurdish political organizations in Germany. Overall, the apparent indifference of German politicians and press toward the new government's more direct treatment of human rights and Kurdish issues has come as a keen disappointment to

the Turkish political and economic elite.[41] The deterioration of bilateral
relations with Germany suggests that the Demirel government's more
liberal approach on human rights matters will not necessarily clear the
way for closer relations with Europe if the Kurdish insurgency continues
to escalate and perhaps develop an urban dimension.

Germany is widely viewed as the one country that could successfully
promote Turkey's application for membership in the EC. The fact that
German policymakers have been unwilling to do so has reinforced the
Turkish sense of frustration over German policy. The principal German
concern in this context has been the prospect of additional Turkish
migrants in Germany if all restrictions on the movement of labor were
to be removed. Indeed, the future of the existing 1.5 million Turks in
Germany is set to emerge as an even more pressing issue in bilateral
relations as migrants from eastern Europe and the former Soviet Union
begin to compete with Turks in the German labor market, and as the
general climate facing foreigners in Germany deteriorates. The return
of substantial numbers of guest workers to Turkey, as a result of official
policy or disinclination to remain in Germany, would pose serious
problems for Ankara. Turkish workers abroad come from predominantly rural and religious backgrounds, and many have developed fundamentalist inclinations in response to their marginal position in
German society (fundamentalist groups, Kurdish nationalists and others have been able to organize and operate with greater ease in emigre
communities than in Turkey). Their return would introduce a body of
unemployed and dissatisfied younger people into the Turkish political
equation, and perhaps strengthen the position of religious and nationalist parties. The loss of foreign remittances would also have an adverse
effect on the Turkish economy.[42]

Germany has been a leading source of foreign investment in Turkey,
and by far the largest source of tourist revenues.[43] Turkish investment
in Germany has also been substantial. The prospects for increased
German investment and aid to Turkey will undoubtedly be limited by
the rise of competing outlets for financial attention in eastern Germany
and eastern Europe.

France, with its long tradition of support for Greece, a highly politicized immigration problem, and its preference for rapid integration
within the existing EC is unlikely to emerge as a champion of Turkish
membership in Europe. Italy and Spain could play a helpful role on the
issue of Turkish membership and improved EC-Turkish relations in general.[44] Certainly, the prompt Italian response to Turkish needs during
the Gulf crisis has been noted in Ankara.[45] The concept of a CSCE
(Conference on Security and Cooperation in Europe) for the
Mediterranean or "CSCM" promoted by Italy and Spain could provide a

useful vehicle for Turkish participation in a framework that is neither too European nor too Middle Eastern.[46] To date, however, CSCM has not evoked much more than passing interest in Ankara, perhaps because of the primacy Turkish policymakers place on the U.S. role in the eastern Mediterranean.

With the end of the Cold War, north-south relations in the Mediterranean have become the focus of growing debate, not only in the southern European countries, but in Europe as a whole. Issues of concern include the developmental and demographic imbalance between north and south and the resulting immigration pressures; the implications of Islamic fundamentalism and political change in the Maghreb; and the continued growth of conventional and unconventional arsenals along the southern and eastern shores of the Mediterranean. The debate on these security and security-related issues is taking place against a background of uncertainty on the broader question of Europe's evolving relationship with the Islamic world—including the Islamic population in western Europe and the Balkans. It is unlikely that Turkey's relations with Europe can remain unaffected by the evolution of this broader relationship. Ozal has hinted at the risks inherent in allowing religion to drive political decisions in Europe's institutions, asserting that if Islam emerges as an overt bar to Turkey's membership in the EC or the WEU, this might drive Turkey into a closer relationship with the Middle East, encourage the spread of fundamentalism, and "send a wrong message to the rest of the Arab world."[47]

Turkish-Greek Relations

Despite broad rhetorical support in Ankara for attempts to reinvigorate the process of detente launched by Ozal and Papandreou in Davos in 1988, there has been little progress toward this goal.[48] The declining sense of political confidence within the conservative government in Athens has made this a difficult task. Equally problematic are the results of the October 1991 Turkish elections and the return of coalition government. Under these conditions, bold new initiatives in Aegean relations are unlikely. In the absence of political personalities with the confidence and freedom of action enjoyed by Ozal and Papandreou at the height of their political careers, the prospects for a sweeping improvement in Greek-Turkish relations on the pattern of the extraordinary Ataturk-Venizelos detente of the interwar years must be considered limited.

A full discussion of the history and points of contention in the Aegean dispute is beyond the scope of this analysis.[49] A brief list of key issues would certainly include the dispute over military and civil air traffic control zones; the delineation of sovereign rights on the continental shelf; the question of territorial waters claimed by each country; and the fortification of Greek islands in the Dodecanese and the eastern Aegean.[50] Beyond these issues is the separate but related question of the status and treatment of minorities: the residual Greek Orthodox population of Istanbul and the Turkish islands of Gokceada and Bozcaada; and the more substantial Muslim (and predominantly Turkish) minority in Greek Thrace.[51]

Above all, Turkish relations with the West have been most seriously affected by the continuing dispute over Cyprus, where the northern half of the island has been occupied by some 30,000 Turkish troops since the intervention of 1974.[52] The issue of Cyprus looms large in Greek and European perceptions, and has been a consistent impediment to Turkey in its relations with the EC and the United States. In the case of the "Johnson letter" of 1964 and again with the 1974 arms embargo, the Cyprus question has led to a crisis in bilateral relations with Washington.[53] Nonetheless, Cyprus, and the issue of Greek-Turkish relations in general, while relevant to Turkish domestic politics, do not occupy the attention of Turkish policymakers and elites to anything like the extent found in Athens. Ankara simply faces too many competing foreign and security policy issues. By contrast, the Cyprus dispute has enormous symbolic importance in Greek perceptions. Resolution of the Cyprus problem would transform the overall climate of Greek-Turkish relations and facilitate the settlement of more practical questions concerning air and sea space and resources in the Aegean.[54]

In the wake of the Gulf War, the United States adopted an active approach to the Cyprus issue, a policy that resulted in serious negotiations under United Nations auspices.[55] A September 1991 meeting in Paris between then Prime Minister Mesut Yilmaz and Prime Minister Mitsotakis, although a clear display of political goodwill, failed to produce an anticipated agreement on a quadripartite conference. The leading obstacles to progress in this case appear to have been the growing wariness of Turkish Cypriots coupled with impending elections in Turkey which left Ankara with little ability to negotiate.[56] Neither a coalition government in Ankara nor a precarious conservative leadership in Athens (the New Democracy Party rules with a single-seat majority) are likely to risk accusations of having "sold out" the interests of their respective communities on Cyprus. Developments in the former Soviet Union could also affect the prospects for a settlement. Should one or more of the emerging Central Asian republics recognize the Turkish Republic of Northern Cyprus, ending its isolation, Turkish and Turkish Cypriot policy might harden.

Finally, there is a certain amount of inertia associated with an apparently tolerable status quo. The Republic of Cyprus and the Turkish Republic of Northern Cyprus both enjoy a higher standard of living than mainland Greece or Turkey. Indeed, a post-settlement Cyprus would be a prime candidate for EC membership.[57] In the absence of progress toward a Cyprus settlement, Greek opposition continues to serve as an impediment not only to Turkish membership in the EC, but also to a significant deepening of relations at the current level. As noted earlier, Greece has consistently used its veto power within the EC to prevent the release of more than $800 million in financial assistance earmarked for Turkey in 1986, pending movement toward the withdrawal of Turkish troops from northern Cyprus.[58]

Opinion in Ankara regards the conservative government in Athens with some suspicion precisely because of its comparative popularity elsewhere in the West after a decade of socialist rule. In short, it is feared that the Mitsotakis government will use its support in the United States and Europe to pursue a more aggressive policy toward Turkey, including new pressure on the Turkish minority in Thrace.[59] The presence and position of this minority constitutes a leading source of risk in contemporary Greek-Turkish relations. Whereas territorial and resource disputes in the Aegean may ultimately be amenable to discourse and compromise between governments, frictions in Thrace, like those on Cyprus, are more likely to be driven by the perceptions of residents whose behavior may or may not be controllable from Ankara and Athens. With the deepening crisis in and around Yugoslavia, there is a further danger that Thrace will be caught up in broader Balkan strife.

There are roughly 200,000 Muslims, mostly ethnic Turks, in Greek Thrace, a community that is growing rapidly by Greek standards. Indeed, the Greek government has sought to offset this progressive change in the ethnic balance by resettling in Thrace ethnic Greek immigrants from the Pontus region of the former Soviet Union.[60] To the extent that the Turkish minority in this economically underdeveloped region looks to Turkey as its natural protector, Athens fears that the conditions may exist for a new Cyprus-like intervention. This concern is reinforced by the existence of broader cleavages between Orthodox and Muslim communities elsewhere in the Balkans. (The implications of these cleavages are explored in detail in Chapter 4 of this book.) The status of Muslim minorities in Greek Thrace, Kosovo, Macedonia, and Bulgaria is of direct concern to Ankara, not least because of public anxiety about the prospects of further migration from the Balkans (as well as the Caucasus and the Middle East). The experience of 1989, in which some 320,000 Bulgarian Turks fled to Turkey, remains in the minds of many Turks who view it as an indication of the potential consequences of too close an involvement in neighboring regions.[61] In the post-Cold War environment, key issues in Turkish-Greek relations are increasingly tied to the broader evolution of ethnic and interstate problems in the Balkans.

Of the many points of contention in the Aegean, one of the most pressing from the Turkish perspective has been the presence of Greek forces on islands close to the Turkish coast in the eastern Aegean. Ankara has consistently opposed the introduction of these forces, which began in earnest in the 1960s, as an illegal remilitarization of territory demilitarized under the Treaty of Lausanne (1923). Turkish strategists and policymakers are concerned about preserving unimpeded movement through the Aegean archipelago, both as a practical commercial and strategic matter, and as part of a less tangible sense of geopolitical vulnerability. In this context, Turks are keenly aware of the history of Greek operations in Anatolia in 1922, and the continuing debate in Greek political and intellectual circles on the "Great Idea," the quest for reunification of former Greek territories around the Aegean basin.[62]

A recent Greek proposal for the demilitarization of borders in Thrace, supported by Bulgaria, was rejected by Ankara, ostensibly because it failed to embrace Greek forces in the Aegean islands.[63] Greek and Bulgarian interests in the Balkans would clearly be served by arms-control arrangements which would encourage a shift in the center of gravity of Turkey's strategic orientation from Europe to Asia. Despite the existence of competing strategic requirements on its Middle Eastern borders and the evaporation of the Warsaw Pact threat to Thrace, Turkish military and civilian leaders can be expected to react warily to future proposals affecting forces in Thrace, not least because of the perceived value of Turkish military superiority in deterring the mistreatment of Muslim minorities in Bulgaria, Greece, and elsewhere in the Balkans. The evaporation of the Soviet threat to Thrace has allowed Greek defense planners to shift their attention to Turkey, completing a trend observable since the Cyprus crisis of 1974.[64] Greek and Bulgarian concerns about the effect of allied equipment transfers to Turkey as a result of the CFE (Conventional Forces in Europe) Treaty, and the potential concentration of forces in the "exclusion zone"—including the port of Mersin from which the Turkish garrison in Cyprus is supplied—allowed under the agreement, have been reinforced by the Gulf crisis and the prospective modernization of Turkish forces.[65]

The prospects for Turkish-Greek relations remain highly uncertain. Cyprus, the Aegean, and Thrace will remain potential flashpoints and pose a continuing problem of crisis prevention for Europe and the United States. The Greek sense of insecurity in relation to a neighbor of continental scale and uncertain strategic orientation is certain to persist, and will be supported by deep rooted cultural and historical factors.

Should Turkey continue to be isolated from the process of European integration and the development of new defense arrangements, the outlook for peaceful relations in the Aegean and Thrace will very likely worsen. More optimistically, there are tentative signs that Athens and Ankara have recognized that expressions of animosity may no longer serve the interests of either country in a less tolerant post-Cold War environment. The balance of incentives may well be changing for both parties as they seek to bolster relations with the United States.[66] But conflicting interests in the Balkans will remain a leading source of risk in Turkish-Greek relations.

As NATO moves through a period of uncertainty, the idea that Turkish involvement in the EC could serve to anchor and stabilize Turkish-Greek relations, widely discussed in moderate circles in Athens and Ankara, may gain momentum. Members of the business community in both countries are among the strongest advocates of Aegean detente as a means of improving relations with the EC and as a source of opportunity in its own right.[67] Ironically, as the incentives for Greek opposition to Turkey within the EC may be declining, there is a growing perception in Turkey that Europe as a whole tolerates and even fuels Greek-Turkish enmity as a pretext for holding Turkey at arm's length.[68]

The Security Dimension

A shift of Turkey's strategic priorities from traditional lines in the Balkans and the Caucasus to address new risks in the Middle East, including those emanating from Iran, Iraq, Syria, and the activities of Kurdish separatists in southeast Anatolia, may encourage a further separation of Turkish and European security interests.[69] Nonetheless, Turkey will retain a strong interest in European security arrangements, and will look to its ties with the United States and NATO to ensure itself of a continuing role. The success of this approach will depend in large measure on the evolution of Western perceptions of Turkey's strategic importance and the implications of prospective defense improvements.

Turkey and NATO

Turkey shares with the United States a strong interest in the preservation of existing security structures and relationships, not least the NATO link. Traditionally, this observation has applied to most of the NATO Southern Region countries (Portugal, Spain, Italy, Greece, and Turkey), but the Turkish stake in the maintenance of the institutional status quo is especially pronounced since the alternative of a European defense identity remains closed to Turkey. Germany's response in the context of the NATO decision to send allied reinforcements to Turkey during the Gulf crisis, referred to earlier, has also left lingering doubts about the dependability of the NATO guarantee in the absence of a Soviet threat. Yet, the NATO connection retains tremendous symbolic and material importance. Above all, participation in the alliance is seen, rather like the prospect of EC membership, as a symbol of Turkey's membership in the Western democratic "club." It also gives Ankara a greater voice than it might otherwise have in international affairs. Equally important in relation to developments in Europe and the Gulf, is NATO's ability to provide a multilateral and Euro-Atlantic framework for defense cooperation that might otherwise appear too heavily weighted toward the bilateral relationship with the United States and Middle Eastern security. Indeed, this may take on even greater importance for the Demirel government as the Turkish political debate reflects growing sensitivity on these points.

Despite the new attention to Mediterranean security within NATO, including the risks facing Turkey, it is worth considering how useful the Southern Region framework will be in assessing Turkey's future position within the alliance.[70] Traditionally, Turkey has shared certain characteristics with NATO's other southern allies. Leaving aside the Italian case which is somewhat unique, these characteristics have included a lower level of economic and defense-industrial development, the experience of a recent democratic transition, and a relatively low level of military capability despite high manpower levels. Unlike its Southern Region allies, Turkey has never seen the Soviet threat as distant and diffuse, but rather as an historically potent and pressing reality.[71] Indeed, until quite recently, Ankara has retained a very conservative view of developments in the Soviet Union and the strategic implications of East-West disengagement in Europe. As late as the spring of 1990, it was still possible for a visitor to the Turkish ministries of foreign affairs and national defense to hear the "Soviet threat" described in traditional terms, in striking contrast to the official mood elsewhere in the Southern Region (and in NATO headquarters).

Turkey stands apart from the trend toward Europeanization that is driving the evolution of foreign and security policies across the Southern Region. In strategic terms, this has meant that countries such as Portugal and Greece are increasingly unwilling to adopt positions on security issues, including defense cooperation with the United States, that are at variance with their European partners. Southern Europe looks first to Brussels in these as in other matters in a general movement toward convergence with the European mainstream.[72] Turkey's isolation from this process alone suggests that the Turkish position within the Southern Region—indeed within NATO as a whole—is becoming more rather than less distinctive.

Ankara retains a wary attitude toward the development of an "out-of-area" role for NATO. In practice, a formal expansion of the alliance's area of responsibility is both unlikely for NATO and problematic for Turkey. In the Turkish perspective, the defense of Turkey's Middle Eastern borders is clearly an in-area responsibility for the alliance. Although the NATO treaty leaves no doubt that Turkey is correct on this point, the experience of the Gulf crisis, in particular the debate over AMF reinforcements, has undermined Turkish faith in the NATO guarantee outside East-West contingencies. Ankara can have little interest in the growth of a debate about out-of-area, or worse "gray area," responses. Turkish sensitivities on this point include the possibility of being called on to provide forces or more automatic access to bases for the support of operations in the Middle East. NATO's adoption of a more active role outside Europe would severely complicate Turkey's already delicate relations with the Arab world.

CFE and Nuclear Issues

Even in the wake of the disintegration of the Soviet Union, Ankara retains a rather conservative view of the residual military threat to Turkey from this quarter. This approach to the implications of recent developments in East-West relations is, as noted earlier, a product of Turkish historical experience. It also reflects a natural attachment to a strategic view that has served Turkey very well throughout the Cold War, and more tangible concerns. The security benefits of the Soviet withdrawal from eastern Europe and the CFE agreement are less direct, and even ambiguous in the Turkish case. The large conventional (and unconventional) arsenals facing Turkey in the Middle East fall outside current arms-control initiatives, a risk only partially offset in Turkish perceptions by the exclusion zone in southeastern Turkey provided for by the CFE agreement. Moreover, Turkey's proximity to former Soviet forces behind the Urals, could leave Turkey in a relatively unfavorable position within the alliance after implementation of the CFE accords.

The announced reductions in NATO's sub-strategic nuclear forces, including those based in Turkey, will ensure that Turkey remains within the alliance mainstream on nuclear matters.[73] The new initiative will result in the removal of all nuclear weapons in Turkey with the exception of those carried by aircraft.[74] The continued presence of these forces in Turkey as short-range weapons are withdrawn from Europe would have raised the prospect of Turkey's "singularization." This would be as politically unattractive in Turkey as in Germany, or elsewhere in the alliance.[75] Over the longer term, however, Turkish attitudes on nuclear questions will be influenced by the extent of the proliferation threat on

Turkey's Middle Eastern borders. Ankara will need to pursue policies designed to deter the threat of weapons of mass destruction without giving additional encouragement to regional proliferators.

Extra-European Security Concerns and Their Effect

Turkey's armed forces are the second largest in NATO, totaling 579,000 in active service (almost 500,000 of which are conscripts), with over one million in the reserves. The defense budget for 1991 was $4.8 billion, a marked increase from the 1990 figure of $3.4 billion, which itself represented a virtual doubling of the previous year's budget even prior to the Iraqi invasion of Kuwait.[76] Defense spending currently represents roughly 12.5 percent of the Turkish budget. These figures are a tangible reflection of two realities. First, Ankara remains wary of the longer-term implications of instability on its border with the former Soviet Union and, above all, sees a range of serious security risks flowing from the Middle East. These include the challenge of an increasingly aggressive Kurdish insurgency led by the PKK, with its bases in Iraq and Syria. Second, Turkey is now addressing in earnest its longstanding military modernization needs, an imperative highlighted and given new urgency by the experience of the Gulf War.

The Iran-Iraq war and the process of militarization affecting Turkey's neighbors, including Syria, had stimulated a progressive shift in Turkish defense priorities away from traditional lines in Thrace and the Caucasus and toward the south and east. Consideration of Turkey's strategic vulnerabilities and assets in relation to security on its Middle Eastern borders also began to receive increased attention.[77] As an example, from the mid-1980s, Turkish defense officials had begun to pay close attention to the mounting dependence of Iraq on Turkish pipelines and road transport for the export of oil during the war with Iran. The Gulf War and its aftermath have simply confirmed and reinforced emerging perceptions about the regional ambitions and expanding arsenals across Turkey's borders, not least the growing threat from weapons of mass destruction, including ballistic missiles of increasing range and accuracy.

The prospect of a revived Iraq posing a conventional and unconventional threat to Turkey is an obvious source of concern in light of Turkey's prominent role in the coalition against Baghdad. The recent upsurge in PKK activity from bases in Iraq, and the Turkish cross-border operations aimed at suppressing it, have drawn Turkey more directly into the problem of Iraq's future and raised new concerns in Europe about Turkey's policy toward the Kurds.[78] The prospects for additional European (especially German) security assistance to Turkey may well be affected by the perception that Turkey's defense requirements are being driven by the Kurdish insurgency, which has caused at least 5,000 civilian and military deaths in southeastern Anatolia since 1984. Indeed, many critics point to Ozal's activist stance in the Gulf as a leading source of the deepening Kurdish problem as well as a very uncertain outlook for Turkey in the Middle East as a whole.

Above all, Turkey faces longer-term security risks from Iran, with its competing aims in Azerbaijan and active interest in nuclear and ballistic missile technology, and Syria. Points of risk with regard to Syria include a territorial dispute over Turkish Antioch, continuing Syrian support for the PKK (the PKK and Dev Sol, the leftist terrorist organization, have been allowed to establish training bases in the Syrian controlled Bekaa Valley), and the growth of the Syrian arsenal. Turkish population centers in the southeast are already vulnerable to Syrian SS-21 and Scud missiles.[79] To these issues, one might add the ongoing friction over Turkey's control of the Tigris and Euphrates waters. Syria and Iraq have alleged that the Ataturk Dam, under construction as part of Turkey's Southeast Anatolia Project, will severely restrict the downstream flow.[80] The aggressive strategy which Turkey has adopted toward the Kurdish insurgency, including cross-border operations in Iraq, involving large-scale ground operations and extensive air strikes, and the establishment of a de facto "security zone" inside Iraqi territory, may eventually affect Turkey's relations with Syria.[81] Some Turkish observers have even speculated on the possibility of a Turkish strike against PKK and Dev Sol bases in the Bekaa Valley. Short of this, a "hot pursuit" incident on the Syrian border, against the background of long-standing frictions on other matters, would pose a serious risk of escalation.

Defense Improvement and Gulf Lessons

Given the nature of the security challenges facing Turkey in the Middle East (Turkish officials like to use the metaphor of "living in a tough neighborhood"), the impetus for continuing and expanding Turkey's defense modernization program will be strong. Turkey is scheduled to be the recipient of substantial CFE-surplus armaments "cascaded" under NATO's Equipment Transfer Program. The transfers will include roughly 1,050 M-60 and Leopard tanks, 700 armored combat vehicles, 70 110mm artillery pieces, 40-F-4 fighters, Cobra attack helicopters, and Roland surface-to-air missiles. Turkey has also concluded agreements for the purchase of additional ex-Soviet helicopters, and the purchase and coproduction of U.S. helicopters. These arms will make a significant contribution to the modernization of Turkey's forces while satisfying the reduction requirements of the treaty.[82] The scale of the armaments acquired in this manner, together with other prospective transfers in the wake of the Gulf War, have raised questions about the future of Turkey's own defense industrial programs as well as the operations and maintenance burden of these weapons.[83]

The Gulf crisis has had the effect of reinforcing a trend already under way toward the reorientation of Turkey's defense priorities from Thrace and the Caucasus to the Middle East. The experience of the crisis has also influenced the thinking of Turkey's strategic elite in other ways. In contrast to the experience elsewhere in NATO's Southern Region, where, as a rule, the enthusiasm of the military for active participation in the coalition operations was tempered by the conservatism of the political leadership, the Turkish General Staff adopted a very cautious approach to military involvement in the Gulf. Their conservatism can be explained, in part, by their adherence to Ataturk's precepts against foreign adventurism and compromising Turkish sovereignty. Beyond this, however, the military leadership apparently had serious doubts about Turkey's ability to deploy and sustain forces beyond their own territory, or even to conduct large-scale mobile operations on the border with Iraq. In short, close observation of the campaign in the Gulf confirmed the unpreparedness of the Turkish armed forces to wage modern conventional warfare. It has even cast doubt on the value of the relatively modern equipment to be acquired from the allies as a result of the CFE agreement.

The deployment of 100,000 Turkish troops along the border with Iraq (posing the threat of a second front and an important contribution to the coalition strategy in the Gulf) required the largest movement of forces since the 1974 invasion of Cyprus. Difficulties encountered in this operation and more general observation of Gulf "lessons" have led the General Staff to undertake a series of sweeping reforms aimed at improving the operational ability of the Turkish military. Land forces are to be reduced by roughly one-third, to 350,000 by July 1992. The division system is to be eliminated entirely and replaced by a system of brigades with the aim of improving mobility. Airborn refueling operations practiced with American forces during the Gulf crisis (Turkish aircraft remained within Turkish airspace) have led to plans for the acquisition of two tankers, dramatically increasing the operational range of Turkish fighters and allowing them to be based at less vulnerable bases away from Turkey's borders.[84]

Not surprisingly, air defense, including the acquisition of Patriot and additional F-16s (Turkish F-16 strength will eventually reach the impressive total of 320 coproduced aircraft) has emerged as a leading priority. In the absence of these systems, Turkey will remain vulnerable to air and ballistic missile attack, a vulnerability that could affect Turkey's willingness to permit foreign military operations from Turkish bases in non-NATO contingencies. Indeed, Turkey's inability to defend itself against the Iraqi Scud and conventional air threat, and the consequent need to allow the presence of NATO air defense forces on Turkish territory as a deterrent, has been seen as a double blow to Turkish sovereignty. Nonetheless, the expansion of Turkish airpower and ground-based air defenses to a level commensurate with the scale of forces facing Turkey in the Middle East (Syria deploys some 650 combat aircraft) will inevitably raise questions about the military balance in the Balkans. These questions will not be limited to air defense. The restructuring and modernization of Turkey's land forces will, as noted earlier, be driven by the need to develop a capacity for mobile operations in the Middle East, rather than a positional defense against a Soviet threat in Thrace or the Caucasus. The net result of this strategic and operational reorientation will be an increase in the offensive capability of the Turkish armed forces from the Aegean to the Iraqi border.[85]

Turkey and the United States

The relationship between the United States and Turkey dates from the first quarter of the nineteenth century, when the U.S. presence in the Mediterranean began to expand eastward, spurred by the attractions of the "Turkey trade" and the lure of bases in the Levant. The deepening of ties between the United States and Ottoman Turkey was at the same time limited by popular American enthusiasm for Greek national aspirations and a reluctance to become embroiled in the "Eastern Question," specifically the problem of containing Russian power in the eastern Mediterranean as an element of the European balance (the contrast with post-1945 attitudes is striking). Economic ties with the Ottoman Empire did however grow steadily through the turn of the century. In a curious reversal of the current situation, petroleum products actually made up a large percentage of American exports to the eastern Mediterranean and the Levant before 1900. Ottoman Turkey was a large purchaser of surplus weapons and ammunition from the American Civil War.[86]

Relations with the Ottoman Empire were severed following the U.S. entry into World War I, and were not fully restored with the new Turkey until 1927. The Treaty of Lausanne establishing postwar arrangements for the former Ottoman territories, of which the United States was a signatory, was not ratified by Congress until 1930. Turkish observers often refer to this extended delay in ratification as the first serious setback in bilateral relations, noting that the obstacles to smoother relations have hardly changed since 1930: perceptions of Greek-Turkish and

Armenian-Turkish issues. Turkish neutrality during World War II ensured that bilateral ties remained at a modest level through 1945, after which Turkey emerged as a key actor in the early years of the Cold War. Indeed, the Cold War and the strategy of containment could be said to have had their origins in the eastern Mediterranean with the Truman Doctrine and the U.S. commitment to bolster the "Northern Tier" of Greece, Turkey, Iran, and Afghanistan as a bar to Soviet adventurism in the Middle East.[87] Thus began the cycle of strategic perception in which Turkey's importance in American eyes has been defined alternately in Middle Eastern, European, and, again, in the aftermath of recent developments in the Gulf, Middle Eastern terms.[88] The first bilateral military aid agreement, signed in June 1954, provided the basis for more extensive security assistance and set a precedent for numerous subsequent agreements on defense and economic cooperation.

The perception that Turkey has long been treated unfairly at the political level in the United States, particularly in Congress, is pervasive among the Turkish elite. The experience of the 1964 "Johnson letter" warning against a Turkish move against Cyprus, and the arms embargo of 1975–1978 imposed following the Turkish occupation of northern Cyprus, is still vivid in Turkish minds. More recently, congressional and executive treatment of the Armenian issue has been the source of frustration and dismay in Ankara. Congress did not approve a resolution on the Armenian genocide introduced in 1990, but the administration's comments in the spring of 1990 (actually intended to defuse the issue) struck a negative chord in Turkey. President Bush's statement was understood as implicating the modern Turkish state as well as the Ottoman government, setting a possible precedent for U.S. policy toward an independent Armenia. An argument common in Europe, but rarely heard in Ankara, is that the Armenian issue will remain an impediment to Turkish policy internationally, and can be overcome only through the direct acknowledgment of the Turkish government. Thus, it is argued that in an era in which Moscow can admit Katyn, and the former German Democratic Republic could admit the Holocaust, surely Turkey can acknowledge events of the Ottoman period. For reasons closely bound up with Turkish political culture, an admission of this sort is extremely difficult. The development of tentative ties with the Armenian Republic may well necessitate and facilitate this process. In the meantime, the Kurdish problem and the broader issue of human rights in Turkey is likely to emerge as a more immediate obstacle to Turkish policy in Washington and Brussels. In certain quarters, notably the Turkish Foreign Ministry, it is argued with growing conviction that the success of Turkey's policy toward the West will depend on a complete overhaul of Ankara's approach to human rights.[89]

To the extent that Turkey is frustrated in its efforts to join Europe, the bilateral relationship with the United States should, in theory, acquire greater significance. An important longer-term question concerns the degree to which Turkish public and elite opinion will distinguish between Turkey's difficult relations with Europe and relations with the West as a whole. In the absence of a dramatic expansion of bilateral cooperation across the board—and this is unlikely for a variety of reasons—it may prove difficult to insulate U.S.–Turkish relations from the adverse effects of a European rebuff.[90] Although the Gulf crisis has resulted in a great deal of good will toward Turkey at the official level, and a greater awareness of Turkey and its regional problems among the informed public, a measured expansion of economic and security cooperation may fail to satisfy heightened expectations in Ankara. The change of leadership in Washington, and Demirel's disinclination to pursue bilateral relations with quite the same zeal as Ozal, introduces new elements of uncertainty.

Two broad features of the post-Cold War, post-Gulf War bilateral relationship have already emerged. First, the consensus for maintaining a viable defense relationship with the United States will almost certainly hold, but there will be little interest in the formal expansion of existing arrangements. A second and related feature is Ankara's emphasis on building a new and more diversified "strategic relationship" in which economic and political cooperation plays a leading role and defense issues are subjected to closer scrutiny. Both trends were visible prior to the elections—in fact they developed in full during the Gulf crisis—and are likely to prove durable.

A Window for Expanded Defense Cooperation?

The window for expanded defense cooperation that some had foreseen in the wake of the Gulf crisis has almost certainly closed, if indeed it was ever open. Developments in the Gulf provided some incentives for Turkey to consider a more active security relationship with the United States: a heightened sense of insecurity with regard to the Middle East; more evident security assistance needs; and, above all, a sense that the NATO commitment to Turkey might not be ironclad in all cases. Yet, the prospects for a formal increase in U.S.–Turkish defense cooperation remain limited. Ozal's willingness to provide bases for U.S. and allied forces during and after the conflict provoked strong domestic opposition from quarters as diverse as the Turkish left, the nationalist and fundamentalist right, and the military leadership itself.[91] The latter, although thoroughly pro-Western and champions of bilateral security cooperation as an essential element in the modernization of the armed forces, regarded the large scale use of Turkish facilities by foreign forces as an affront to Turkish sovereignty. Moreover, many senior officers were inclined to distrust Ozal's motives in the Gulf (relations between Ozal and the military have never been particularly warm in any case), suspecting a link between his active support for the Gulf monarchies and his tactical courting of the religious right in domestic politics. The net result of this experience has been heightened sensitivity across the political spectrum on sovereignty-related issues, including security cooperation with the United States. Turkey's decision to extend for another year the bilateral Defense and Economic Cooperation Agreement (DECA), which was due to expire in December 1991, effectively postponed any question of a formal change in the ground rules for U.S. access to facilities, the presence of U.S. personnel, or the prepositioning of materiel (special arrangements outside the DECA involving the use of Turkish facilities for non-NATO purposes will remain possible).[92]

The United States, for its part, is unlikely to seek an expansion of its permanent presence in a period of force reductions and economic stringency. An expansion of this presence would, of course, also send inappropriate signals to Moscow and the southern republics. Indeed, Turkish officials are more likely to be confronted with modest reductions in the U.S. presence. Turkey has given strong support to NATO plans for maintaining a land-based U.S. tactical air presence in the Southern Region following the departure of the 401st Tactical Fighter Wing from Torrejon in Spain. Ankara regards this presence as a contribution to regional deterrence and evidence of a continued alliance commitment to Turkey (the bulk of the 401st TFW had traditionally been earmarked for the reinforcement of Turkey, and elements of the wing rotated periodically to Incirlik). Turkey is, however, unlikely to accept the "permanent" presence of U.S. aircraft.

The possibility of placing substantial prepositioned stocks of U.S. equipment in Turkey as a means of facilitating the rapid deployment of forces to the region has been the subject of some discussion. Although doubtless a more acceptable alternative to the permanent deployment of U.S. forces (a political impossibility under current conditions), extensive prepositioning would raise problems of its own. For contingencies in eastern Anatolia, stocks held afloat at Izmir or Iskenderun would be of doubtful value, while prepositioning in the southeast might actually limit flexibility (it would also place these stocks and associated personnel in the middle of an active insurgency).

The problem of an adequate quid pro quo for any expansion of the bilateral security relationship will persist, despite the increase in aid as a result of the Gulf War in which U.S. security assistance to Turkey was raised from $553.4 million to $635.4 million in 1991 appropriations. Most of this aid will be in the form of outright grants, and additional emergency assistance is likely. If CFE-related transfers are included, Turkey will be the recipient of roughly $8 billion in U.S. and German equipment. Although Congress has shown no sign of abandoning the informal "7:10 ratio" under which Greece has received seven dollars worth of assistance for every ten dollars given to Turkey, the prospect of further "emergency" assistance and the essentially fungible nature of economic and security assistance funds suggest that the future significance of the 7:10 ratio will be largely symbolic. But the symbolism of the ratio matters a great deal in political terms to both Greece and Turkey and will remain an important issue on the trilateral agenda. Leaving aside the current windfall resulting from CFE and the Gulf War, Turkish observers are aware of the declining enthusiasm for security assistance in Congress, although Turkey will certainly continue to be among the strongest claimants for future funding even at lower levels (barring, of course, a debacle over Cyprus, the Balkans, or the Kurdish problem).

The United States has been instrumental in raising international support to compensate Turkey for the economic costs of the Gulf War. The closure of the oil pipeline from Iraq, together with the loss of Middle East trade is estimated to have cost Turkey up to $9 billion in lost revenue. The pipeline closure alone will cost Turkey some $500 million per year. Prior to the Gulf crisis, trade with Iraq had accounted for 10 percent of Turkish exports.[93] Roughly $3 billion in oil, grants, and loans have been raised thus far from Saudi Arabia, Kuwait, the United Arab Emirates, Japan, France, and the EC. Taken together with the potentially large role of Turkish enterprises in the reconstruction of Kuwait, the economic costs of the Gulf crisis may be covered or perhaps exceeded by compensatory arrangements and arms transfers.[94] Nonetheless, many Turks argue with conviction that their country is unlikely ever to be adequately compensated for the short- and longer-term security consequences of its cooperative role in the Gulf crisis, not least the deepening Kurdish insurgency in the southeast.

The prospects for U.S. access to Turkish facilities in non-NATO contingencies will be influenced by the waning of Ozal's ability to influence the Turkish security debate, and the natural conservatism of the military leadership regarding foreign forces on Turkish soil (and in Turkish airspace).[95] Turkish interests in the Middle East will also encourage a careful approach. As in the past, Turkey's leadership will be compelled to consider the regional effects of too close and too visible cooperation with the United States outside the NATO context. Turkish policy in future crises may well resemble its restrained behavior in relation to the Middle East conflicts of 1967 and 1973 rather than the recent and perhaps unique experience of the coalition against Iraq. Even prior to the October 1991 elections, evidence of a return to a more cautious policy could be seen in then Prime Minister Yilmaz's comments ruling out the use of Turkish bases for renewed air strikes against nuclear facilities in Iraq.[96] Demirel was similarly reserved in his discussions with President Bush in February 1992, warning against the use of force to topple Saddam Hussein.[97]

A New Strategic Relationship?

Over the next decade, Ankara can be expected to place great emphasis on the development of a "more mature" relationship with the United States in which security assistance and defense cooperation play a less prominent role and political and economic ties are strengthened. This interest has already taken the form of calls for what the Turkish elite like to describe as a broader or expanded "strategic relationship." The term strategic, in this case, is meant in the broadest sense. Increased trade and investment is at the heart of Turkish proposals for a diversified relationship.

Through the 1970s, the total volume of bilateral trade averaged $500 million per year. The growing export orientation of the Turkish economy in the 1980s, of which Ozal was the leading architect, produced a marked increase in the level of economic activity between the United States and Turkey. During the 1980s, the volume of bilateral trade more than tripled, from $846.4 million in 1981 to $3.25 billion in 1990. Despite the growth in volume, Turkey has registered consistent deficits in this bilateral trade.[98] Negotiations spurred by the Gulf crisis have led to a doubling of the U.S. quota for Turkish textile imports through 1993. But with a relatively small share of the U.S. market to begin with, the effect of such apparently large increases remains incremental. The prospects for further quota adjustments of this scale must be considered limited, especially in the very sensitive area of textile imports. During his visit to Washington in March–April 1991, Ozal proposed a free trade agreement between the United States and Turkey. Few observers regard this as a serious proposal. Certainly, the United States has too many pressing issues on its trade agenda, including the future of GATT and arrangements for a North American Free Trade Area, to consider opening negotiations on this front. From the Turkish perspective, the proposal is perhaps a useful vehicle for keeping economic issues at the forefront of the bilateral relationship.

Defense industrial cooperation is one area in which the pursuit of a broader strategic relationship merges with strategic issues of a narrower and more traditional sort. Existing co-production arrangements with U.S. firms for the manufacture of F-16s and armored fighting vehicles are seen in Ankara as important contributions to Turkey's security, economic development, and international prestige. Turkey will also produce 46 F-16s for the Egyptian Air Force by 1995. Overall, Turkey is pursuing an active program of collaborative defense procurement with its NATO allies, and defense-industrial development will be a leading consideration in future Turkish proposals for bilateral cooperation.[99] In the short-term, Turkey looks to an expansion of its defense-related exports to the United States under the free trade provisions of the DECA.[100]

Finally, Turkey will seek U.S. support for its regional policies and initiatives as part of an active strategic relationship. Support for the Black Sea plan and Turkey's application for EC membership will be priorities for Ankara, although the prospects of influencing European attitudes on the latter from Washington will be extremely limited. Short of this, the United States may be in a stronger position to press for Turkey's inclusion in emerging European security arrangements. Yet, as U.S. interests in Turkey continue to focus, for valid strategic reasons, on that country's role in Middle Eastern and Central Asian security, the task of promoting Turkey's role in the new European security order will be a difficult one. The reorientation of Turkey's own security concerns and defense policy toward the southeast will further reinforce Western perceptions in this regard.

More problematic may be Ankara's desire for U.S. backing in its policy toward the Kurdish insurgency. A hard-line response to increasingly severe PKK attacks could prove an impediment to closer relations with the United States as well as Europe, where Turkey's human rights record has long been the subject of scrutiny.[101]

The reassertion of Turkey's regional role in the Balkans, around the Black Sea, in the Caucasus, Central Asia, and the Middle East would introduce an entirely new and less predictable element into relations between Ankara and Washington. Given the (probably healthy) disinclination on both sides to view Turkey as a Western gendarme in regional matters, the emergence of Turkey as a regional power raises the important question of whether U.S. and Turkish interests will be divergent or convergent over the longer term. Some Turkish commentators have already raised this issue in relation to the "new strategic relationship," questioning whether Turkey's local and regional interests will be compatible with the global interests of the United States in all cases.[102] U.S. interests in the stable evolution of political and economic systems around the Black Sea and in the Middle East, and in preventing the emergence of regional hegemonies (e.g., Iran) are broadly compatible with Turkey's regional preferences. In the Balkans, Turkey's interest in safeguarding the well-being of Muslim minorities is not incompatible with U.S. interests in the region, but the West as a whole may well give higher priority to ensuring that ethnic conflicts in the Balkans do not threaten the European order. It is difficult to imagine a Turkish intervention of any sort finding support in the United States, unless it was part of an EC or NATO operation. In the Aegean, the potential for a divergence of interests and approaches is more substantial. Even here, however, the United States and Turkey share a substantial overall interest in crisis avoidance. One of the very few points of agreement between Ankara and Athens has been on the stabilizing role of the U.S. presence in the Eastern Mediterranean.

Barring a sweeping change in the character of Turkey's domestic political orientation—an unlikely development—a fundamental clash of interests must be considered remote. The Western orientation and natural conservatism of Turkey's foreign and security policy elite is probably too strong to countenance a deliberate policy of confrontation. Nonetheless, as with Cyprus in 1974, the potential for serious friction on regional matters will remain should the Turkish leadership confront what it perceives to be a basic challenge to Turkey's security and well-being. The United States, both bilaterally and through its role in NATO, will remain the best guarantor of Turkish security in relation to the most dangerous risks facing Ankara over the longer term (i.e., those emanating from Syria, Iran, and Iraq), and this will necessarily influence the shape of Turkey's foreign and security policy. The threat from the Middle East may not entirely replace the containment of Soviet power as a unifying element in Turkey's external relations, but it will exert a powerful influence on its cooperative relationships. Turkey's continued exclusion from Europe will inevitably put increased pressure on the relationship with the United States To the extent that a new strategic relationship between the United States and Turkey can be placed in the context of broader Western cooperation, it is likely to prove more resistant to the vagaries of domestic politics and regional change.

Overall Observations and Conclusions

The changing character of the strategic environment will pose substantial problems of adjustment for Turkey in its relations with the West. Long-standing priorities are being critically examined in light of the end of the Cold War, instability in the Middle East and the Balkans, and new opportunities and challenges in the Black Sea and Central Asia. At the same time, Europe and the United States will need to reassess the pattern of relations that had been dictated by the strategy of containment and the traditional perception of Turkey's role in European security.

Turkey's basic Western orientation will almost certainly hold. The October 1991 elections suggest a substantial strengthening of the center in Turkish politics. Groups on the left and the religious and nationalist right espousing anti-Western policies have not registered significant gains. The political and economic elite, as well as the military, remain deeply attached to the Western-looking, Ataturkist philosophy.

Turkey will remain outside of Europe. The prospects for Turkey's joining Europe in the formal, institutional sense have not improved in the wake of the Gulf War and Turkey's active support for coalition policy. Ironically, the prospects for Ankara's EC application probably worsened as Europeans found confirmation for existing perceptions about Turkey's importance and exposure in the Middle East. The longer-term outlook for Turkey in Europe will turn on the future character of the community itself. An expanded EC might be more amenable to closer ties with Turkey, but a wider EC that still refuses to entertain Turkish membership will only reinforce the sense of frustration in Ankara. In the meantime, and in the absence of closer ties with Europe, Turkey's political and economic elite is looking to new areas of opportunity outside Europe or on the European periphery (e.g., the Black Sea).

Most significantly, the prospects for Turkish inclusion in new European security arrangements will remain poor. To the extent that Europe moves toward a common foreign and security policy, Community members will be increasingly unwilling to accept the immediate and additional exposure in the Middle East which Turkey's full participation in the WEU (or other European security arrangements) would imply. As a result, Turkey will continue to share with the United States a pronounced interest in the viability of the Atlantic Alliance as the dominant European security institution.

At the same time, Turkey will become increasingly distinctive and perhaps isolated within the alliance. As Turkey remains outside the process of Europeanization affecting the rest of NATO's Southern Region, and if its strategic importance is defined largely in Middle Eastern rather than European terms, Turkey, the United States and NATO will face a difficult problem of adjustment even without an expansion of NATO's current area of responsibility.

To the extent that Turkey is frustrated in its relations with Europe, the bilateral relationship with the United States will acquire additional significance. Even as Turkey pursues new initiatives around the Black Sea and elsewhere, Ankara will look to the United States as a source of strategic reassurance and political and economic cooperation. The bilateral relationship will also be the subject of closer political scrutiny in the wake of the Gulf experience. The "post-Ozal" era is likely to be characterized by a more reserved approach to bilateral defense matters. Ankara will seek a diversified "strategic relationship" in which increased trade and defense-industrial cooperation are given priority.

Despite continuing risks for crisis management in the Aegean, U.S. and Turkish interests are likely to remain broadly congruent as long as Ankara does not begin to view Europe as an opponent in key areas such as the Balkans and Central Asia. In this context, perceptions in Turkey—indeed the prospects for Turkey's relations with the West—will be driven to a great extent by the future character of relations between Europe and the Islamic world as a whole. Should southeastern Europe come to be seen as a strategic glacis insulating the Community from turbulence and risks in the Middle East (including those affecting or emanating from Turkey), the United States will be faced with more difficult dilemmas in its policy toward Turkey.

Implications and Recommendations for U.S. Policy

The United States, as a global power, should strive to promote the strategic importance of Turkey in Europe as well as in the Middle East and Central Asia. Movement toward a new European security order that excludes Turkey (or actively opposes it in the Aegean) would contribute to instability in the Balkans and work against the longer-term convergence of Turkish and Western interests. It would also pose substantial dilemmas for U.S. policy in the Aegean and the Middle East. The United States should continue to support Turkish efforts to participate in the process of European integration (formally or informally), not least the creation of a European defense identity.

The United States need not press Ankara for a formal expansion of bilateral defense cooperation which would, in any case, present substantial problems of political acceptance. From the U.S. perspective, the current situation on Turkey's Middle Eastern borders, and the prospect of an increasingly violent Kurdish insurgency in southeast Anatolia, does not suggest the need for a large and visible presence. The key objective for the United States should be to maintain a healthy, broad-based political relationship that will enhance the prospects for Ankara's support, including access to Turkish facilities and air space, in non-NATO contingencies.

New security initiatives involving Turkey should, to the extent possible, be pursued in a multilateral context; that is, through NATO or in cooperation with individual European allies. This would promote Turkey's importance in Europe; pose fewer political challenges for Ankara and thus contribute to the durability of security ties; and, not least, contribute to "burdensharing" within the alliance. Similarly, new initiatives on the political and economic fronts should be given a trilateral (U.S.–Turkish–European) character wherever possible.

The United States should work to dispel Turkish doubts about the predictability of the NATO security guarantee, and the emergence of a "gray area" debate within the alliance. On a practical level, the maintenance of a U.S. tactical air presence in the Southern Region (with periodic rotations to Turkey) will contribute directly to the reassurance of Turkey. Turkey should be encouraged to participate in new multinational rapid response initiatives for the Southern Region, as well as the development of a standing naval force in the Mediterranean.

The longer-term interests of both the United States and Turkey will be served by the development of a more mature, diversified relationship, in which security assistance of the traditional sort is accompanied by an expansion of political and economic cooperation. Leaving aside the proposal for a bilateral free trade agreement, priority should be given to new trade and investment incentives, support for Turkey's regional economic initiatives, and a wider program of cultural and educational exchanges. The growing interest in Turkey should not be limited to the strategic and foreign policy communities.

In developing U.S. policy toward the independent republics of the former Soviet Union, consideration should be given to the potential role of Turkey in supporting political and economic initiatives. This would build on the increasingly active Turkish involvement in the region and contribute to the continued convergence of Turkish and Western interests. Specifically, the United States (and the EC) might use Turkey as a base for a more direct program of aid to the Caucasian and Central Asian republics. Similarly, the United States should lend its active support to Ankara's plan for Black Sea cooperation.

The United States should continue to play a role in promoting negotiations on Cyprus, as circumstances allow, both as a contribution to resolving the dispute and as tangible evidence of a continuing interest in the Aegean balance. The clear concern of Ankara and Athens in assuring themselves of secure relations with the United States after the Cold War has reinforced the already substantial stabilizing role of the United States in the eastern Mediterranean.

Notes

1. An early glimpse of the Demirel government's views on external and security issues can be found in the text of the foreign policy section of the prime minister's news conference of December 11, 1992. See "Demirel's Comments on Foreign Policy Reported," *FBIS-West Europe Report*, December 18, 1991, p. 44.

2. Chris Hedges, "Results of Turkey's Election May Mean Basic Policy Shifts," *New York Times*, November 18, 1991; "The Blur in Turkey," and "Turkey Steps back to Demirel," *The Economist*, October 26, 1991.

3. A geopolitical analysis of Turkey's position in Europe and Asia is offered in Ferenc A. Vali, *Bridge Across the Bosporus: The Foreign Policy of Turkey*, Baltimore: Johns Hopkins Press, 1971, pp. 42–48.

4. The growing prominence of religion in Turkish society can be seen in the growth of religious schools and organizations, more frequent references to Islam as a component of civil and private life, and such visible manifestations as the growing popularity of headscarves for women in urban areas (the later is attributable, at least in part, to the influx of rural population to Istanbul and Ankara).

5. "Turkey, even at its lowest ebb, was never called the 'Sick Man of Asia.'" From the text of a speech delivered by then Foreign Minister Mesut Yilmaz to the Twelfth Conference of Directors and Representatives of the European Institutes of International Relations, Istanbul, June 1–2, 1989, published in *Dis Politika*, Quarterly Review of the Foreign Policy Institute, Ankara, Vol. xiv, Nos. 3–4.

6. The clash of Spanish and Ottoman power in the Mediterranean is treated extensively in Fernand Braudel, *The Mediterranean and the Mediterranean World in the Age of Philip II*, New York: Harper and Row, 1976, first published in 1949.

7. Duygu Bazoglu Sezer, "Turkey's Strategic Dilemma," paper prepared for the RAND-IAI Conference on The Southern Region of Europe and the Middle East: New Challenges and New Hopes, Rome, September 16–17, 1991.

8. Philip Robins, *Turkey and the Middle East*, New York: Royal Institute of International Affairs, 1991, p. 14.

9. The ICO has been the forum for recent criticism of Turkey's cross-border operations against the PKK (Kurdish Workers' Party). See "Cross Border Attacks Continue: ICO Reacts," *FBIS-West Europe Report*, August 22, 1991, p. 45. The Council of Europe has been a focus of European debate on Turkey's human rights record.

10. Robins, *Turkey and the Middle East*, p. 14.

11. See, for example, Soreyya Yocel Ozden, "Turkey as a Gateway to Eastern European Markets," paper prepared for the Annual Conference of the Turkish–U.S. Business Council, New York, October 30–November 1, 1991; and the speech by President Ozal, stressing opportunities in the Balkans and the Black Sea, presented to this conference on October 31, 1991.

12. Sukru Elekdag, "Black Sea Economic Cooperation Region Project," draft paper for *Turkish Economy and Dialogue*, May 1991.

13. "Agreement Reached on Black Sea Economic Cooperation Project," *FBIS-West Europe Report*, July 16, 1991, p. 42; and "Ozal Opens Meeting on Black Sea Cooperation," *FBIS-West Europe Report*, February 4, 1992.

14. Speech by President Ozal to the Annual Conference of the Turkish–U.S. Business Council, New York, October 31, 1991.

15. The volume of two-way trade with the Soviet Union as a whole has grown dramatically, from $477 million in 1987 to roughly $3 billion in 1991.

16. M. Ali Birand, "An Important USSR Request from Anakara," *Milliyet*, Istanbul, in *FBIS-West Europe Report*, September 27, 1991, p. 27.

17. Elekdag, *"Black Sea Economic Cooperation,"* p. 8.

18. I am grateful to RAND colleague Paul Henze for this suggestion. The large amount of aid shipped via Turkish airfields as part of Operation Provide Hope in February 1992 reinforces this point.

19. Jonathan Eyal, "Ozal Aims to Revive Turkish Power," *The Guardian*, April 21, 1991. See also Daniel N. Nelson, "North from the Bosporus: Turkey's Relations with the USSR," *National Interest*, Spring 1990. On strategic cooperation between Greece and Bulgaria, see Paul Anastasi, "Greek-Bulgarian Tactics for Turkey," *New York Times*, February 7, 1991.

20. A recent study entitled "Turkey in the Year 2020," sponsored and published by *Cumhuriyet*, surveyed the opinions of 32 leading members of the Turkish political and intellectual elite on a range of issues, including the prospects for Turkey in Europe. The results suggest a solid consensus on the durability of Turkey's western orientation. Only a third of the participants thought that Turkey would be a member of the European Community by the year 2020. "Intellectuals View Future of Economy, Regime," *Cumhuriyet*, March 26–30, April 2–5 and 9–13, 1991, published in full in *FBIS-West Europe Report* (Supplement), June 25, 1991.

21. See Jasper Mortimer, "Please Let Us In, We Promise We'll Behave," *The Middle East*, January 1989; and by the same author, "No Room in Europe," *The Middle East*, February 1990. See also Stephen Hugh-Jones, "Turkey: Half Inside, Half Out," *The Economist*, June 18, 1988; "Are Its Goals in Europe Being Ignored, Turkey Asks," *New York Times*, December 12, 1989; and Edward Mortimer, "Problem Awaiting a Solution," *Financial Times*, May 8, 1991.

22. Mesut Yilmaz, "Turkish Foreign Policy," *Dis Politika*, Vol. XIV, Nos. 3–4, p. 13.

23. The history of these trading relationships is described at length in Braudel, *The Mediterranean and the Mediterranean World*.

24. Eberhard Rhein, "Turkey and the New Europe," remarks presented at a conference organized by the *International Herald Tribune*, Istanbul, November 14, 1990, p. 10.

25. Seyfi Tashan is President of the Foreign Policy Institute, Ankara. Quoted in *The Economist*, June 18, 1988, p. 29.

26. "Trade Cooperation Agreement Signed with EFTA," *FBIS-West Europe Report*, October 18, 1991, p. 4.

27. Ali Bozer, "Turkish Foreign Policy in the Changing World," *Mediterranean Quarterly*, Summer 1990, pp. 17–18.

28. See John Murray Brown, "Turkey, EC in New Push for Customs Union," *Financial Times*, December 6, 1991, p. 3.

29. The original Association Agreement was concluded in 1963, and envisioned a three-stage movement toward full membership over twenty-five years. The agreement is now in its second or "transitional" stage. The stagnation of Turkish–EC relations in the 1970s, and efforts to revitaize these ties in the late 1970s and again following the return to civilian rule in 1983, are described in Ismail Erturk, "Turkey and the European Community," *International Relations*, November 1984. See also David Barchard, "Turkey and Europe," *Turkish Review*, Autumn 1989.

30. Turkey first applied for full membership in the WEU in 1987.

31. Speech to the Western European Union, Paris, June 5, 1991. Quoted in Reuters. On the WEU role in Mediterranean and Middle Eastern security, see Roberto Aliboni, *European Security Across the Mediterranean*, Paris: WEU Institute for Security Studies, 1991.

32. See Charles Eliot, *Turkey in Europe*, London: Frank Cass, 1965.

33. "Giray Views of EC Moves for Military Union," *FBIS-West Europe Report*, October 24, 1991, p. 28.

34. The results of the Maastricht summit are widely interpreted as a setback for Turkish ambitions in Europe. See Sami Kohen, "Inauspicious for Turkey," *Milliyet*, Istanbul, December 12, 1991, in "Commentary on Decisions Reached at Maastricht," *FBIS-West Europe Report*, December 18, 1991, p. 49.

35. The alternative Anglo-Italian proposal preserves a leading role for NATO and insists on the full participation of non-EC NATO members in new European security arrangements.

36. Sezer, "Turkey's Strategic Dilemma," p. 20.

37. A notable period in this history is addressed in E. M. Earle, *Turkey, the Great Powers and the Baghdad Railway*, New York: Macmillan, 1924.

38. Germany also provided air defense equipment and deployed a large portion of its navy to the Mediterranean in support of coalition operations; see Jonathan T. Howe, "NATO and the Gulf Crisis," *Survival*, May/June 1991, p. 251.

39. In an interview of January 24, 1991, broadcast on German television, Ozal termed Germany "an unreliable NATO ally" that had been protected by the alliance for forty years and was "now unwilling to stand by Turkey in its time of need." Ozal went on to note the role of German firms in supplying chemicals to Iraq. BBC World Service, January 24, 1991.

40. *Turkish Briefing*, December 23, 1991, p. 10.

41. "Kurdish Issue Raises Tension in Turkish Ties," *Frankfurter Allgemeine*, December 9, 1991, in *FBIS-West Europe Report*, December 26, 1991, p. 8.

42. Workers' remittances totaled over $3 billion in 1989. International Monetary Fund, *Balance of Payments Statistics: Yearbook*, Washington: IMF, 1989.

43. Germany currently accounts for slightly over 10 percent of foreign investment in Turkey, ranking fourth after Britain, Switzerland, and the United States. Germany accounted for over 18 percent of foreign arrivals in Turkey in 1990. See *Turkey 1991: An International Comparison*, Istanbul: Foreign Economic Relations Board, 1991.

44. Portugal has adopted a less enthusiastic attitude to Turkish membership and EC enlargement in general. Portugal has expressed its particular concern about competition from the Turkish textile industry, and worries about the diversion of EC development assistance funds from southern Europe. See David Buchan, "Greek Veto on EC Aid to Turkey," *Financial times*, March 5, 1991.

45. Italy deployed six RF-104Gs to Turkey as its contribution to the AMF-A reinforcement.

46. See the joint "non-paper" and other documents on the CSCM concept assembled in *The Mediterranean and the Middle East After the War in the Gulf: The CSCM*, Rome: Ministry of Foreign Affairs, March 1991.

47. Quoted in Clyde Haberman, "Turkey Remains Confident It Will Join European Community," *New York Times*, March 17, 1990.

48. See the Joint Statement by Prime Minister Turgut Ozal and Prime Minister Andreas Papandreou of January 31, 1988, summarizing agreements on political and economic relations and confidence-building measures, published in *Turkish Review*, Spring 1988.

49. On the outlook for Greek-Turkish relations generally, see Monteagle Stearns, *Entangled Allies: U.S. Policy Toward Greece, Turkey and Cyprus*, New York: Council on Foreign Relations Press, 1992. See also *Aegean Issues: Problems and Prospects*, Ankara: Foreign Policy Institute, 1989; James Brown, *Delicately Poised Allies: Greece and Turkey—Problems, Policy Choices and Mediterranean Security*, London: Brassey's, 1991; and Dimitri Constas, ed., *The Greek Turkish Conflict in the 1990s: Domestic and External Influences*, New York: St. Martin's Press, 1991, with contributions by Greek and Turkish authors.

50. For a detailed discussion of these issues, see Andrew Wilson, "The Aegean Dispute," in Jonathan Alford, ed., *Greece and Turkey: Adversity in Alliance*, New York: St. Martin's Press, 1984.

51. The Greek Patriarchate in Istanbul was the scene of anti-Greek demonstrations in the fall of 1991. Anti-Turkish incidents flared in Greek Thrace in the same period.

52. A comprehensive survey of the dispute is offered in Robert McDonald, *The Problem of Cyprus*, Adelphi Paper No. 234, London: IISS, Winter 1988/89.

53. The "Johnson letter" of 1964 warned against a Turkish move over Cyprus, and suggested that if such a move encouraged Soviet action against Turkey, the United States and NATO might not feel obliged to respond.

54. F. Stephen Larrabee, "The Southern Periphery: Greece and Turkey," in Paul S. Shoup, ed., *Problems of Balkan Security: Southeastern Europe in the 1990s*, Washington: Wilson Center Press, 1990, p. 188.

55. See Maureen Dowd, "Bush Names the Next Challenge: Cyprus," *New York Times*, July 19, 1991.

56. See "Greek, Turkish Prime Ministers Meet in Paris," *FBIS-West Europe Report*, September 12, 1991; and Kerin Hope and John Murray Brown, "Ankara Denies Agreement to Return Territory in Cyprus," *Financial Times*, August 8, 1991.

57. Turkish Cypriot leaders insist, however, that Cyprus can only join international organizations in which both Greece and Turkey are members. See "Denktash Calls Cyprus EC Membership Last Move," *FBIS-West Europe Report*, September 3, 1991, p. 34.

58. Buchan, "Greek Veto on EC Aid to Turkey."

59. The status and treatment of this and the much smaller Greek minority in Turkey have been the subject of complaint and counter-complaint on both sides. See the discussion in Chapter 4.

60. Some Turkish observers have likened this policy to the situation in Israel and the West Bank.

61. Roughly half of these refugees have returned to Bulgaria, encouraged by the liberalization of the new Bulgarian regime's policy toward its Turkish population. See "Mass Migration and International Security," *Strategic Survey 1990–1991*, London: IISS/Brassey's, 1991, p. 43.

62. See Oral Sander, "Turkish-Greek Relations After World War I: A Vicious Circle of Sixty Years," *Turkish Review*, Winter 1985–86, Vol. 1, No. 2. Greek geopolitical concerns are treated in Yorgos A. Kourvetaris, "The Southern Flank of NATO: Political Dimensions of the Greco-Turkish Conflict Since 1974," *East European Quarterly*, January 1988.

63. "Northern Demilitarization Proposal Discussed," *FBIS-West Europe Report*, August 7, 1991, p. 55.

64. See Thanos Veremis, "Greece and NATO: Continuity and Change," in John Chipman, ed., *NATO's Southern Allies: Internal and External Challenges*, London: Routledge, 1988.

65. On Greek perceptions of CFE and the Aegean balance, see Yannis G. Valinakis, *Greece and the CFE Negotiations*, Ebenhausen: Stiftung Wissenschaft und Politik, June 1990.

66. See Maureen Dowd, "Bush Names the Next Challenge: Cyprus," *New York Times*, July 19, 1991. On the general question of "ripeness" and the U.S. role in international disputes, including Cyprus, see Richard N. Haass, *Conflicts Unending: The United States and Regional Disputes*, New Haven: Yale University Press, 1990.

67. See Faruk Sen, "The Opportunities for Economic Cooperation Between Turkey and Greece," *Turkish Review*, Spring 1989. A joint Turkish-Greek business council has been established to explore avenues for cooperation.

68. John Murray Brown, "Turkey Survey," *Financial Times*, May 20, 1991.

69. The rise of competing security interests in the Middle East had begun to affect Turkish perceptions even prior to the Gulf crisis. See Duygu Sezer, "Turkey's Security policy, Challenges of Adaptation to the post-INF Era," *RUSI Journal*, Winter 1989; and Alain Gresh, "La Turquie Ebranlee par les Mutations Regionales," *Le Monde Diplomatique*, July 1991, pp. 16–17.

70. NATO's new "strategic concept" refers explicitly to the growing importance of security problems around the southern and eastern shores of the Mediterranean. See "The Alliance's New Strategic Concept, Agreed by the Heads of State and Government Participating in the Meeting of the North Atlantic Council in Rome on 7th-8th November, 1991," *NATO Press Communique* S-1(91)85, pp. 3–4.

71. The history of Ottoman imperial decline is in large measure the story of Turkish retreat in the face of Russian power. See Paul B. Henze, *Turkey, the Alliance and the Middle East: Problems and Opportunities in Historical Perspective*, Washington: International Security Studies Programs, the Wilson Center, Working Paper No. 36, 1981. See also, Stanford J. Shaw and Ezel Kural Shaw, *History of the Ottoman Empire and Modern Turkey*, Cambridge: Cambridge University Press, 1976; and W.E.D. Allen and Paul Muratoff, *Caucasian Battlefields: A History of the Wars on the Turco-Caucasian Border, 1828–1921*, Cambridge: Cambridge University Press, 1953.

72. On this and other trends affecting the Southern Region, see Ian O. Lesser, *The United States and Southern Europe After the Cold War*, P-7679, RAND, Santa Monica, CA, 1990; and *Mediterranean Security: New Perspectives and Implications for U.S. Policy*, R-4178-AF, RAND, Santa Monica, CA, 1992. See also Diego Ruiz Palmer, "Paradigms Lost: A Retrospective Assessment of the NATO-Warsaw Pact Military Competition in the Alliance's Southern Region," *Comparative Strategy*, Vol. 9, 1990; and Ellen Laipson, "Thinking About the Mediterranean," *Mediterranean Quarterly*, Winter 1990.

73. NATO has announced cuts of roughly 80 percent in its stocks of shorter-range nuclear weapons in Europe. See "Rome Declaration on Peace and Cooperation," NATO Press Communique S-1(91)86, November 8, 1991.

74. See Hadi Uluengin, "Reduction of Nuclear Arms and Turkey," *Hurriyet*, Istanbul, October 1, 1991, in *FBIS-West Europe Report*, October 7, 1991, p. 44.

75. See Duygu Sezer, "Turkish Foreign Policy in the Year 2000," in *Turkey in the Year 2000*, Ankara: Turkish Political Science Association, 1989.

76. IISS, *The Military Balance 1990–1991*; and Kuniholm, "Turkey and the West," p. 43.

77. The prospects for Turkey's relations in the Middle East are assessed in Chapter 2 of this book.

78. See "German Envoy Denies Alleged Support for PKK," *Cumhuriyet*, Istanbul, August 21, 1991, in *FBIS-West Europe Report*, August 26, 1991, p. 43; and Chris Hedges, "Iraqis Are Arming the Rebel Kurds in Turkey's South," *New York Times*, October 20, 1991.

79. On ballistic missile proliferation trends affecting Turkey's security, see Janne E. Nolan, *The Trappings of Power: Ballistic Missiles in the Third World*, Washington: Brookings, 1991; Martin Navias, *Ballistic Missile Proliferation in the Third World*, Adelphi Paper No. 252, London: IISS, 1990; and W. Seth Carus, *Ballistic Missiles in the Third World: Threat and Response*, Washington: Center for Strategic and International Studies, 1990.

80. See "En Turquie, Ce Barrage Qui Commande Tout," *L'Express*, August 16, 1991. Turkish efforts to organize a "water summit" to discuss the future use of the Tigris and Euphrates and the Water for Peace initiative have been postponed pending the outcome of the Middle East peace talks in Madrid. See "Turkey's Giray Announces Water Summit Postponed," *FBIS-West Europe Report*, October 3, 1991, p. 1.

81. See John Murray Brown, "Turkey Sets Up a Buffer Zone in North Iraq to Curb Rebels," *Washington Post*, August 8, 1991; and "Turks Raid Rebel Kurds in North Iraq," *New York Times*, August 8, 1991.

82. Greece will also be a substantial recipient of equipment under the program. See *Jane's Defence Weekly*, July 6, 1991, pp. 18–19; Gen. Dogan Gures, "Modernization and Restructuring of the Turkish Land Forces," *NATO's Sixteen Nations*, February–March 1990; and an October 6, 1990, interview with then Minister of Defense Safa Giray, quoted in *FBIS-West Europe Report*, November 16, 1990, p. 36.

83. See John Murray Brown, "Arms Windfall Dilemma for Turkey," *Financial Times*, June 27, 1991, p. 6.

84. Ertugrul Ozkok, "Important Decisions in the Turkish Army," *Hurriyet*, Istanbul, August 2, 1991, in *FBIS-West Europe Report*, September 9, 1991.

85. "Circular Promises Improvements in Armed Forces," *FBIS-West Europe Report*, July 30, 1991, p. 29.

86. See James A. Field, *America and the Mediterranean World, 1776–1882*, Princeton: Princeton University Press, 1969; and Frank Gervasi, *Thunder Over the Mediterranean*, New York: David McKay, 1975.

87. The evolution of Western policy toward the Northern Tier is assessed in detail in Bruce Kuniholm, *The Origins of the Cold War in the Near East: Great Power Conflict and Diplomacy in Iran, Turkey and Greece*, Princeton: Princeton University Press, 1980.

88. Turkey became a member of NATO in 1952. Two years earlier, the deployment of a Turkish division in Korea under UN command had a very favorable effect on U.S. opinion (it has also contributed to a certain mythology within the alliance concerning the ferocity of Turkish troops).

89. See "Turkey's New Government: The Art of the Compromise," *The Economist*, November 23, 1991, p. 56.

90. Notably, only a small number of the respondents in the *Cumhuriyet* "Turkey in the Year 2020" survey thought that Turkey would have closer relations with the United States than Europe through the end of the century and beyond. *FBIS-West Europe Report*, June 25, 1991, p. 33.

91. Opposition within the military leadership to Ozal's activist stance in the Gulf crisis reached a peak with the resignation of Turkey's chief of staff, General Necip Torumtay, in December 1990. See "Torumtay's Resignation Seen as a Blow to Ozal," *Briefing*, Ankara, December 10, 1990, p. 4. See also the critique offered by Bulent Ecevit in Norman Frankel, "Conversations in Istanbul: An Interview with Bulent Ecevit," *Political Communication and Persuasion*, Vol. 8, No. 1, 1991; and "Public Opinion: Approval for the War but Not for Turkish Role," *Briefing*, Ankara, January 28, 1991.

92. "Defense, Economic Pact with U.S. Renewed," *FBIS-West Europe Report*, August 30, 1991, p. 27; and September 17, 1991, p. 25.

93. "Foreign Ministry on Failure to Sell Iraqi Oil," *FBIS-West Europe Report*, November 1, 1991, p. 41.

94. On the potential for Turkish infrastructure and construction contracts in Kuwait and elsewhere in the Middle East, see Feyyaz Berker, "Infrastructure and Construction in Turkey and the Middle East," paper presented at the Annual Conference of the Turkish-U.S. Business Council, New York, October 31, 1991.

95. On the Turkish military's sensitivities in this area, see John Murray Brown, "Kurds Seek to Prevent Allied Pullout from Turkish Border," *Financial Times*, September 18, 1991.

96. "Bush Says Iraq Is Mistaken to Bar Access to Nuclear Arms Programs," *New York Times*, July 29, 1991. Turkey also insisted upon detailed consultations on military operations mounted from its territory as part of Operation Provide Comfort. Patrick Tyler, "U.S. Has Trouble Maintaining Unity of Allies on Iraq," *New York Times*, July 28, 1991.

97. Barbara Crossette, "Turkish Leader, on Visit, Cautions Bush on Toppling of Hussein," *New York Times*, February 13, 1992.

98. Turkish exports to the United States in 1990 represented only .42 percent of imports. Leading exports to the United States are tobacco, textiles, and iron and steel; leading imports from the United States are iron and steel, boilers and machinery, and tobacco. Turkish-U.S. Business Council, *Turkish-American Relations*, Istanbul, 1991.

99. See Lale Sariibrahimoglu, "Building an Industry: The Turkish Dimension," *Jane's Defence Weekly*, November 9, 1991, pp. 881–890.

100. Turkish exports of defense goods to the United States under the DECA "Memorandum of Understanding" amount to roughly $185 million annually.

101. See M. Ali Birand, "Someone Is Doing Something Wrong," *Milliyet*, Istanbul, *FBIS-West Europe Report*, October 24, 1991.

102. Comment by Oral Sander, quoted in *Briefing*, Ankara, April 1, 1991, p. 8.

4

Turkey: Back to the Balkans?

J. F. Brown

The upheavals in what was once Yugoslavia and the threat of more in the Balkan peninsula have raised the question of Turkish reaction—not so much *whether* Turkey will react, but in what form. The stability that prevailed since the end of World War II in the Balkans has now been shattered. The region has returned to the instability for which it was traditionally noted. Turkey will influence, and be influenced by, what occurs there.

Between the end of the fourteenth century and the beginning of the eighteenth, the Ottoman Empire dominated the Balkan peninsula. For the next two centuries, it was steadily pushed back until, with the final collapse of the empire after World War I, its European territory was restricted to a small area in Thrace, centered on Istanbul, the historical capital.[1] Istanbul, straddling two continents, became unique, with its downtown in Europe and its growing suburbs, across the Bosporus, in Asia. The new Republic of Turkey, founded by Mustafa Kemal, Ataturk, with its new capital in the Anatolian city of Ankara, jettisoned Balkan ambitions along with many other pieces of the Ottoman baggage. Turkish attention abroad now became riveted on western Europe with the aim of education and emulation.[2] After World War II, in the context of the Cold War, this Turkish preoccupation with adherence to the West broadened, evolving into a close alliance with the United States, membership in NATO, association with the European Community (EC), and the subsequent application for full membership in it.

Turkey's twentieth-century diplomatic revolution brought a drastic change in its relationship with the successor states of its former Balkan dependencies. After massive population transfers negotiated with Greece following Greek victory in the Greco-Turkish war of 1919–1922, Turkey actively sought reconciliation with Athens. This was achieved with remarkable success by Ataturk and the dominant Greek politician of the interwar period, Eleftherios Venizelos.[3] There still remained serious unsettled questions between the two countries, but these were to reemerge only after World War II.

With the other Balkan countries—Albania, Bulgaria, Romania, and Yugoslavia—the new Turkey pursued correct bilateral relations, although relations with Bulgaria were occasionally strained, mainly because of repatriation questions affecting the Turkish community in Bulgaria and the pervasive memory of the past. However, apart from the spectacular rapprochement with Greece, Turkey's most notable diplomacy in the Balkans during the interwar period was on the multilateral, rather than the bilateral, level. Turkey took part in four Balkan conferences between 1930 and 1933 and signed the "Pact of Balkan Entente," or Balkan Pact, in February 1934, the other signatories being Greece, Romania, and Yugoslavia. A newly founded Balkan Chamber of Commerce actually had its headquarters in Istanbul.[4] But these prewar attempts at Balkan cooperation came to nothing. Albania and Bulgaria never joined, and, in any case, German and Italian encroachments in southeastern Europe soon exposed the frailty of such attempts.

After World War II

Turkey's neutrality during World War II enabled it to escape the devastation and dislocation the other Balkan nations suffered. But it now found itself on the front line of the incipient Cold War, with Stalin pressing demands for territorial concessions, for a revision of the 1936 Montreux Convention regulating navigation through the Straits, and even for a naval base on the Bosporus. It was this that led Turkey into alliance with the United States and membership in NATO in 1952.[5] Greece, too, torn by civil war—and with its neighbors, Albania, Yugoslavia, and Bulgaria, now hostile Soviet satellites—also needed American protection. This was provided to both countries under the terms of the Truman Doctrine of 1947. Turkey and Greece, therefore, became allies or, more correctly, Cold War companions.

They were soon to be joined by Yugoslavia. Tito broke with Stalin in 1948, and for several years Yugoslavia faced every form of pressure, except military, from Moscow and its allies. Yugoslavia also became dependent on the West, particularly American military support, for survival. As a communist state, however, it could hardly join NATO or be eligible for assistance under the Truman Doctrine. There were no obstacles, however, first to a rapprochement and then to active cooperation with Greece and Turkey. Thus, in quite different circumstances, these three countries reassumed the cooperation that had begun in the 1930s.

This time, though, the emphasis was on defense against the Soviet-directed threat. In 1953, the three countries concluded in Ankara a Treaty of Friendship and Cooperation, and a year later they signed a treaty containing a formal pledge of mutual military assistance in case of attack.[6]

But this treaty, though supposed to last twenty years, almost immediately fell into desuetude. First, the enmity between Turkey and Greece, interrupted for over a quarter of a century, now resumed. This time the main issue was Cyprus. The first serious postwar crisis over Cyprus occurred in 1955 and led to rioting against the still large Greek community in Istanbul. From then on, Turkish-Greek relations deteriorated to the point where, by the middle of the 1970s, these two nominal allies regarded each other as the principal enemy. Yugoslavia, too, quickly lost interest in the Balkan Pact. In 1955, on the initiative of Stalin's successors, Yugoslav-Soviet relations greatly improved, thereby reducing the need Yugoslavia may have had for the Pact. In any case, Tito now also began his long association with the "nonaligned movement" of neutral states which he helped to found.

The Balkan Pact, therefore, though it was never formally revoked, simply fell apart. From the middle of the 1950s, Turkey ceased any active Balkan diplomacy. It maintained correct relations with all the Balkan communist countries and, in 1968, finally managed to come to agreement with Bulgaria on the further repatriation of Bulgarian Turks to the homeland. This issue had bedeviled Turkish-Bulgarian relations since Bulgaria achieved independence in 1878 and, soon after World War II, almost brought them to a complete breaking point.[7] But for almost twenty years, Turkey virtually turned its back on the Balkans. It continued to depend on NATO and on the United States for military support, and this was mainly what prompted it to reject Soviet-inspired Romanian and Bulgarian overtures for detente and a Balkan nuclear-free zone in the second half of the 1950s. However, in the 1960s, largely as a result of the offense it took over American policy toward Cyprus,[8] Turkey began to diversify its foreign portfolio, cultivating better relations with the Soviet Union and with the Arab states, most of them former parts of the Ottoman Empire. By the early 1970s, Turkey also began developing closer bilateral relations with the Balkan countries.[9]

With Greece, however, relations continued to deteriorate, and in 1974, in the most serious Cyprus crisis so far, Turkish troops invaded the island and the two countries came very close to war. It was the Cyprus crisis, however, that led to the overthrow of the Greek military regime in Athens and the return to power of Constantine Karamanlis as the head of a democratic government. As a result of Greek disappointment over what had been perceived as too much American support for the Greek colonels and too little for the Greek cause over Cyprus, it was now time for Karamanlis to diversify Greece's foreign portfolio. This included developing relations with the Soviet Union; its two Balkan allies, Bulgaria and Romania; and with Albania and Yugoslavia, the two independent Balkan communist states.[10]

Karamanlis also set about reviving multilateral cooperation in the Balkans after an interval of some forty years. The Balkan conference held in Athens in early 1976 was, however, quite different from its pre–World War II predecessors. These had been rather grandiose in concept, tending to ignore the major problems that still divided the participants. Karamanlis was determined to proceed quietly, step by step, concentrating on "non-controversial" topics such as agriculture, health, transport, and tourism. Turkey, however, remained cool to the multilateral idea, arguing that it was necessary to solve "controversial" bilateral problems first. But it continued to participate in subsequent meetings, and it was Hoxha's Albania, comprehensively isolationist, and Bulgaria, reflecting traditional Soviet suspicions of multilateral cooperation in the region, that were the main obstacles to practical progress.[11]

Balkan Instability

Despite these developing contacts, the Balkans were not one of Turkey's main foreign policy interests. These continued to be western Europe and the EC, the United States and NATO, followed at some distance by the Soviet Union and several Arab states. Turkish perspectives remained fairly constant until the international, political, and social stability in the Balkan region began to crack.

The Ottoman Empire at its height had given the Balkans a certain stability; this, though, began to be disrupted at the end of the seventeenth century by the encroachments of the Hapsburg Empire. The Ottomans were pushed back from the northern regions of the Balkans, which fell under the permanent control of Austria and, after the *Ausgleich* in 1867, of Austria-Hungary.[12] These Hapsburg advances led to a long period of standoff stability as the two empires faced each other along a north-south "Theodosian" line, a situation somewhat similar to the east-west divide across Europe caused by the Cold War in the second half of the twentieth century. But from the beginning of the nineteenth century the Ottoman Empire began to weaken irreversibly as a result of the successive independence struggles of its subject nations. These began with Serbia and Greece and continued right to the eve of World War I.[13]

It was during this period, particularly in the second half of the nineteenth century, that the Balkans got their reputation for chronic, violent instability. This continued during the interwar period when the small successor states to both the Ottoman and Hapsburg empires, despite the efforts at cooperation previously noted, were often divided by historical enmities and irredentist ambitions.[14] These divisions culminated in the bloodshed of World War II, when, particularly in Yugoslavia, the war against the foreign occupiers was complicated by internal struggles among and even within the different nations of the region.

After World War II, however, the interaction between communism and Soviet domination, or the threat of it, led to a stability unknown for centuries. Tito's victorious partisans imposed a combination of socialism and federalism on Yugoslavia. Albania became communist under Enver Hoxha. Both these countries had freed themselves from Axis occupation, largely without Soviet help. Bulgaria and Romania were overrun by the Red Army, Greece came perilously close to being overrun by its own communists, and the integrity of Turkey was being threatened by the Soviets. All in all, it was a situation inducing concentration on the perils of the present rather than the grudges of the past. This led to overall restraint in the region, and it persisted after Yugoslavia, Albania, and, in part, Romania had rejected Moscow's tutelage. The combination of international tension and domestic rigidity served to dull the historical antagonisms.

With the weakening of communist rule and Soviet power in the 1980s, this phase of Balkan stability was coming to an end. Nationalism had, in any case, never been far below the surface.[15] Occasionally, national outbursts had erupted, but now it became clear that Balkan history, which the communists had believed would be supplanted by a new order, had simply been lying in wait. This was most evident in the case of Yugoslavia, but every country in the region became increasingly aware of it. During the period 1989 to 1991, when communism was routed or in retreat, when Soviet control disappeared and when the Cold War ended, Balkan history not only returned, but also seemed to be making up for lost time.[16]

Muslim Flashpoints in the Balkans

By the middle of 1991, Yugoslavia was disintegrating in civil war. In the opening "Slovenian phase" of disintegration and conflict, however, there was nothing that directly affected Turkey. Nor in the bloody war between Serbia and Croatia were any Turkish interests and concerns directly affected.[17] But Bosnia-Herzegovina was entirely different. It is the most northerly and westerly region in the Balkans where there is a large concentration of Muslims. Out of a total republic population in April 1991 of about four million, about 43 percent were

Muslim. About 33 percent were Orthodox Serb, and over 17 percent Roman Catholic Croat. It was this mixture that had led Bosnia-Herzegovina to be considered not only a microcosm of Yugoslavia as a whole, but also as essential to any present or future concept of Yugoslavia. Yugoslavia's Muslims, converted to Islam during the Ottoman Empire, were considered solely a religious group until 1968, when Tito allowed Bosnia's Muslims (but not the Albanian Muslims in Kosovo) to be classified as a nation. He did this because of their numerical weight in this pivotal republic and to prevent Serbs and Croats from claiming them—as historically they had—as members of their own nation. The granting of nationhood to the Muslims of Bosnia-Herzegovina gave them a self-confidence they had previously lacked, and, as the power of Islam increased on the international scene, this strengthened their assertiveness vis-à-vis the Serb and Croat communities, which (especially the Serbs) had always regarded them with barely disguised contempt.

In the Sandjak of Novi Pazar, most of it in Serbia itself but part in Montenegro, there are over 200,000 Muslims. These Sandjak Muslims identify with their coreligionists in Bosnia and after 1990 became increasingly restive. Serbia therefore, even excluding Kosovo, was itself never entirely free from the dangers of Muslim disaffection.[18]

In the province of Kosovo, an autonomous province of the Republic of Serbia, there are nearly two million Muslims who are not, as indicated above, accorded the status of nation, but rather are considered a minority. Ethnic Albanians, they constitute about 90 percent of the entire Kosovo population, the rest being Serbs and Montenegrins. These Muslim "Kosovars" have the fastest rate of population growth in Europe. After 1989, the Serbian central government in Belgrade began whittling down the powers of the provincial authority in Kosovo, and in 1990 a new Serbian constitution placed both Kosovo and Serbia's other autonomous province, Vojvodina, directly under central control. The Kosovo Albanians claimed, with justice, that their province had been reduced to colonial status by the Serbs.

Kosovo was the center of the great medieval kingdom of Serbia, and Kosovo Polje is the site of the historic defeat by the Turks which in Serbian legend became transfigured into a heavenly victory. Kosovo also contains several Serbian Orthodox monasteries, which Serbs consider the cradle of their nation, faith, and civilization.[19] As one Serbian Orthodox bishop put it, "Kosovo is our Jerusalem."[20] Hence, despite the Serbs having shrunk to a tenth of Kosovo's population, largely through migration to other parts of Serbia over the last three centuries, this is still holy ground for all Serbs. Ever since the end of 1989, tension in the province had been running very high. By the middle of 1992, there had already been much violence and many casualties, many of them probably unrecorded. There was a great danger of open warfare between the Serbian army and the Kosovars.

In Macedonia, the republic neighboring Kosovo in southern Yugoslavia, there are estimated to be at least 500,000 Muslims—the vast majority Albanians, but including perhaps about 80,000 ethnic Turks—in a total population of about two million. Their proliferation in recent years, due to a high birth rate and to considerable emigration from Kosovo, led to serious tension with the Macedonian Slav majority. Macedonian nationalism had, itself, begun to grow markedly in the previous years, and this had only been sharpened by what was perceived as the growing "Muslim menace."[21] The extreme nationalist Internal Macedonian Revolutionary Organization (IMRO), the reincarnation of the legendary Macedonian national movement of the same name, finished first in the Macedonian republican parliamentary elections in November 1990 mainly because of the public fear of the Muslim Albanians' voting strength.[22]

In September 1991, Macedonia declared its full sovereignty and independence. The Muslim minority generally supported this move but objected to certain articles in the new republic's constitution it regarded as discriminatory. In January 1992, the Albanians of Macedonia held a referendum which resulted in a nearly 75 percent majority in favor of territorial autonomy for themselves. The vote was not binding on the government, which regarded it as invalid and refused to act on it. But it could be a portent. If central governmental authority weakened in Macedonia, either through serious economic deterioration or through its failure to achieve international recognition due to Greek objections— backed by both the United States and the EC—to its "usurping the name of Macedonia," then the demands for autonomy or even the incorporation of some Albanian Muslim districts into "Greater Albania" might increase. This would provoke a violent response from IMRO and probably cause increased local support for it.[23] Macedonia, with common borders with Greece, Albania, Kosovo, Serbia, and Bulgaria, could become yet again an apple of discord in the Balkans, at worst a replay of Bosnia-Herzegovina. Perhaps, though, Bosnia-Herzegovina might itself constitute a deterrent. In any case, the Macedonian Question is back, and demands comprehensive answers.

Moving beyond Yugoslavia, Albania itself had a population of over three million in the middle of 1992, of which nearly 70 percent were Muslim. By the end of the century, the total population was expected to have risen to four million, with the Muslim proportion almost certainly having become greater. (The population growth rate in Albania is second in Europe only to that in Kosovo.) The danger to Balkan stability in this high and rising Muslim population lies in the gradually growing probability of agitation in both Albania and Kosovo for a union of these two lands, both overwhelmingly Muslim by religion and ethnically Albanian. (They were briefly united in World War II, under Axis control.)

The Albanian revolution came about a year after the revolutions in most parts of Eastern Europe. Its first free election in March 1991 resulted in a victory for the reformed communist party, but the second, almost exactly one year later, produced a resounding democratic victory. The difficulties facing the new Albania seemed overwhelming. In many respects, the situation was hardly attractive for Albanians in either Kosovo or Macedonia. But at least these Albanians were not being victimized or persecuted simply because of their nationality. If the situation in Kosovo deteriorated any further, and if, in Macedonia, it deteriorated drastically, merging into Albania could well be the most promising choice from among the unsatisfying options available.[24]

Albania's relations with Greece, historically tense, began deteriorating seriously again during 1991. Though they have been officially set aside, Greek claims to parts of southern Albania (in Greek, northern Epirus) are historical. Successive Greek governments, backed by public opinion, the military, and the Orthodox Church, have been increasingly concerned about the fate of the Greek minority there (60,000 according to the Albanians; 300,000 to 400,000 according to some Greeks; probably about 100,000). The breakdown of order in Albania in 1991, together with the deteriorating economic situation, caused an influx of thousands of Greek-Albanian refugees to an alarmed Greece. The Albanians, in their flush of freedom, began, for their part, to refer to the condition of their own "Cham" minority in parts of northern Greece—"Chameria" as some Albanians were now beginning to call it. The billowing of Greek nationalism in 1992 over Macedonia could add a dangerous dimension to Albanian-Greek relations, as could the Greek government's overall sympathy for Serbia in the Yugoslav civil war (despite joining in the condemnation of Belgrade and the sanctions against it).[25] Of particular concern to the Albanians is Athens's refusal to countenance the idea of an independent Kosovo, let alone reunion with Albania.

In Bulgaria, the Muslim population was probably over a million in the middle of 1992. It was very largely of Turkish ethnic origin, descendants of settlers from Anatolia during the 500-year Ottoman occupation. During the time of the empire, there had been large Turkish settlements in other parts of the Balkans, too, but many of these had been resettled back in Turkey after World War I. A large number had also transferred back from Bulgaria itself.[26] But this large community, making up over one-tenth of the entire population, remained.

The discrimination and subsequent repressive measures against the Bulgarian Turks during the 1980s became a subject of international outrage. But there had already been strong efforts to assimilate the approximately 150,000 Pomaks in Bulgaria. These were ethnic Bulgarians who had been converted to Islam during the Ottoman period (but they continued to speak Bulgarian). The overt repression against the Bulgarian Turks that began in the 1980s was part of the drive for a unitary state that became Bulgarian (and Romanian) policy from the 1960s onward. It was now claimed that these Turkish Muslims were not Turkish at all but were the descendants of ethnic Bulgarians who had been converted to Islam while Bulgaria was under the "Turkish Yoke," and subsequently "Turkicized." It was time, therefore, to "Bulgarize" them back again! At the end of 1984 and in early 1985, a brutal campaign was launched to force them to officially give up their Turkish names and adopt Bulgarian ones. They were also forbidden to speak Turkish in public. In the northeast and southeast of the country, where most of the Turks lived, there was considerable resistance and many Turkish casualties.

Some four years later, when the ferment that was to lead to the downfall of communism in eastern Europe began to affect Bulgaria, there was renewed Turkish resistance to continuing official repression. It was this that prompted the Zhivkov regime in Sofia to begin expelling some of the Turkish resistance leaders and then strongly "encouraging" Bulgarian Turks to leave for Turkey. Much pressure, even terror, was used to induce Turks to leave. It was estimated that toward the end of 1989 well over 300,000 members of the minority had crossed the border into Turkey, stretching to breaking point the Turkish government's ability to accommodate them.

Subsequently, after the deposition of Todor Zhivkov in November 1989 and the official rescinding of all the anti-Turkish measures since 1984, over 150,000 Bulgarian Turks returned to their homeland. The situation of the Turks has continued to improve in post-communist Bulgaria despite the difficulties of many returning Turks in regaining their land and property. Politically, their influence burgeoned when, as a result of the elections in October 1991, the Turkish Rights and Freedoms Party held the balance in the parliament between the victorious democrats and the reformed communists.

But several factors still threatened ethnic harmony in Bulgaria. Among these were continuing bureaucratic difficulties (many of them deliberate) in regaining land and property; Bulgaria's serious economic situation; continuing, deep Bulgarian suspicions of Turks and Turkey; the still-powerful reform communists' strategy of playing the nationalist card by, among other things, keeping anti-Turkish feeling alive; and the general Muslim unrest in the Balkans.[27]

Unlike every other Balkan country, Greece has been virtually ethnically homogeneous (98.5 percent) since the 1920s, after the massive transfers of populations with Turkey in the post-World War I period.[28] But, still, in Greek Thrace, the northeastern part of the country bordering onto European Turkey, there were in 1991 about 200,000 "Greek citizens of Muslim religion," as they were officially described, many of whom were unquestionably of Turkish ethnic origin. Their status and condition were hotly contested by the Greek and Turkish governments, the former claiming that the Muslims were well treated, the latter insisting they were not.

The bitterness with which the dispute was being conducted reflected the growing hostility between Athens and Ankara over Cyprus and a whole range of Aegean issues. Representatives of the minority itself, who were also affected by this growing hostility as well as by the ethnic and religious ferment in the Balkans as a whole, insisted that they were treated as second-class citizens by the Greek government. Their claim obviously had some validity, and subsequently signs appeared that the Greek government was moving to redress some of the minority's grievances.[29] Greece, therefore, whether it admitted it or not, had a growing "Turkish problem."[30]

Traditionally, of course, the Greeks had despised their northern neighbors, whether Slav or non-Slav. But during the 1980s, common fear of, and hostility toward, Turkey and Turks forged an alliance of mutual convenience between Greece and Bulgaria. In the early 1990s, however, this alliance cooled, principally because Bulgarian-Turkish relations improved and sharp differences arose between Athens and Sofia over Macedonia. Over the longer run, though, Turkey was likely to remain the big problem for both countries, ensuring, therefore, that they would not move too far apart.

The Turkish Response

The Muslim factor in the Balkans during the 1990s is likely to be divisive and could be decisive. Even before the Bosnian conflict, some observers were expecting a period of widespread Slav-Muslim, Orthodox-Islam confrontation. This confrontation, though, was not expected to result in conflagration but rather an overarching tension punctuated by skirmishing or violent incidents of varying sizes. Nor was it expected immediately: by the end of the century was a generally credible estimate.[31]

The war in Bosnia in 1992 confirmed expectations about a Slav-Muslim confrontation but now in terms of conflagration and with a time-frame much shorter than had previously been thought likely. Turkish concern about the disintegration of Yugoslavia had been evident about a year earlier as the violence in Croatia was already spilling over into Bosnia-Herzegovina, and the Muslim community there was being pressed by the Serbs. Slobodan Milosevic and Franjo Tudjman, the presidents of Serbia and Croatia, had apparently already met secretly to discuss the partition of Bosnia-Herzegovina.[32] As seen from Belgrade and Zagreb, this was beginning to look like the last chance of avoiding all-out war between the two nations. If a mutually satisfactory compromise between Serbia and Croatia could have been reached, it might even have saved the basic integrity of Yugoslavia. Slovenia could have seceded, and Croatian and Serbian interests would have been largely safeguarded. But it would have had to be at the expense of the very existence of Bosnia-Herzegovina and the large Muslim community there. The Bosnian president, Alija Iszetbegovic, had declared more than once that the Muslims would fight any attempts at partition which would lead to the destruction of the Muslim nation. And, if bloodshed occurred in Bosnia, it was widely feared that it would spread to other parts of Yugoslavia—Kosovo almost certainly, and perhaps Macedonia.

Turkish concern and fears, therefore, were growing in 1991, but nobody in Ankara could have expected the disastrous turn of events the following year. In fact, the Balkan situation was far from being one of Ankara's priority issues in the first half of 1992. It was preoccupied with the war between Azerbaijan and Armenia and the Kurdish revolt within its own territory. In the former, it strongly supported the Azeris, and Turkish sabre-rattling from President Ozal on down caused serious uneasiness in the West and a very sharp response from Russia.[33] In their suppression of renewed Kurdish disturbances in March 1992, the Turks also drew unwelcome attention to themselves, and the episode caused a near-rupture in their relations with Germany.[34]

Beyond these pressing developments, Turkey was laying the basis for a growing, influential relationship with the Turkic-Muslim successor states of the Soviet Union, a development that received wide and generally welcoming publicity in the West.[35] It was also preparing its plans for a Black Sea economic cooperation zone (see below), which it did at a meeting in Istanbul in June 1992.

But as the fighting in Bosnia-Herzegovina intensified, Turkish expressions of concern grew.[36] The Balkans could become a major diversion from the new opportunities the world situation had suddenly presented. And while the Turks had genuine feelings of concern for the Bosnian Muslims, they were also aware that the Bosnian situation gave them welcome relief from the deluge of Western criticism they had been receiving earlier in the year on account of Armenia and, especially, the Kurds. In June 1992, Turkey hosted a meeting of the foreign ministers of the Islamic Conference Organization, which promised to support outside military intervention if the United Nations sanctions failed to deter the Serbs.[37] But, still, the Turkish response was relatively muted. There was hope in Ankara and Istanbul (as there was also in the West) that the sanctions might work and that UN and/or EC efforts to end the fighting would succeed. It was also not clear to many what course the fighting in Bosnia-Herzegovina would take, i.e., how far the Serbs were prepared to go in carving out for themselves large parts of the republic, and to what extent Serbs and Croats would agree on dismemberment at Muslim expense.

Very soon, however, with the growing numbers of valid reports about "ethnic cleansing" and then about "detention centers" or "concentration camps," there was no doubt: Muslims were being driven from their homes, deprived of their belongings, and in many cases killed, or incarcerated in cruel or primitive conditions. As for the future, Serb plans would give those remaining from the originally 43 percent Muslim part of the total population of Bosnia-Herzegovina about 5 percent of the former republic's territory—the area around Sarajevo and a few other Bosnian enclaves. There was also enough convincing evidence that Serbs and Croats, however great their own enmity, were carving up the republic.[38]

Pressure on Turkey

With ethnic cleansing and the exposure of the detention camps, the war in Yugoslavia had entered a new phase and had taken on a strengthened and potentially explosive international dimension. Turkey was part of this dimension: It was becoming increasingly involved in a situation it would like to have avoided but now could not. It was being drawn into the Balkan conflagration for several reasons:

1. *The strength of public opinion in Turkey itself.* Although it was too much to speak of the "re-Islamization" of Turkey, there had been enough movement away from Kemalist secularization since the end of World War II to make large sections of the Turkish public responsive to demands (usually from more fully "Islamisized" compatriots) that

something be done in Bosnia. The Kemalist elites in Istanbul and Ankara were still reluctant to see Turkey involved again in the Balkans, but their political power had been considerably weakened over the past quarter of a century. Instead, power lay with moderate Muslims, a fact reflected in the behavior of the True Path and Motherland parties and personified by Prime Minister Suleyman Demirel and President Turgut Ozal. The Social Democrats, led by Adnan Inonu, generally embodied the Kemalist tradition, but they were members of Demirel's coalition government along with his True Path party. Whatever their real inclinations, the Social Democrats knew that a lack of concern about Bosnia would hasten their political decline.

Religion aside, Turks and the Bosnian Muslims generally felt close to one another. After the Austro-Hungarians took control of Bosnia-Herzegovina in 1878, and again during the first part of the twentieth century, many Bosnian Muslims moved to Turkey, and several hundred thousand Turks today are believed to have Bosnian ancestry.[39] Also, Bosnian and Turkish Muslims have generally shared an easygoing attitude to their religious faith. Bosnian Muslims, in particular, were famous for their bending of Islamic rules of behavior.[40] (For this, as well as for their Slavic ethnicity, they were often frowned upon by strict Muslims.)[41]

2. *The lack of a firm Western response to the situation.* The disunity, indecision, and impotence shown mainly by the EC, but also by the United States, in their response to Bosnia-Herzegovina, only seemed to shift responsibility increasingly toward Turkey.

3. *Suspicions throughout Islam that the "West" was ready, or even anxious, to see this Muslim "outpost" in Europe liquidated, an idea lent credibility by (2) above.* Thus, in the Balkan Slav vs. Muslim confrontation that had now turned to conflict, the West was showing its hand by leaving the Bosnian Muslims to the mercy of their much more powerful enemies. The Bosnian Serbs, for their part, were only too glad to pose as the defenders of European civilization against what they claimed to be a new threat from Islam.[42] Muslim suspicions of Western intentions were gathering strength even among some liberals in Turkey. Mehmet Ali Birend, for example, a well-respected, generally pro-Western journalist, said that his whole *Weltanschauung* had been shattered by the recent Balkan developments. "The events in Bosnia-Herzegovina show," he said, "that the West does not want a Muslim country in Europe. Their non-intervention shows this. They are letting the Serbs do their dirty work."[43] Inevitably, the contrast with Western firmness over Iraq's invasion of Kuwait in 1991 was drawn by many Muslim, including Turkish, commentators. It was not just a question of Bosnia-

Herzegovina having no oil. Even more to the point, the argument went, was that nearly half its population were unwanted in Europe because they were Muslim.

Charges of Western complicity in Serbian genocide were being heard throughout the Islamic world, but they were understandably the loudest in the more militant Islamic states, as were the calls for united Muslim action against the Serbs. (A "jihad" was being called for with increasing frequency.)[44] Iran was taking the lead in this agitation, some pronouncements by its leading clerics recalling the uncompromising ferocity of Ayatollah Khomeini's heyday.[45] Just as in the internal Iranian domestic context, where the moderates had to try to keep pace with the extremists, so in the international Muslim context moderate Turkey could not afford to be demonstrably less concerned than extremist Iran.

4. *Pressure from the Muslim sphere.* This was another Muslim context in which Turkish-Iranian rivalry could force Ankara into militancy. The growth of Turkish influence in the Muslim-Turkic republics of the old Soviet Union since the beginning of 1991 had been one of the most important results of the collapse of Soviet communist power. Stabilizing and extending this influence was a means by which Turkey could become a major regional power—perhaps a major world power. These new republics looked to Turkey rather than Iran because (with the exception of Tadjikistan) of a similar ethnic background and because Turkey represented a more modern Muslim outlook bent on technical and economic progress. But both governments and citizens in this huge, developing, Turkish sphere of influence would be watching Turkey's response to the Bosnian crisis very carefully. Again, Ankara could not afford to appear less concerned than Iran. If it could not actually deliver the Muslims in Bosnia-Herzegovina, it must at least take the lead in organizing measures aimed at this.

The result of all these pressures was a feverish Turkish diplomatic activity in the summer of 1992 to try to strengthen Western resolve against Serbia. Turkey also offered to place at least 1,000 troops at the disposal of a combined expeditionary force and urged the bombing of Serbian targets.[46] But the real test of Turkey's commitment to the Bosnian Muslims, at least in the eyes of Islam generally, would be its reaction to any peace or cease-fire agreement arranged by the Western powers which left the Muslims demonstrably worse off in terms of territory controlled. In sum, the situation in Bosnia-Herzegovina was putting Turkey on notice. Turkey wanted to concentrate on other matters but it was being forced back to the Balkans. And if the Yugoslav conflict spread to Kosovo and then spilled over into Albania and Macedonia, Turkey could be in the thick of a conflict it did not want, in a region to which it would have preferred not to return.

Muslims apart, none of the Balkan nations wanted the Turks to return, either. If they did, even as part of a multilateral force, the reaction in Greece and Bulgaria, for example, would be one of unmitigated consternation. Not much would be needed to bring the population of either country to fever pitch with warnings about new waves of "Mehmetçiks" roving the peninsula. Once they got there, would they ever leave? In Bulgaria, especially, with its large Turkish minority, and the recent memory of its persecution, the prospect could be unsettling in the extreme.[47] It would certainly put an end to the promising improvement in relations between Ankara and Sofia which began in 1991. Finally, taking the region as a whole, Turkish reentry in any kind of military capacity would both hasten and broaden the Slav vs. Muslim confrontation already discussed. Some of the early speculation about such a confrontation had centered on whether Turkey would be able to stay aloof from it. That question might be answered much earlier than most had expected.

The Black Sea Project: A Peaceful Initiative

The war in Bosnia-Herzegovina, the plight of the Muslims, and the prospect of Turkish intervention in 1992 put Ankara's relations with the Balkan countries in a new light. It also possibly set them on a quite different course from that which seemed to be developing at the beginning of the 1990s.

Turkey's relations at the official level with the rest of the Balkan countries had varied according to the country concerned. With Greece, as already mentioned, they had seriously deteriorated after the end of World War II, occasionally almost to the point of war. With neighboring Bulgaria, they had also often been strained partly because Bulgaria, as a subservient ally of the Soviet Union, presented a threat to Turkish security. But bilateral history, mainly regarding the Turkish minority in Bulgaria, often injected a special bitterness into relations. With the other three Balkan countries—Romania, Yugoslavia, and Albania, all communist but all achieving various degrees of independence from Moscow—relations ranged from cordial to good. None threatened Turkey. In fact, all three, in their policy of distancing themselves from the Soviet Union, saw Turkey, if not as an ally, then at least as a state whose national interests complemented theirs. With Enver Hoxha's Albania, in many respects an international pariah, Turkey had enjoyed good relations on account of the Muslim and Ottoman connection. Even as militant a communist leader as Hoxha could not totally reject the Turkish legacy, especially when he stood in virtual isolation.

With the revolutions in Eastern Europe in 1989 and the demise of the Cold War—but before the disintegration of the Soviet Union itself—the previous Balkan alliances and alignments collapsed. In 1992, after the Soviet collapse, the situation changed globally. Under Ozal's leadership, Turkey began to engage in both multilateral and bilateral diplomacy aimed at channeling the extraordinary turn of events both constructively and in its own national interests.

Alongside its initiatives in the Turkic parts of the Soviet Union, Turkey also looked to the Balkans, not as a principal area of interest but one where the post-Cold War situation needed both stabilizing and steering toward future forms of cooperation. In this regard, its multilateral initiative, inspired by Ozal himself, known as the Black Sea Cooperation Region Project (BECR), has been the most spectacular and intriguing.

As announced by the Turks, the BECR's main objective was to "create favorable conditions and establish institutional arrangements among the Black Sea countries for the development and diversification of their economic relations by making efficient use of advantages arising from geographical proximity and the complementary nature of their economies."[48] A multinational constituent conference was held in Ankara in December 1990, one year before the final collapse of the Soviet Union. Romania and Bulgaria took part; the Soviet delegation also included deputy foreign ministers from Azerbaijan, Georgia, Moldavia, and Armenia. In the first half of 1991, meetings to discuss the initial stages of the project were held in Bucharest, Sofia, and Moscow. These were designed to help create favorable conditions for both intergovernmental and nongovernmental cooperation. The longer-term aim was to set up a "flexible organization" facilitating "the free circulation of people, communities, capital, and services." The initial fields of intergovernmental cooperation included telecommunications; energy and the extraction and processing of raw materials; environmental protection; scientific and technological research; the establishment of free trade zones; agriculture, agro-industry, and food processing; tourism; and pharmaceutical fields.

Hardly surprising for an Ozal initiative, the project laid great stress on private enterprise in international cooperation. This, the Turks argued, would assist the transition to the free market economy which the Soviet Union, Bulgaria, and Romania were undergoing. The eventual, broader ambition of the project was for the Black Sea region to become an "integral part of the world economy." The BECR, it was claimed, followed on from the end of the Cold War and the breaking down of hostile world blocs, a process which it would help to accelerate.

It was an imaginative project typical of Ozal's resourcefulness and fertile imagination. But the main aim for Turkey was to get into the Soviet market and to have access to Soviet raw materials. The emphasis given to cooperation, not only with the then Soviet center, but also with the individual republics, offered reinsurance against the eventual breakup of the USSR, which was to occur much sooner than expected. The specifically Balkan aspect of the project, however, at first looked rather small. Bulgaria and, particularly, Romania could not be optimistic about early political and economic acceptance by western Europe, but this goal was still given much higher priority than the southern and eastern orientation implicit in the BECR proposal.

The aftermath of the Soviet collapse delayed progress in developing the Turkish initiative. During a period of breakup, and then of new or revived antagonisms and conflicts in parts of the old Soviet empire, any proposals for a new type of regional cooperation were seen by many as, if not visionary, then clearly premature. But the Turks persisted, and in June 1992 eleven heads of government met in Istanbul officially to launch the Black Sea economic cooperation project. Greece and Albania, which are not Black Sea countries and were not initially envisaged as members, were represented, along with Romania and Bulgaria. So were, from the former Soviet Union, Azerbaijan, Armenia, Georgia, Ukraine, Moldova, and Russia, none of them, as *The Economist* put it, "famous for their ability to cooperate."[49] The Black Sea project became a symptom of Turkey's confidence and a reflection of its extraordinary reemergence on the post-Cold War scene.

But the enthusiasm for the Black Sea project had to be tempered by a realistic view of the situation in many of the areas it was supposed to encompass. As long as strife abounded in the former Soviet Union and in the Balkans, the Black Sea project was little more than a framework for the future. It was not a mechanism for settling conflicts but one to facilitate cooperation once the conflicts were sufficiently settled. If they persisted and intensified, the Black Sea project would be stillborn—just another bold idea that never left the ground. And it was precisely those areas where the Turks were trying to stimulate cooperation that were the centers of the most serious conflict. Armenia and Azerbaijan were already at war. Georgia was beset by internal chaos. Russia and Ukraine were poised on the brink of conflict. Moldova was facing problems of secession. These were the problems that could kill the Black Sea initiative.

In fact, the Balkans had always been peripheral to the Black Sea project. Bulgaria's and Romania's geographical situation rather than their geopolitical importance had brought them into the project and, as previously mentioned, their governments were not enthusiastic. Greece and Albania were subsequently included, but what role, if any, they might play remains to be seen.

At the popular level, though, it should be recorded that, by the middle of 1992, Istanbul had become a magnet for many Romanians and Bulgarians, particularly young entrepreneurs who crowded into the old Ottoman capital selling their wares, looking for work or the odd deal—legal or illegal.[50] Thus, while Bulgarian and Romanian politicians, intellectuals, and large-scale entrepreneurs were still looking to the West, thousands of their more "ordinary" compatriots were gravitating to Istanbul. For them, anyway, the old Ottoman capital was returning to its pride of place. This immigration is likely to continue and, over the years, have a marked effect on the geopolitics of the region.

Notes

1. An excellent general history of the Balkans is Barbara Jelavich's *History of the Balkans*, two volumes, Cambridge University Press, 1983. For the Ottoman period, see Vol. I, pp. 38–126. See also Wayne S. Vucinich, *The Ottoman Empire: Its Record and Legacy*, Princeton, N.J.: Van Nostrand, 1965.

2. See Bernard Lewis, *The Emergence of Modern Turkey*, London: Oxford University Press, 1961; also Jelavich, *History of the Balkans*, Vol. II, pp. 126–133.

3. See Richard Clogg, "Troubled Alliance: Greece and Turkey," in Richard Clogg, ed., *Greece in the 1980s* London: MacMillan, 1983 pp. 123–149.

4. See Aurel Braun, *Small-State Security in the Balkans*, London: MacMillan, 1983, pp. 40–44.

5. See Jesse W. Lewis, Jr., *The Strategic Balance in the Mediterranean*, Washington, D.C.: American Enterprise Institute, 1983, pp. 70–72, 155–169; Barry Buzan, "The Status and Future of the Montreux Convention," *Survival*, Nov.–Dec. 1976.

6. Braun, *Small-State Security*, pp. 44–46.

7. See J. F. Brown, *Bulgaria Under Communist Rule*, New York: Praeger, 1970, pp. 293–297.

8. The two most important American slights to Turkey were in October 1962, when, as part of the package settling the Cuban missile crisis, President Kennedy agreed to remove Jupiter missiles from Turkey without having consulted the Turkish government. More serious, however, was the offense caused by President Johnson's letter to President Ismet Inönü in June 1964, warning him that, if Turkey invaded Cyprus, NATO would not automatically come to Turkey's aid if the Soviet Union used the opportunity to attack Turkey.

F. Stephen Larrabee gives succinct analyses of American involvement with both Turkey and Greece in "Balkan Security," Adelphi Paper No. 135, London: IISS; and "The Southern Periphery: Greece and Turkey," in Paul W. Shoup, ed., and George W. Hoffman, Project Director, *Problems of Balkan Security: Southeastern Europe in the 1990s*, Washington, D.C.: Wilson Center, 1990, pp. 174–302.

9. On this "diversification," see Udo Steinbach, "Türkei: Diversifizierung der Aussenpolitik," *Aussenpolitik*, No. 4, 1973.

10. See John O. Iatrides, "Greece and the United States: The Strained Partnership," in Clogg, *Greece in the 1980s*, pp. 164–170.

11. Braun, *Small-State Security*, pp. 51–53.

12. See Jelavich, *History of the Balkans*, Vol. I, pp. 59–63; Vol. II, pp. 127–168.

13. See Jelavich, *History of the Balkans*, Vol. I, pp. 79–105.

14. See Jelavich, *History of the Balkans*, Vol. II, pp. 134–243.

15. The best work on the interaction of communism and nationalism in the Balkans remains Paul Lendvai, *Eagles in Cobwebs: Nationalism and Communism in the Balkans*, New York: Doubleday, 1969.

16. See J. F. Brown, *Eastern Europe and Communist Rule*, Durham, N.C.: Duke University Press, 1988, pp. 263–293, 317–383, 415–444; and the same author's *Surge to Freedom: The End of Communist Rule in Eastern Europe*, Durham, N.C.: Duke University Press, 1991, pp. 181–245.

17. One of the best running commentaries on the Balkans in recent years has been by Viktor Meier in the *Frankfurter Allgemeine Zeitung* and by Alexander Oplatka and Cyrill Stieger in the *Neue Zurcher Zeitung*. For an excellent article, see F. Stephen Larrabee, "Long Memories and Short Fuses: Change and Instability in the Balkans," *International Security*, Vol. 15, No. 3, Winter 1990–1991. For a succinct review, see "Welcome to the Seething South," *The Economist*, March 2–8, 1991.

18. Viktor Meier, "Das Serbien Milosevic's schafft in Sandzak ein zweites Kosovo," *Frankfurter Allgemeine Zeitung*, June 25, 1991.

19. On Kosovo, see Brown, *Surge to Freedom*, pp. 226–228.

20. Bishop Amphilocius of Pecs, in an interview with Thomas Ross, *Frankfurter Allgemeine Zeitung*, November 6, 1989.

21. Viktor Meier, "Wieder die Mazedonische Frage," *Frankfurter Allgemeine Zeitung*, June 22, 1990.

22. The new IMRO leader, Ljupco Georgievski, was warning that by 1991 an independent Macedonia would be negotiating its future with both Greece and Bulgaria; see interview with Carl Gustav Strohm, *Die Welt*, January 4, 1991. On IMRO's origins and development see Duncan M. Perry, *The Politics of Terror: The Macedonian Revolutionary Movements, 1893–1903*, Durham, N.C.: Duke University Press, 1988.

23. See Duncan M. Perry, "Macedonia: A Balkan Problem and a European Dilemma," *RFE/RL Research Report*, Vol. 1, No. 25, June 19, 1992.

24. "Albaniens ungelöste nationale Frage," *Neue Zurcher Zeitung*, April 6, 1992.

25. On the reasons for the Greek refusal to recognize Macedonia, see Howard La Franchi, "Greeks United in Opposition to Independent Macedonia," *Christian Science Monitor*, June 24, 1992. Many studies agree that the best overall coverage of this issue was by the *Neue Zurcher Zeitung*. "Mazedoniens Recht auf seinen Namen," June 22, 1992; and "Athens mazedonische Angste," June 25, 1992. For the Greek attitude on Kosovo and the Balkans generally see the two articles by Viktor Meier, "Europa hat die Wahl zwischen Athen und Skopje" and "Grosse Schwierigkeiten mit Mazedonien," *Frankfurter Allgemeine Zeitung*, June 9 and 10, 1992.

26. See Huey Louis Kostanick, "The Geopolitics of the Balkans," in Charles and Barbara Jelavich, eds., *The Balkans in Transition*, Berkeley: University of California Press, 1963, p. 40.

27. On the anti-Turkish measures in Bulgaria, see Brown, *Eastern Europe and Communist Rule*, p. 427, and *Surge to Freedom*, p. 195. In 1991 and 1992, some 140,000 Bulgarian Turks went to Turkey as guest-workers because of economic depression in Bulgaria; Reuters, Sofia, August 3, 1992. The figure of 140,000 may be exaggerated, but it should be noted that the enormous, short-term migration to Turkey had begun in the summer of 1991; BTA, July 26, 1991.

28. See Jelavich, *History of the Balkans*, Vol. II, p. 176.

29. See statement by Greek Premier Mitsotakis to *Hurriyet*, Istanbul, June 15, 1991, *FBIS-WEU*-91-118, June 19, 1991, p. 33.

30. There is considerable Greek-Turkish polemical literature on western Thrace with the Turks on the offensive and the Greeks responding. For a substantial Turkish criticism see Dr. Sadik Ahmet's interview in Nokta, Istanbul, April 14, 1991, *FBIS-WEU*-91-108, June 5, 1991, p. 53. (Sadik Ahmet sits as a deputy in the Greek parliament for the city of Komotini in western Thrace.) For the rapidly dwindling Greek minority in Turkey, see Alexis Alexandris, "Political Expediency and Human Rights: Minority Issues Between Greece and Turkey," paper delivered at the conference on Minority Rights—Policies and Practice in southeast Europe, in Copenhagen, March 30–April 1, 1990. (This paper was provided by the Embassy of Greece, Washington, D.C.)

31. See, for example, J. F. Brown, "The East European Agenda," in Ivo John Lederer, ed., *Western Approaches to Eastern Europe*, New York: Council on Foreign Relations Press, 1992, pp. 30–31.

32. See Judy Dempsey, "Secret Talks over Yugoslav Borders to Be Restarted," *Financial Times*, July 10, 1991; Tim Judah, "Creation of Islamic Buffer State Discussed in Secret," *The Times*, London, July 12, 1991.

33. See Maria Dejevsky, "Turkey Is Warned of War Risk," *The Times*, London, May 21, 1992; Gerd Höhler, "Säbelrasseln in Ankara," *Frankfurter Rundschau*, May 22, 1992; Nicole Pope, "La Turquie estime qu'une intervention militaire entamerait son crédit international," *Le Monde*, May 22, 1992.

34. See Chris Medges, "Kurds in Turkey Seem to Be Nearing Full-Scale Revolt," *New York Times*, March 30, 1992.

35. See Wolfgang Günter Lerch, "Pantürkismus oder Europa," *Frankfurter Allgemeine Zeitung*, April 27, 1992; Hugh Pope, "Demirel Woos Turkish-Speaking States," *The Independent*, April 27, 1992.

36. Turkish concern had begun to be evident about a year before. Iszetbegovic visited Turkey in July 1991 and received strong unofficial expressions of support for an independent Bosnia-Herzegovina. At least two Istanbul newspapers were urging that Turkey "protect" Bosnia's and Macedonia's Muslims (*Hurryet* and *Cumhurryet*, both July 12, 1991). But months were to elapse until the fighting really began in Bosnia.

37. On the Islamic Conference, see Judy Dempsey, "Islamic Nations Press UN on Force," *Financial Times*, August 7, 1992.

38. Tim Judah, "Sarajevo's Plight Conceals Stealthy Partition of Bosnia," *The Times*, London, July 8, 1992.

39. See, for example, Ömer Erzeren, "Türkei: Bomben auf serbische Stellungen," *Tageszeitung*, Berlin, August 11, 1992.

40. As one Bosnian Muslim official put it, "We are blond Muslims. We are part of European culture and European civilization. About 70 percent of the Bosnian Muslims don't know anything about Islam. They drink alcohol, they eat pork." Quoted by Peter Maas, "Serbs Say They're Fighting Islamic Fundamentalism in Bosnia," *New York Times*, August 11, 1992; the gist of this quotation is right, but it contains a good deal of rhetorical exaggeration.

41. Michael Binyon, "Iran Urges Islamic States to Intervene," *The Times*, London, August 6, 1992.

42. Maas, "Serbs Say They're Fighting Islamic Fundamentalism."

43. Erzeren, "Turkei."

44. See Amir Taheri, "Die islamische Welt ruft zu Dschihad gegen Serbien auf," *Die Welt*, August 10, 1992. See also Fred Halliday, "Bosnia and the Sword of Islam," *The Guardian*, August 10, 1992.

45. See Wolfgang Kohler, "Iran fur eine 'Islamische Armee'," *Frankfurter Allgemeine Zeitung*, August 12, 1992.

46. See Jonathan Rugman, "Turkey Offers 1,000 Troops for UN Force," *The Guardian*, August 17, 1992.

47. See Wolfgang Gunter Lerch, "Und wenn die Turken kamen?" *Frankfurter Allgemeine Zeitung*, August 12, 1992.

48. On the BECR, see the unpublished paper entitled, "Black Sea Cooperation Region Project," by Dr. Sukru Elekdag of the Turkish Ministry of Foreign Affairs, May 9, 1991. Quotations about the project are taken from this source.

49. "Black Sea Zone—Black Hole," *The Economist*, June 27, 1992.

50. Rudiger Wischenbart, "Auch die Osmanen hatten ihr Reich auf den Balkan hin ausgerichtet," *Der Tagesspiegel*, Berlin, August 9, 1992.

5

Conclusions: The Growing Role of Turkey in the World

Graham E. Fuller

Quite unexpectedly, the world at the end of the twentieth century has been sharply buffeted by geopolitical change unparalleled in scope since World War I. The collapse of communism and the dissolution of the Soviet Union have not only spawned fifteen new states in the world, but have brought the global Cold War to an end, unleashing major new waves of nationalism and separatism in many other states, of which Yugoslavia is only the most dramatic example. These regional events have gone on to generate massive ripple effects elsewhere in the world among a large number of noncommunist states; the process of fracture and disintegration of the basic concept of the nation-state is perhaps only beginning.

Turkey has been among those states most immediately affected by the changing environment. Located in geopolitical terms in the southeastern corner of Europe for so many decades, Turkey now lies at the center of a rapidly evolving new geopolitical region of Turkish peoples from Eastern Europe to western China—in which it will be the central player.[1] These geopolitical shifts, combined with Turkey's new prominence in international events, will have a major impact on the way Turkey sees itself, deals with others, and is perceived by others.

The emergence of a whole new "Turkic world"—similar to the Arab world in size and distance spanned—has come as a surprise to much of the world. A huge Turkic belt has now revealed itself, stretching from the Balkans across Turkey, Iran, and Central Asia, up into the Russian heartland of Tatarstan and into western Siberia, deep into western China, and to the borders of Mongolia, comprising in all some 150 million people. The concept of a shared sense of Turkishness is widespread among nearly all of them.[2]

The degree of political cohesion that will emerge from these close cultural and ethnic ties may well be limited. But the existence of a new "Turkic belt" has to be a major element in geopolitical thinking about Asia from now on—perhaps comparable to the special relationships that exist among the Arab states. The degree of distinctiveness among the Central Asian states, while a political reality, will always be viewed by intellectuals as somewhat artificial and perhaps susceptible to political union sometime in the future.

If one can generalize at all about the historic experience of ethnic groups, one observation is that the Turkic peoples, coming originally out of a nomadic background, have traditionally been a "martial" people who have almost invariably dominated wherever they have moved, variously controlling large parts of China, Mongolia, Central Asia, Russia, Iran, and Anatolia as they migrated in various groups from east to west over a period of some 1,500 years. The Turks have honed the skills of empire for long centuries and are accustomed to the practice of rule, statecraft, and geopolitics. This long historical experience has given them a certain "gravity" of conduct, a distinct self-confidence in comparison to the historical experience of many other Middle Eastern peoples, such as the Persians and Arabs, who indeed developed rich and sophisticated urban civilizations, but who nonetheless remained under the control of other peoples for long periods of their history. This experience as the dominated, rather than the dominant, often lends the political culture of such societies greater wariness and suspicion about the manipulative role of outside forces. While these generalizations can only be taken with extreme caution, they do suggest that the newly liberated Turkic peoples could become a significant political force in the heart of Asia, eventually looking towards ethnically based state building. The Turks' traditions of power suggest they may be less inclined toward radicalism and will have less historical basis for nurturing anti-Western inclinations.

How Does Turkey Matter to the United States?

In what ways does Turkey matter to the United States in a sharply changing world? The question is less easy to answer today, when U.S. interests themselves are in a state of major flux with the end of the Cold War. The Cold War often lent many far-flung countries major, if transitory, geopolitical significance resulting from their role in Western competition with the Soviet Union: such diverse states as Afghanistan, Angola, and Nicaragua took on special weight in U.S. calculations precisely because of Soviet or pro-Soviet activities there. Turkey historically derived its importance to the West from its strategic location on the southern flank of the Soviet Union; its guardianship of the Bosphorus and Dardanelles straits, which controlled access to the communist-dominated Black Sea; and its explicit commitment to the Western security cause, demonstrated as early as the Korean War, in which Turkey fought. Thus, geopolitics and Turkey's pro-Western orientation rapidly won Turkey a prominent role within NATO.

That role has now shifted drastically. Even though the end of the Cold War sharply diminishes the place of NATO, Turkey's growing importance today is much more powerfully defined by its centrality to regions of major instability and conflagration in which the long-range policies of Turkey could undergo significant and unprecedented change. The policies adopted by Turkey will have a great impact on many key problems, with Turkey serving either as a stabilizing force or as a complicating and exacerbating factor, in accordance with newly perceived national interests. This new centrality of Turkey in relation to a huge geographical region, analyzed at length in the four regional studies in this project, emerges vividly in the following significant areas:

- Turkey may play a significant role in the seething Balkans, where old states are collapsing, new ones are being formed, new hostilities and new political alliances are emerging, and a large (9 million) Muslim population (especially in Bosnia, Albania, Macedonia, and Bulgaria) increasingly looks to Turkey as a potential ally in the unfolding struggle among new national movements in the region. Major Turkish involvement would tend to place the Balkan confrontation along more starkly religious lines, reactivating the traditional Eastern Orthodox-Islam schism that so long dominated the region, poising Serbia, Greece, and potentially Bulgaria against Turkey. Some Russian nationalist circles have even expressed solidarity with this historical Orthodox grouping of nations.
- Turkey's more assertive role in the Balkans and Greece's increasing insecurities about the new Balkan politics could serve to increase Greek-Turkish frictions in the Aegean, now less constrained with the end of the East-West struggle. Aegean confrontation would present both Washington and Europe with a serious problem.
- Turkey has been unavoidably drawn into the volatile new politics of the Caucasus, where Armenia and Azerbaijan are locked in a seemingly unresolvable and potentially expandable war, where Georgian politics are highly unstable, and where other Muslim peoples agitate to break away from the new Russian federation. Turkey can, for example, act as regional powerbroker, offering its good offices to mediate in regional strife. Far less constructively, it can take sides by joining the Turkic Azeris against Armenia. An

overt and permanent Azerbaijani-Turkish alliance against Armenia would damage Turkey's standing as a regional great power, negatively affect Turkey's international standing and influence, draw in Iran, and broaden the conflict substantially.

- New conflict could emerge with Syria over water rights; Syrian long-term support for the Kurdish separatist-terrorist organization (The Kurdish Workers Party, or PKK) in Turkey is highly volatile. Conversely, improving Turkish ties with Syria could help lead the northeast Arab region into a period of dramatic new stability, especially if such ties were linked to progress on Arab-Israeli-Palestinian issues.

- A new and ever-deepening Turkish rivalry with Iran is emerging over influence in the new states of Central Asia and especially Azerbaijan. The independence of former Soviet Azerbaijan threatens to stimulate a parallel separatist movement in northern Iran (Iranian Azerbaijan) that could provoke Iran into severe, high-stakes conflict with Turkey—even if Ankara does not seek to provoke it.

- Unprecedented new Turkish confrontation with Iraq has developed as a result of the Gulf War and Turkey's role as an active belligerent against Saddam Hussein. Turkey is deeply disturbed by Iraq's quest for weapons of mass destruction and will be a key country in limiting future Iraqi expansionism in the Gulf area.

- The Gulf War and the emergence of an increasingly autonomous Kurdish region in northern Iraq have inexorably drawn Turkey into the increasingly complex and destabilizing aspects of Kurdish nationalist politics, affecting the territorial integrity of at least three states. The Kurdish problem threatens Turkey with a potential separatist movement that could draw Turkey into conflict with Iran and Iraq as well, especially if these states seek to exploit or exacerbate Turkey's ethnic vulnerability—as they have already done.

- Turkish involvement in the evolving politics of Central Asia could have a major impact, especially where broader Turkic nationalism has the potential to play a growing regional role. While cultural pan-Turkism does not have to be a negative element in the development of these states (especially if it can serve to establish useful regional federal relationships), even limited moves toward Central Asian Turkic unity will exacerbate competing national feelings among Russians and Iranian peoples (Persians, Afghan Tajiks, Tajikistan's Tajiks). These same Central Asian ethnic movements are already reinforcing separatist yearnings among the Turkish peoples of Chinese Turkestan (Xinjiang Province) and have the potential to unleash further separatist or breakaway movements in northern Afghanistan and, in counter-reaction, even in Pakistan. Beijing has already reacted by dusting off certain irredentist claims of its own in Central Asia (although they enjoy no regional support).

- If relations should deteriorate between the millions of expatriate Russians living in Central Asia and the native Turkic peoples, the confrontation is likely to intensify extreme nationalist feelings in Russia itself, strengthening less moderate elements and leading to a more explicit "Christian-Muslim" confrontation in the region. Russia already feels vulnerable because of the breakaway tendencies among the Tatars and other Turkic and Muslim peoples within Russia. Turkish association with these movements, however indirect, will serve to resuscitate the grand old geopolitical and religious confrontation between Turkic and Russian peoples from several centuries ago—Tsarist Orthodox Russia vs. the Muslim Ottoman Empire. Resurgent extreme nationalism among Russians would work directly against moderate, pro-Western forces in Russia.

- Turkey maintains an abiding interest in gaining full membership in the European Community (EC) and the Western European Union (WEU), a quest that is facing increasing problems from at least two sources: the emergence of independent states in Eastern Europe that themselves seek membership in the EC, and the anxiety of several European states, especially Germany, that new activist Turkish policies in the East could indirectly embroil NATO and the EC in undesirable conflicts thousands of miles from Europe. Yet Turkish exclusion from what may be perceived as a "Christian club" in Europe could lead to negative and anti-Western inclinations in Turkey itself.

Turkey's centrality to these issues has thus, quite unexpectedly, mushroomed overnight as a result of post-Cold War change, making Ankara's views and policies now of great importance to the region. Turkey is one of the countries that has gained importance in the new world environment as the importance of other players, especially the major Soviet client states, has diminished. Consultation with Turkey on these issues is essential to Western policymaking in the region. In fact, Turkey's own national interests are perhaps more immediately and vitally affected in some of these areas of conflict than are Western interests themselves.

Turkey is also of major significance as the preeminent model of a secular Islamic state in the Middle East—a factor that takes on increasing prominence with the current intensification of Islamic politics in key

Arab countries. Turkey was actually the first Muslim state in Islamic history to declare secularism as the basis of the state—it did so as early as 1924. This decision, perhaps rather casually noted by the West at the time, now takes on far greater significance given the place Islamic fundamentalism has now so vividly assumed in the Western political lexicon and the search for credible secular Muslim models.

But the religious issue is permanently with us: Islamic factors simply cannot be shut out of Middle Eastern politics. The difficulty is how to integrate Islam into politics without destabilizing the state. While the Turkish historical experience differs in several ways from that of other Muslim states in the region, many of the problems of political Islam are still shared by most states. Turkey, after banning explicitly Islamic politics for decades, has for many years now allowed Islamic parties to compete in the political process; this experience has importantly demonstrated that, in the final analysis, the overall appeal of these groups at the ballot box is fairly consistently limited to no more than 15 percent of the population. (This moderate Turkish experience is less relevant in those countries where Islamic parties have burst forth onto the political scene following a period of severe political repression—such as in Egypt, Algeria, or the former Soviet Central Asia—when they have often been one of the few coherent opposition movements capable of winning massive public support in initial free elections.) However, the Turkish experience in the evolution of an interrelationship between democracy and Islam is very important for the future evolution of the whole Muslim world; it needs to be examined for its implications by western policymakers as well.

The Turkish Domestic Debate

Acceptance of a new role in the Balkans, the Caucasus, Central Asia and the Middle East has not come easily to Turkey, for it has required virtual abandonment of a revered and deeply rooted foreign policy legacy left by the father and founder of the modern Turkish state, Mustafa Kemal Ataturk, in the years after World War I. As the new republic rose out of the ashes of the old multinational, multi-sectarian Ottoman Empire, Ataturk warned his countrymen to eschew all irredentist ambitions or foreign policy based on ethnic or religious ties, and to focus on the development and preservation of a new Turkish nation-state within its modern boundaries. Any kind of pan-Turkish or neo-Ottoman interests or aspirations clearly could only lead to dangerous confrontation with nascent Soviet power or with the Western imperial power that dominated most of the Middle East. Ataturk untiringly preached that Turkey must face west, align itself within European politics and culture, and abandon its historic ties with the Middle East. Since then, the Turkish elite has prided itself on being part of a broadly European culture and Western political orientation; even the average Turkish "man on the street" views himself as far removed from the Arab or Persian world for which he has little affection.

Ataturk's overall vision was of course sound at the time, and was largely observed until the collapse of the Soviet Empire, with certain exceptions. While Turkey rigorously avoided any interest in Soviet Central Asian affairs—to the extent that even academic study of the Turkic languages and history of that region was suspect and discouraged for long decades—Turkey did begin to evince growing interests in the welfare of other "overseas Turks" (dis Turkler), first in Cyprus—that actually led to military intervention and partition of the island—and then in Bulgaria. The 1970s oil boom in the Persian Gulf also led to increasing economic ties with the Arab world and a parallel growing Turkish sensitivity to the policies of many Muslim states whose good will was seen as important to Turkish economic interests. Growing trade with the Arab world and the increased presence of Arab investment in Turkey introduced a slightly more acceptable "Islamic orientation" in Turkish foreign policy; the fact that it was anchored in economic reality made the classic Ataturkist elite only slightly less uncomfortable with this modest new "Arab orientation." Increasingly open involvement of avowedly Islamic parties in Turkish politics in the seventies and eighties began to further fray the stricter interpretations of pure Ataturkist secularism.

The liberation of the Turkish republics of the Soviet Union and the emergence of new ethnic politics in the Balkans have brought about further revision of this standing legacy. Indeed, whether Turkey wanted to remain aloof or not, the emergence of the new Turkish states of the region did not permit Turkey to do so, especially as the competition for influence there also broke out among a number of other regional actors, such as Iran, Saudi Arabia, and Pakistan.

The new political developments of the former Soviet Union and the Middle East have therefore opened up painful debates within Turkish society about its future orientation. Most Turks, especially the traditional Ataturkist elite, still believe that Turkey's key interests are to be fulfilled primarily through contact with the West, of which they view themselves as a part. They fear that any new orientation of Ankara toward the Middle East and the Turkic world can only detract from the European character of Turkish society and weaken its very acceptance within the Western political system. Their arguments are strengthened by an observable EC concern, especially in Germany, that Turkey's new foreign policy involvements, starting with the Gulf War against Saddam

Hussein, could end up involving the EC or NATO in security imbroglios far from traditional European interests.

Opponents of any new policies that stress pan-Turkish links also point out that the new states of Azerbaijan and Central Asia have little to offer Turkey in economic terms. Those states are viewed as poor, deeply mired in an internal political struggle to weaken the hold of former Communist party structures and hindered by complex transitions to market economies with very limited economic incentives for Turkey. Turkey has only limited abilities to invest and even less money available for foreign assistance. These opponents argue that Turkey should not get drawn into potential political rivalries and struggles in a region that may be in turmoil for some time. While these arguments make rational sense, the force of regional nationalisms and rivalries will make it almost impossible for Turkey to remain aloof from developments. Turks will find it difficult to eschew a leadership role among the other Turkic states of the world. Turkey's own Islamic parties and groups also stress the need for closer ties with Turkey's Muslim neighbors and preach a cautious view toward the West, which they perceive as hostile to both Islam and Turkey.

This debate over foreign policy—really involving questions of degree rather than of stark alternatives between East and West—is a necessary and healthy one, perhaps the first serious debate over foreign policy since the founding of the republic. Turkey will inevitably have to reconsider its range of priorities now that new opportunities have opened up. From the Western point of view, however, the most negative turn of events may be the possibility of a frustrated Turkey drifting in the direction of more ethnically chauvinistic, adventuristic Turkish nationalism, transforming Turkey into a far less moderate state in the region. Several scenarios could converge to produce this kind of negative effect:

- Turkey is spurned in its search for closer integration into Europe, the EC, and other European institutions.
- Spiraling violence between Armenia and Azerbaijan in the end forces Turkey out of a neutral position and into full military support of Azerbaijan, thereby angering Russia and bringing international pro-Armenian sympathizers into a strong anti-Turkish stance, especially in the United States and Europe.
- Turkish alliance with Azerbaijan lends heightened support to the idea of a "united Azerbaijan" that eventually tears away the important province of Iranian Azerbaijan, plunging Turkey into direct confrontation with Iran.
- Economic conditions deteriorate in Turkey, bringing more radical policies into Turkey's government that might blame the West for

Turkey's economic hardships, especially if Turkey is excluded from the EC and deprived of the former military benefits from NATO membership.

- A clash with Greece leads Turkey toward further estrangement with Europe, especially if Greece gains European support.
- The position of Turkish workers (Gastarbeiter) in Germany leads to deterioration of Turko-German relations that have already been damaged by German tendencies toward sympathy for the Kurdish minority in Turkey and by the potential rivalry for geopolitical position in the Balkans.
- Turkey is drawn into military conflict with Greece over the Turkish minority in Greek Thrace and over Macedonia if the Yugoslav civil war sparks ethnic conflict there as well.
- Continuing deterioration of the Kurdish situation inside Turkey leads to growing civil unrest, violence, a perception in the outside world of broad Turkish human rights violations, and, ultimately, to the deterioration of Turkey's relations with Western states, including the United States. Widespread popular Turkish perception that the West sparked Kurdish nationalism with the Gulf War and then "turned against Turkey" could open the way to more extremist views, nationalist or Islamic.
- Increased Turkish nationalism additionally exacerbates the Kurdish situation, creating strong anti-Kurdish sentiment within Turkey and complicating the opportunity of Kurds to participate fully in the political life of Turkey.
- Islamic fundamentalism in Turkey, while historically often at odds with secular nationalism, joins the fray as a powerful quasi-nationalistic factor. Islamists support Turkey in an anti-Western policy direction, encourage deep suspicions of Western policies and intentions toward Turkey, and reinforce any native trends toward xenophobia. Appeals made to Turkey by Balkan Muslims receive a powerful emotional response from both the Islamist and the nationalist blocs.

If several or all of these conditions converged, Turkey's foreign policy could end up embracing more extreme Turkish nationalism/chauvinism, with uncertain effects on the remaining Turkish states of the region.

While many aspects of some of the scenarios above could come to pass, it is important to recognize that a chauvinist anti-Western Turkey does not represent the more likely course of future events. Turkish political common sense and balance over the years, combined with deeply rooted Westernization within the Turkish upper and growing middle classes, should help maintain balance and proportion in Turkey's poli-

cies and outlook. Turkey's foreign policy establishment is highly professional, experienced, and very Western oriented. Turkey's very professional military has always sought to avoid foreign entanglements, but its
tradition of sober leadership and policies could gradually be altered by a
change of complexion in the civilian leadership of government that pursues a more blatantly pan-Turkist or interventionist foreign policy.
Turkish economic interests overwhelmingly lie to the West rather than to
the poorer Turkish world. Turkey is unlikely to want to divert significant economic resources to an Eastern policy if doing so will harm the
overall economic foundations and social stability of the state. But it is
also important for the West to recognize that a disgruntled Turkey has
far greater negative implications for the region today than ever in the
past. If the region is in turmoil, Turkey is unlikely to sit idly by as other
states are seen to intervene in areas of interest to Ankara.

The expanding character of the Kurdish problem in Turkey is deeply
disturbing for Turkey, its allies, and for the region. Although the Kurds
made their distinctive ethnic feelings very clear during uprisings in
southeastern Anatolia in 1925 and after, basically the Kurdish areas had
been free of any major uprisings for long decades. The Turkish security
presence there has kept order, but it has done nothing to meet the population's grievances about often harsh police methods or its desire for cultural and linguistic rights and a greater share in the economic prosperity
of Turkey. In the past decade, with the emergence of the PKK's ideologically driven, Marxist-Leninist "national liberation movement," the level
of armed confrontation has risen dramatically and—some might argue—
decisively.

The Gulf War greatly exacerbated the Kurdish problem through
Saddam Hussein's gross depredations against the Kurdish people; the
flood of over a million Kurdish refugees into Turkey from Iraq; the creation of a UN-protected Kurdish autonomous zone in northern Iraq; the
holding of elections for an autonomous Kurdish government, under
Western protection, in northern Iraq; the establishment in the fall of 1992
of a "federal" Kurdish state within Iraq; and the continuing moves of the
Kurds toward de facto administrative autonomy and de facto "foreign
relations" with Turkey. Not only has the international plight of the
Kurds risen dramatically before the world, but Turkish domestic policy
has been in the process of an unprecedented shift toward greater liberal-
ism and the recognition of the existence of a Kurdish minority and that
minority's right to use its language.

While Turkey has now recognized officially that there can be no permanent military solution to the Kurdish problem in Turkey, and that
development of the Kurdish regions must be the centerpiece of any

effort to pacify the region, the PKK has also taken advantage of the new circumstances to step up armed struggle, carrying terrorism into the cities and against the civilian population in an effort to polarize the situation. These terrorist actions greatly complicate the government's ability to solve the problem through more enlightened economic and social policies. A major Turkish offensive against the PKK inside northern Iraq with support from the Kurdish administration there in late 1992 dealt a major blow to the PKK military infrastructure and guerrilla strength, but the problem of Kurdish unrest cannot ultimately be resolved without also creating alternative, meaningful political vehicles for the expression of Kurdish grievances and aspirations within Turkey. Kurdish separatism within Turkey is hardly a foregone conclusion as of now, but a refusal to face grievances will only strengthen the forces for separatism.

Unfortunately, these events are not taking place in a vacuum, but in a world in which separatism is a growing phenomenon. Sadly, there can be no guarantee that even liberal and enlightened policies in the Kurdish areas of Turkey can guarantee that the Kurdish population may not now seek to move toward autonomy at a minimum. While most Kurds probably do not view the PKK as the ideal vehicle for Kurdish aspirations in Turkey, it is the only "national" movement the Turkish Kurds so far have, and as such it enjoys at least the sympathy of a large number of Kurds who see it as a means of improving their situation in Turkey. In brief, liberalized policies may now be too late to stem a historical move toward self-determination by the Kurds in all three countries of Iraq, Iran, and Turkey. While there is nothing inevitable about Kurdish separatism in Turkey, it cannot remain untouched by the far more advanced and rapidly evolving separatist movements in Iraq.

Any tendency by the Kurds in all three countries to move to full autonomy, subsequent independence, or even eventual unity will be highly destabilizing to the region. Such a tendency may now also be unstoppable, at least in Iraq. Only time, regional events, and the wisdom of state policies will tell. If Ankara ultimately sets out to stop a process that may not be historically reversible, then the turmoil and cost to Turkey will be very high. Such an attempt will not only involve the loss of a considerable portion of Turkish territory, it will also inevitably unsettle ethnic relations more broadly over the rest of Turkey, where perhaps half the Kurdish population is widely distributed, well away from their ethnic zones of the southeast. Kurdish events thus may yet have a massive impact on the stability and future of Turkey, the character of its role in the region, and its relationship with the West and the United States.

Turkey's National Interests

With this sweeping geopolitical change in the world, Turkey's own national interests have likewise changed accordingly. The old Soviet threat may be gone, yet new instabilities have emerged all around Turkey, both more real and more destabilizing than the Soviet threat was.

The central fact determining Turkey's policies toward the former Soviet Union is that modern Turkey came into existence almost simultaneously with Bolshevik Russia in the early 1920s. The existence of a large and primarily hostile USSR has therefore shaped Turkey's view of the world from the outset, impelling it after World War II to join Western defense arrangements. In the post-Cold War world of today, Turkey no longer even borders the Soviet Union or Russia. The character of its relations with the Soviet Union has now been disaggregated into a whole series of separate bilateral and regional relationships that are far more complex and, in some cases, present conflicting interests.

The nature of Turkey's relationship with the United States may have now changed as well. The global character of the Cold War required the United States to adopt a global strategy that postulated a direct American interest in any country relevant to the East-West conflict. As a result, it was important for Turkey to coordinate closely with Washington on nearly all issues that could affect their joint interests. Today, the global character of U.S. interests has sharply diminished; the inherent importance of any region is no longer augmented by East-West rivalry. But the urgent character of local political conflict around Turkey's own periphery has raised the geopolitical stakes for Turkey while diminishing them for the United States. Turkey is therefore certain to be far more outspoken with Washington about the character of its own interests, and less likely to consider or defer to diminished U.S. interests in the region.

One sign of Turkey's shifting orientation is its recent interest in the formation of new blocs of states for economic or political ends. Most of these new blocs are formed out of the newly liberated states of Eastern Europe or the Soviet Union. Many of them are tentative in character, may not long survive, or may regroup into yet other blocs.

American interest in the formation of these blocs remains to be seen. On the one hand, they may offer a desperately needed coherence to groups of new states that would otherwise be hard put to exist on their own in economic and security isolation. They could provide building blocks of stability in regions that are still in the process of determining their own new national interests. On the other hand, they could also lead to the weakening of Western or American influence in the region.

Ultimately, the integrative character of new blocs should outweigh most negative considerations.

The Black Sea Consortium (BSC)

Formed at Turkish suggestion, the BSC includes all riparian states of the Black Sea: Turkey, Bulgaria, Romania, Ukraine, Russia, Georgia, plus Greece, Moldova, Armenia, and Azerbaijan (not actually riparian). While the Black Sea had served commercial purposes even during the Cold War, it was dominated by Eastern bloc powers, and East-West trade was relatively limited; the sea also was the center of much rival military activity. Today, the Black Sea has come into its own, linking states commercially in peacetime, many of which had neither existed as separate entities nor had separate trading policies. The BSC could emerge as a significant regional trading bloc, usefully assisting in the closer integration of trade in a region that did not think of itself as a coherent trade zone in the past. On the other hand, many of these states are poor and are not likely to provide a major new stimulus to the economies of the region. While Turkish membership in the BSC could in principle complicate Turkish entry into the EC, the EC does in fact favorably view the BSC as providing some alternative to EC membership to states that may not yet be "ready" for admission to the EC, and as serving to strengthen the economies of these states on the EC border. Lastly, the successful functioning of this bloc could also help establish economic relations between the BSC and the EC over time.

The Economic Cooperation Organization (ECO)

This organization was founded over a decade ago by Turkey, Iran, and Pakistan. It has recently been expanded at Iranian initiative to include four of the five Central Asian states (excluding Kazakhstan) and Azerbaijan. It represents an attempt to draw the Central Asian states into the orbit of the Muslim world. Iran in particular hopes to strengthen its own ties with the region by this means. Pakistan has also shown keen interest, since this is a major means for extension of its trade toward the West and for gaining access to Central Asian markets. Despite political differences among these states, all of them view the ECO as an institution that serves their mutual interests.

The Caspian Sea Organization

This organization, based in Tehran, was established in 1991 by Iran, partly in response to Turkey's Black Sea initiative. The Caspian organization of course excludes Turkey, but includes Azerbaijan, Iran,

Turkmenistan, Kazakhstan, and Russia. It remains to be seen how significant the organization will be—especially alongside the ECO—beyond any coordination of policy toward the use of the Caspian.

The Union of Turkic States

Turkey has also proposed the creation of a Union of Turkic States that would unite all the Turkic states of the region—Turkey, Azerbaijan, Turkmenistan, Uzbekistan, Kazakhstan, Kyrgyzstan, plus Tajikistan on an honorary basis—in a loose commonwealth for common benefit. Turkey would obviously be the most powerful and influential member of this grouping. Based as it is on purely ethnic grounds, this union would stir opposition from Iran, Afghanistan, Pakistan, and those who see it as a Turkish effort to gain dominance over the region. Kazakhstan and Uzbekistan have also stated that they do not favor membership in an organization that it based on ethnic or religious grounds, but their leaders have so far attended meetings, even while keeping the organization in low profile.

Turkey and Russia

With the death of communism and the collapse of the Soviet Empire, Turkey has far less reason to fear Russian aggression than in the past. Turkey today no longer even has borders with Russia. From the Russian side, too, the bugaboo of "pan-Turkism," so long touted by a Soviet Union fearful of the implications of resurgent internal nationalisms, has now seen the worst happen: The empire has in fact collapsed before resurgent nationalism. Newly liberated Russian foreign policy thinking therefore was initially inclined to see Turkey as a now positive player in the region: As a moderate secular state, it could help direct the newly independent Turkish states of the former Soviet Union in a moderate and secular direction. Indeed, Turkey was seen by Russia as a successful and useful model of a state that had itself undergone a partial "perestroika" in the eighties, moving out of a statist economic system and toward increased privatization and integration in the world economy.

Initially optimistic interpretations, however, are now beginning to be overshadowed by creeping reassertion of at least some aspects of classic Russian-Turkish geopolitical rivalries. With the end of the Cold War and ideological struggle, and an end to the colonial era, this old rivalry is likely to be far less meaningful than in the last century. Any serious recrudescence of friction between the two states would stir some concerns in the West that it presaged potential Russian expansionism.

Russia still would like to preserve as much as possible of the Commonwealth of Independent States (CIS) structure, which de facto tends to reassert the Russian position of primus inter pares and also provides a useful structure for the adjudication of inter-republican relations in areas such as security and economic affairs. Russia also seeks retention of the ruble zone as a way of broadening and strengthening its own economy. Turkey, with its increasing involvement in the Caucasus and Central Asia, is the single greatest rival (not to say threat) to Russian great power preeminence in these southern regions. Turkish proposals for a Turkic commonwealth or union tend to pull these states out of the Russian orbit—undesirable although not intolerable to Russian interests.[3]

This division of the former Soviet Union into more explicitly Muslim and non-Muslim commonwealths could pose threats to the region and the West. Central Asian politics under any circumstances already involve tensions between the former Russian "masters" of the region— now transformed into often privileged minorities—and the titular native population of each republic, especially in Kazakhstan. If increasing discrimination or bloodshed should result, Russia will be under growing pressure to intervene on behalf of the Russian people and interests that still remain there. If these confrontations should take on an increasingly Muslim vs. Christian character, Islamic fundamentalism will unquestionably grow and could strengthen the hands of imperialist, xenophobic elements still present in Russian politics. Such an eventuality would be very undesirable for the West.

Under more optimistic scenarios, Turkey will indeed play a moderate role in the Muslim regions of the former USSR, will support secular government, and will seek close ties with Russia as well as with the Turkish republics—with a search for maximal overlapping of interests. Turkish-Russian mutual interest in maintaining peace in the Caucasus and Central Asia and in regional cooperation in the Black Sea is considerable, and the importance of these states to each other could prove to be greater than that of their bilateral ties to the other Turkic states (except for the very important Russian-Kazakh relationship).

Even if the more optimistic scenarios for the Turkish role emerge as most likely, Central Asia is still destined to be caught between two other great powers, Russia and China. Historically, Sino-Russian rivalry has in part played out along the western borders of China. There is no reason to assume that these historic rivalries will entirely disappear simply because the Cold War is over. Under these circumstances, the Central Asian states will be caught between these two forces and compelled to some extent to take sides, especially if China is suppressing the quest for nationalist self-determination among the Turkish peoples of western China (Xinjiang, or Chinese Turkestan). Turkey cannot remain entirely aloof from that struggle either.

Turkey, Europe, NATO, and the United States

Turkey continues to place great value upon NATO as its leading security and political link to the West over the past forty years, a tangible
badge of membership in a democratic Western club. As the importance
of NATO diminishes in European strategic calculations, Turkey is
exhibiting concern that a formal Turkish role in Europe is being eroded.
This is even more the case as the WEU grows in stature, accepting
Greece as a full member but granting Turkey only associate status.
Indeed, the prospects for Turkish acceptance into the EC have likely
diminished over the past several years with the emergence of independent states in Eastern Europe that themselves now seek membership in
the EC, especially Poland, Hungary, and the Czech Republic. Moreover,
as Europe moves to develop a common foreign and security policy,
Europeans will be reluctant to accept the political and security exposure
that Turkey brings with it.

Ironically, as European politics grow more complicated in the post-
Cold War world and with the emergence of Eastern Europe, tensions
among European states may grow, suggesting that NATO may perhaps
end up playing a greater role in brokering quarrels among its members
than in focusing on its original mission of regional security. Certainly, in
the case of Turkey, several issues emerge involving direct Turkish interests. Turkish-Greek relations might be further tested over several traditional issues as well: Greece's militarization of the Greek islands just off
the Turkish coast; conflict over air and nautical boundaries between the
two countries; the position of the Turkish minority in Greek Thrace; the
problems raised by the declaration of independence by Macedonia and
especially Bosnia with its large Muslim population;[4] Turkish sympathy
for the Muslim Albanians in their struggle in Kosovo against the Serbs;
and possible Greek-Turkish differences over shifting Balkan politics and
alliances, especially after the collapse of Yugoslavia.

Turkish-German relations are also likely to face increasing strain stimulated in particular by the uncomfortable position of 1.5 million Turkish
guest-workers in Germany—some 2 million in Europe altogether—and
sharp German public opposition to Turkish policies against the Kurds in
Turkey. This latter problem caused the Germans to stop military aid to
Turkey in March 1992 and provoked a storm of recriminations and
counterattacks at the highest level of German and Turkish governments.
Germany also showed the greatest reluctance among major NATO powers to support Turkey militarily during the Gulf War, an omission that
particularly stung Ankara. And whereas Germany and Turkey were in
alignment up to and during World War I, the new Balkan politics con-
ceivably could find Germany and Turkey as rivals for influence in the

Balkans. The unprecedented and unpredictable position of an independent Ukraine as a new player in Balkan politics is also likely to affect Turkish-German relations in the Balkans in unforeseeable ways. If Russian nationalists should come to power in Moscow and pursue Russia's historical interests in supporting Orthodox Christian states in the Balkans (such as Serbia, Romania and Bulgaria), will Ukraine thus lean toward Turkey and Germany in an anti-Russian, anti-Orthodox stance?

Germany therefore may become the major state complicating the Turkish quest for integration into Europe, and the one state within NATO most concerned about the potential for unwanted European involvement in the unstable political situation surrounding Turkey in the East. In simplest terms, many Germans do not want EC borders to be extended to adjoin Iraq, Syria, Iran, Azerbaijan, and Armenia.

Whatever the fate of full Turkish membership in the EC, Turkey's relationship with the West does not ride exclusively on this issue. Turkish businessmen are still determined to focus on the European and American markets as the single most lucrative, and are determined to maintain close ties on whatever level with Europe. Turks are not likely to go to Baku, Tashkent, or Alma Ata for vacation; they will continue going in large numbers to Germany, France, and England, partly to visit relatives working there, but mostly because that is the source of the cultural pull. The Western orientation remains strong and will continue to shape political, economic, and security policy for some time, even as Turkey's political options grow more multifaceted.

As NATO's role becomes less certain and Turkish membership in the EC becomes more elusive, Turkey will likely look increasingly to the United States as a security partner, source of military assistance, and political support. Yet that military assistance, at least in a NATO context, is also likely to diminish because the Russian threat has diminished. Ankara will remain intent on supporting and maintaining NATO as its chief vehicle of European status, but it may be an uphill battle as western Europe begins to place new emphasis on European security arrangements, including a focus on Franco-German military cooperation.

Turkey is undoubtedly entering a very trying and demanding period. Its old foreign policy anchor of Ataturkism and the world that three generations of Turks knew is now gone. Challenges are breaking out around Turkey in nearly all directions. The nation will be sorely tried in coping with the very complex Kurdish problem, many aspects of which are heavily conditioned by events that involve Iraq and Iran as well as Turkey. Under these circumstances, Turkey will seek some kind of mainstay in its security relations. That mainstay almost surely is not to be found any longer in Europe. The United States is the most logical remaining partner because of its long historical relationship with Turkey and its abiding global interests—however diminished after the Cold War.

The American relationship with Turkey need not focus exclusively on security issues. Increasingly, both Washington and Ankara are interested in expanding the relationship to include enhanced trade relations (Turkey has sought a U.S.-Turkish free trade area), technical cooperation, and cooperation on policies relating to neighboring areas. Turkish-American cooperation in channeling aid to the Central Asian republics, for example, is high on Turkey's list of interests. In the new era, Washington itself, however, will increasingly view these broadened areas of cooperation from a narrower perspective of American interest rather than as part of an extended security relationship in a polarized world.

Despite the fact that its relationship with the United States and NATO has been basically good, Turkey has historically been sensitive to issues affecting its sovereignty. American policy on Cyprus and the U.S. desire to use Turkish military facilities during various Middle East crises in the past have provoked questions in the minds of Ankara's policymakers, including during the Gulf War. While Turkey has been ready to assist where it saw no threat to its own broader interests, each of these past efforts to use Turkish facilities has raised Turkish concerns about whether U.S. goals were compatible with Turkish ones in the region, and whether Washington was not taking Turkey for granted and intruding on Turkey's sovereign interests. These questions were raised most sharply during the Gulf War, when many Turks saw UN protection for the Iraqi Kurds as leading directly toward Kurdish autonomy, if not independence in northern Iraq, greatly to the detriment of Turkey's own Kurdish problem. While Ankara will probably seek American support for many of its own regional policies, it will remain sensitive to any suggestion that it must toe Washington's line in order to maintain U.S. support.

As the United States struggles to redefine its own national interests in the new political environment of the post-Cold War world, the new geopolitics must increasingly take into account the nature of the potential ethnic and religious fault lines that exist in the world. These fault lines provide clues to potential breakaway states, drives for national unification, or even irredentist movements that may take place in the coming decades—in a context in which political and territorial change is no longer fraught with the global implications of the past. Turkey is one of the states that has the potential to impact a broad portion of the world based on its theoretical primacy in the newly emerging, far-flung Turkish world.

As noted above, Turkey is now more likely than ever before to pursue its interests with less regard for American interests, simply because most issues will be far more important to Turkey and far less important to the United States in the broader scheme of things. As Turkey assumes a more activist role, there are unquestionably greater complexities for all states that maintain security associations with it, simply because Turkey is now more likely to become involved in one way or another with regional conflict—in the Balkans, the Caucasus, and Central Asia, and with Iran and Iraq. There is every reason to believe that conflict will grow, rather than diminish, in most of these regions.

Western allies might well then ask—as perhaps some of them already do—whether Turkey has not in fact become a less desirable security partner, given that the old Soviet threat is gone and the new regional chaos is hardly inviting to the West. Yet the emergence of these regional problems, crises, and conflicts is not, of course, of Turkey's own doing. They emerge from the end of the Cold War, the collapse of empire, and the creation of a major geopolitical vacuum. Because Turkey quite literally sits along the borders of this vacuum, it is impossible for it not to be drawn in. The question to be posed, then, is not whether the West wishes to maintain such close ties with Turkey any more, but whether the Turkish presence and involvement in these regions are in fact in the Western interest.

The reality is that conflict in the region around Turkey is going to exist, probably for a very long time. Given Turkey's past track record of identification with and support for a large variety of the values and interests of the West, is it not still desirable for Turkey to play a role in these regions of crisis? Turkish moderation, responsibility, and general commitment to the international order, to democracy, and to a free market economy are all valuable qualities that have developed significant roots in Turkey over a long period. Would the United States rather have Serbia as arbiter of the Balkans? Iran or Iraq as arbiter in the Caucasus? Iran as arbiter in Central Asia? Turkey's presence in these troubled regions will in the end most likely exert a moderating influence, even when Turkey is pursuing its own goals.

It is quite possible that American goals may cross with Turkish goals to some extent on some issues. But channels for discussion and arbitration of these issues have existed for a long time, and the West is familiar and comfortable with a dialog with Turkey. The regions surrounding Turkey are indeed likely to be more chaotic in the decades ahead, but American interests will not likely be lessened because Turkey is attempting to cope with the problems. The most specific areas of potential U.S.-Turkish conflict are likely to be

- Armenia and Azerbaijan if events, however rightly or wrongly, force Turkey into full alliance with Azerbaijan, thus turning international Armenian public opinion, especially in the United States, against Turkey.
- Turkish conflict with Greece, in which case, regardless of the issues of the case, Washington will be under strong pressure from Greek political groups in the United States, and under pressure to contain the damage to NATO.
- Harsh measures by Turkey against its own Kurdish population, which will automatically invoke American and international human-rights concerns.
- Significant rivalry between Russia and Turkey in Central Asia in which Russia, rightly or wrongly, perceives that the United States is supporting Turkey at Russia's expense. It would not be in the U.S. interest to be pushed into opposition with a democratic Russia if that scenario should emerge.

It will be in the U.S. interest to understand the Turkish vision of the Turkish world and to consult with Ankara on its perception of the character of problems and potential change in and around the Turkish world. Washington is under no obligation to accept the Turkish vision of regional politics, but it must surely cope with that vision as one of the new realities. Of all the states in the region, Turkey is certainly the most desirable "model" for such a central role in the affairs of this pivotal region. That is why the U.S. relationship with Turkey, despite massive changes in the region and in the world, should remain strong and positive in the decades of challenge ahead.

Notes

1. The average Turk is impressed by the vast similarities among the Turkic languages across Asia. In linguistic terms, most of the languages differ no more at most than Italian from Spanish, or Russian from Ukrainian. A Turk from Istanbul can communicate with an Uzbek in basic terms within a few hours and, with study, can read and understand Uzbek almost fully, say, within a month. Azerbaijani or Turkmen is almost fully comprehensible to an Istanbul Turk within a few days of "adjusting the ear" and noting the use of words unique to the new language/dialect. On the other hand, for serious discussions, Turks in Central Asia and Central Asians in Turkey require an interpreter for full and correct understanding. Cultural differences between the Turks of Turkey and those of Central Asia are more profound given the seventy-five years of communist

culture that has separated them. Unfortunately, there is no established Turkic lingua franca among all Turkic peoples, although Turkish aspires to that role; Turkey is shrewdly assisting in providing communication and media services to the region that would help disseminate a knowledge of Turkish among the broad population.

2. Old suspicions about Western intentions toward Moscow also reappear when the United States is seen to tout Turkey heavily as the "model" for the Muslim regions of the old USSR, suggesting that Turkey could now become the instrument of the West to supplant Russia in this classic area of its influence. And deep within the Turkic-Tatar-Slavic psyche lie memories of past struggles for control over Russia, first by the Mongol-Tatar hordes and later by a resurgent medieval Russia over the Tatars. Even today, this element cannot be entirely erased from the psychological backdrop for both sides.

3. Although the Muslim population of Bosnia is basically Muslim Slav, popular opinion in Turkey often views the Bosnians as "Turks." Indeed, the Muslims of Bosnia themselves early on looked to Turkey for diplomatic support in their struggle for independence and protection.

4. Turkey's adherence to these values may perhaps be imperfect, but how many other states in western and eastern Europe also fall short in some respect or another?

About the Book

With the astonishing transformations in the geopolitics of the world since the collapse of the Soviet Union, Turkey has been profoundly affected by the changes on its periphery. For the first time since the beginning of the century, a Turkic world has blossomed, giving Turkey potential new foreign policy clout from the Balkans across the Caucasus and into Central Asia and Western China.

These geopolitical opportunities have dramatically changed the character of Turkey itself, once an isolationist, Eurocentered NATO ally. At the same time, Turkey has undergone an internal evolution over the last decade, making it an attractive model of Middle Eastern development because of its increasingly free market, democratic governance, and secularist outlook.

This book explores the character of the new Turkey, assessing its foreign policy options and interpreting the significance of those choices for the Middle East, Central Asia, Europe, and the United States.

About the Authors

Graham E. Fuller is a Senior Political Scientist at RAND. He served 20 years as a foreign service officer, including three years in Istanbul, and was the National Intelligence Officer for long-range Middle East forecasting at the CIA. His degrees include a B.A. and an M.A. from Harvard University. Mr. Fuller speaks fluent Turkish and Russian and is finishing a study on modern Turkey as seen through the eyes of its novelists. Among his publications are RAND studies on Islamic fundamentalism in Turkey, Iran, Afghanistan, and Pakistan. He is the author of two books: *The "Center of the Universe": The Geopolitics of Iran* (Westview, 1991) and *The Democracy Trap: Perils of the Post-Cold War World* (Dutton, 1992).

Ian O. Lesser is a member of the International Policy Department at RAND, specializing in European and Mediterranean affairs. Prior to joining RAND, he was a Senior Fellow in International Security Affairs at the Center for Strategic and International Studies, and has also been a Senior Fellow of the Atlantic Council and a staff consultant at International Energy Associates in Washington D.C. A graduate of the University of Pennsylvania, the London School of Economics, and the Fletcher School of Law and Diplomacy, he received his doctorate from St. Antony's College, Oxford. Dr. Lesser is the author of *Resources and Strategy* (St. Martin's Press, 1989), as well as numerous publications on the foreign and security policies of southern European countries and the Mediterranean.

Paul B. Henze is a long-time Resident Consultant at RAND. He has occupied a considerable variety of senior government positions, including two tours in the American Embassy in Ankara. He was Staff Officer of the National Security Council from 1977 to 1980 with responsibility for several countries, including Turkey. Mr. Henze speaks Turkish, has worked closely with the Institute of Turkish Studies in Washington D.C., and has been a trustee of the American Turkish Foundation for almost a decade.

J. F. Brown was a Senior Staff member at RAND between 1989 and 1991. Educated at Manchester University and the University of Michigan, he is a former head of Radio Free Europe (RFE) Research and was Director of Radio Free Europe itself. He has taught at Berkeley and UCLA and has been a visiting research associate at Columbia University and St. Antony's College, Oxford. He is the author of *Eastern Europe and Communist Rule* and *Surge to Freedom: The End of Communist Rule in Eastern Europe*, both published by Duke University Press. His latest book is *Nationalism, Democracy, and Security in the Balkans* (Dartmouth Publishing Company, 1992). At present he is Distinguished Scholar in Residence at the RFE/RL (Radio Liberty) Research Institute in Munich and is working on a study of post-communist Eastern Europe.

Index